Medaka Kuroiwa is Impervious to My Charms

3

Ran Kuze

CONTENTS

Chapter 19 ★ Nursing That Jerk

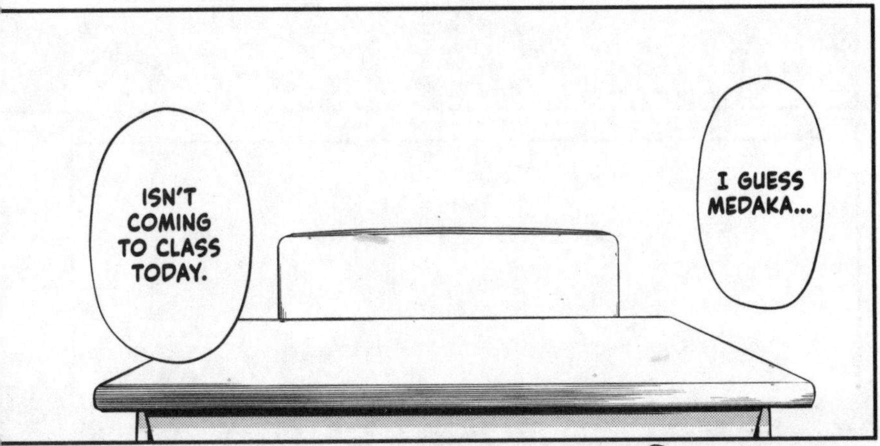
I GUESS MEDAKA...
ISN'T COMING TO CLASS TODAY.

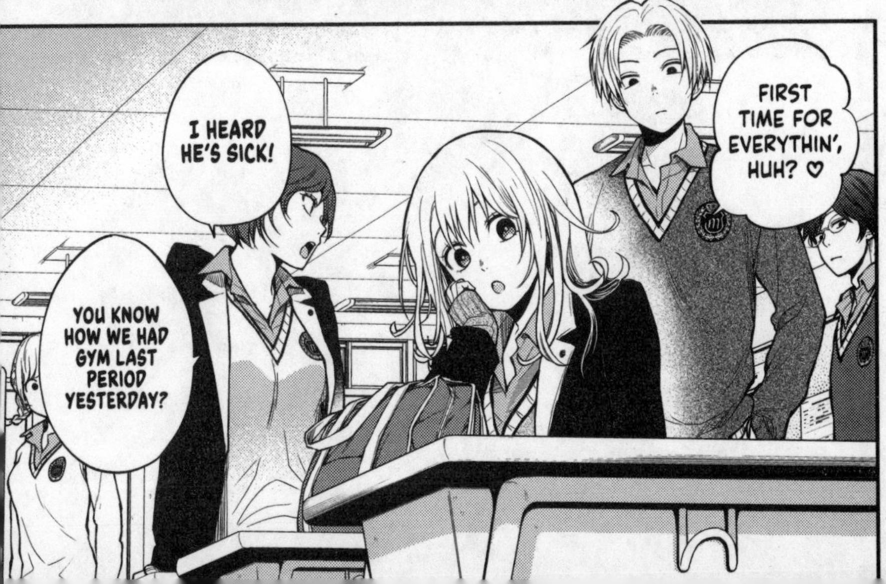
FIRST TIME FOR EVERYTHIN', HUH? ♡
I HEARD HE'S SICK!
YOU KNOW HOW WE HAD GYM LAST PERIOD YESTERDAY?

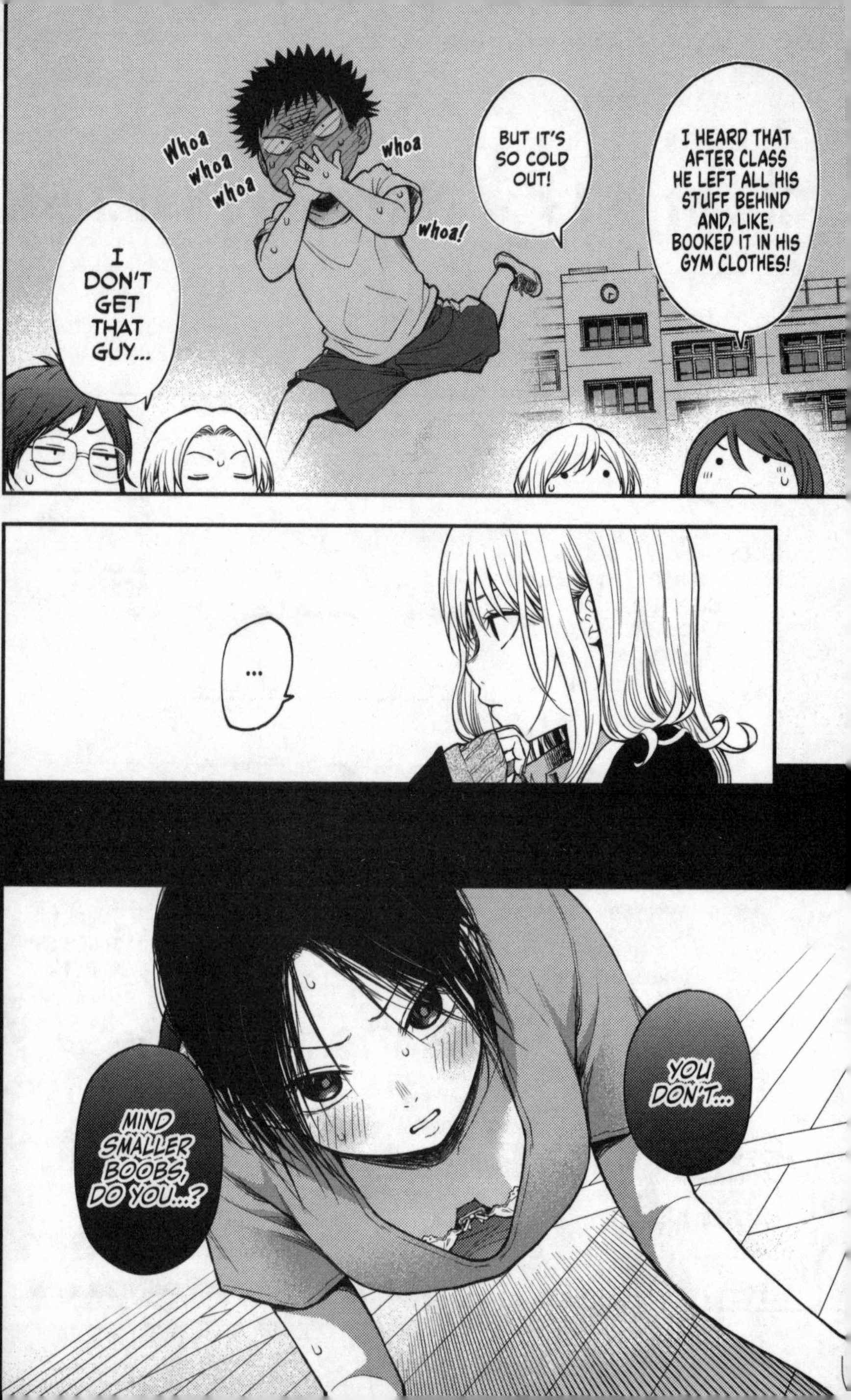

I HEARD THAT AFTER CLASS HE LEFT ALL HIS STUFF BEHIND AND, LIKE, BOOKED IT IN HIS GYM CLOTHES!
BUT IT'S SO COLD OUT!
whoa
Whoa whoa whoa
whoa!
I DON'T GET THAT GUY...
...
YOU DON'T...
MIND SMALLER BOOBS, DO YOU...?

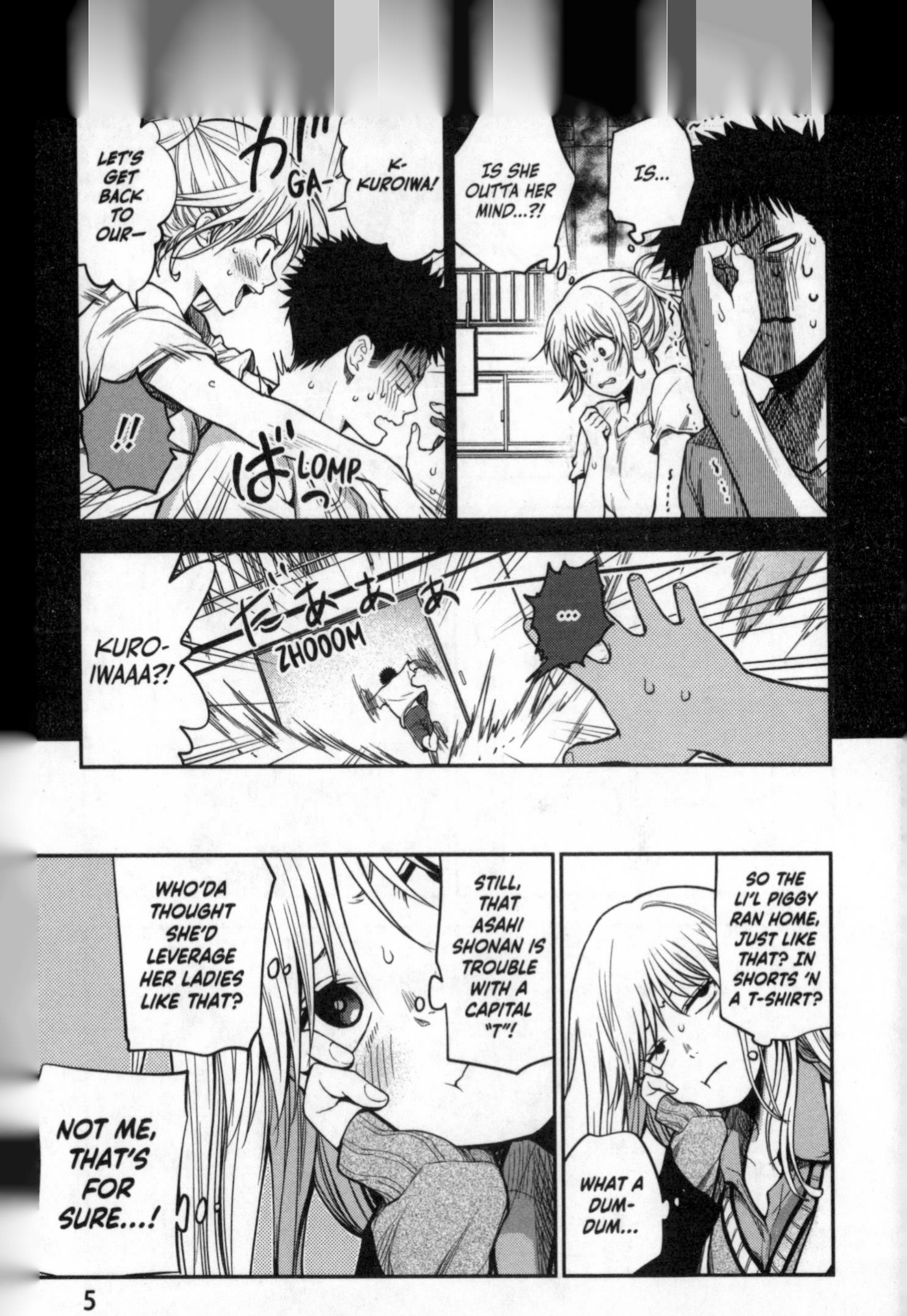
IS...
IS SHE OUTTA HER MIND...?!
K-KUROIWA!
GA-
LET'S GET BACK TO OUR—
!!
LOMP
...
ZHOOOM
KURO-IWAAA?!
SO THE LI'L PIGGY RAN HOME, JUST LIKE THAT? IN SHORTS 'N A T-SHIRT?
WHAT A DUM-DUM...
STILL, THAT ASAHI SHONAN IS TROUBLE WITH A CAPITAL "T"!
WHO'DA THOUGHT SHE'D LEVERAGE HER LADIES LIKE THAT?
NOT ME, THAT'S FOR SURE...!

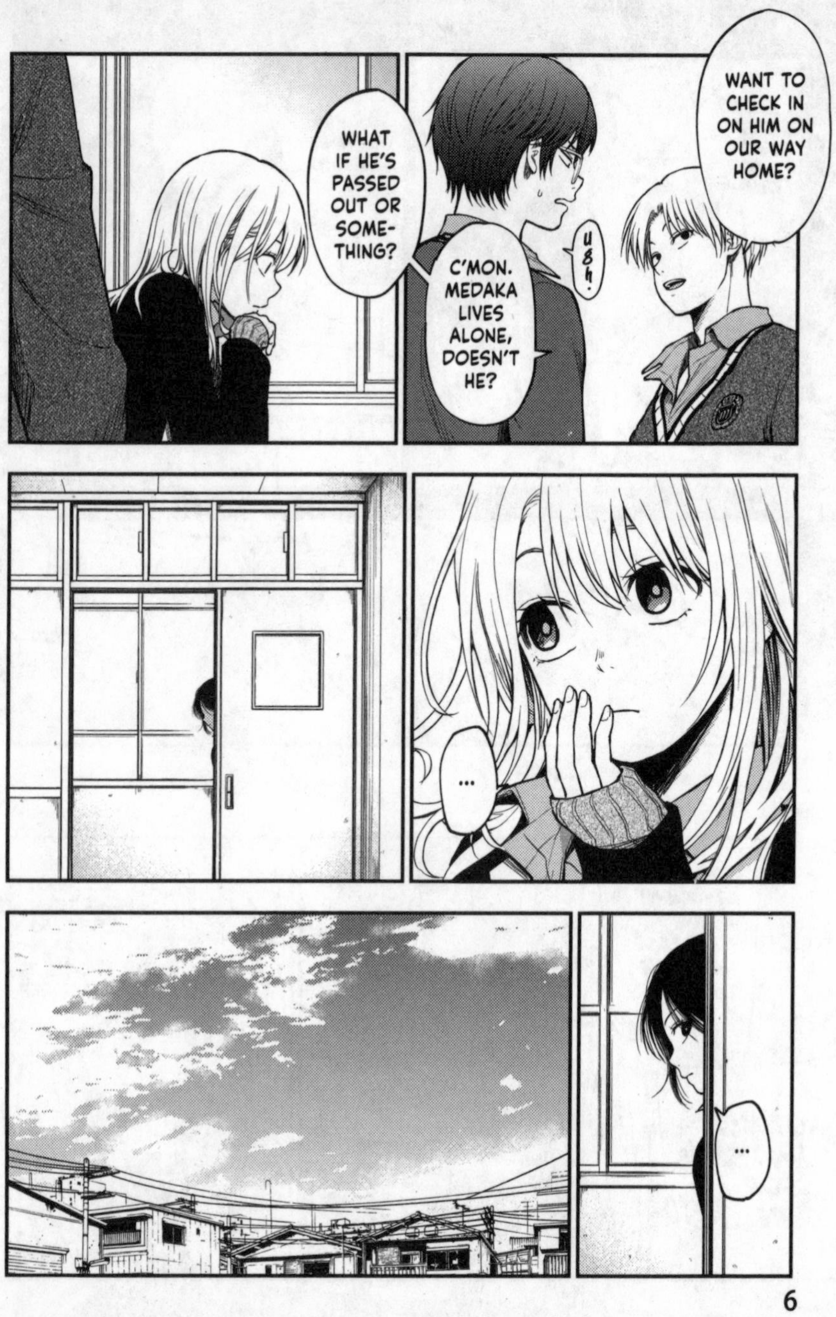
WANT TO CHECK IN ON HIM ON OUR WAY HOME?
UGH.
C'MON. MEDAKA LIVES ALONE, DOESN'T HE?
WHAT IF HE'S PASSED OUT OR SOME-THING?
...
...

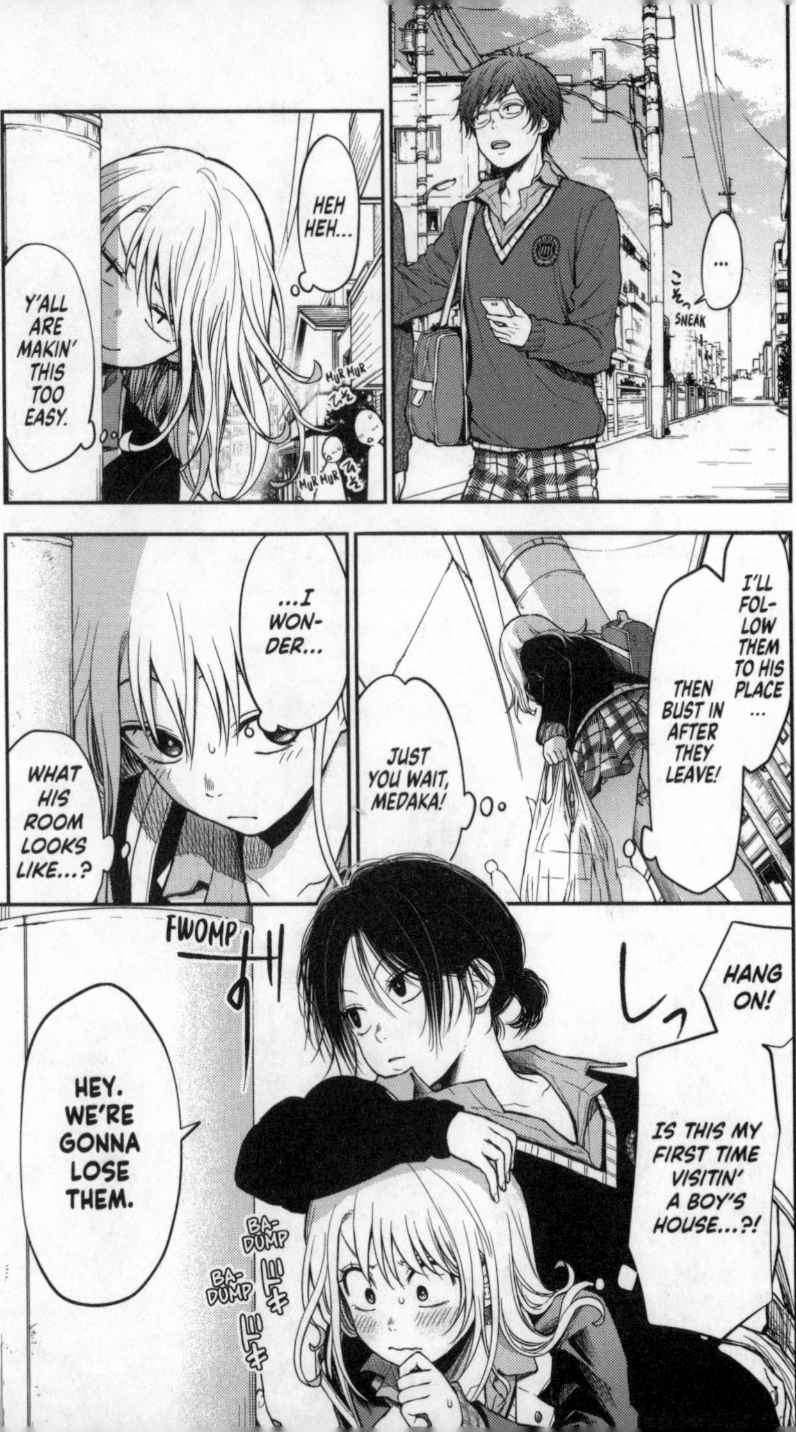
...
SNEAK
HEH HEH...
Y'ALL ARE MAKIN' THIS TOO EASY.
MUR MUR
MUR MUR
I'LL FOL-LOW THEM TO HIS PLACE...
THEN BUST IN AFTER THEY LEAVE!
JUST YOU WAIT, MEDAKA!
...I WON-DER...
WHAT HIS ROOM LOOKS LIKE...?
HANG ON!
IS THIS MY FIRST TIME VISITIN' A BOY'S HOUSE...?!
FWOMP
HEY. WE'RE GONNA LOSE THEM.
BA-DUMP
BA-DUMP

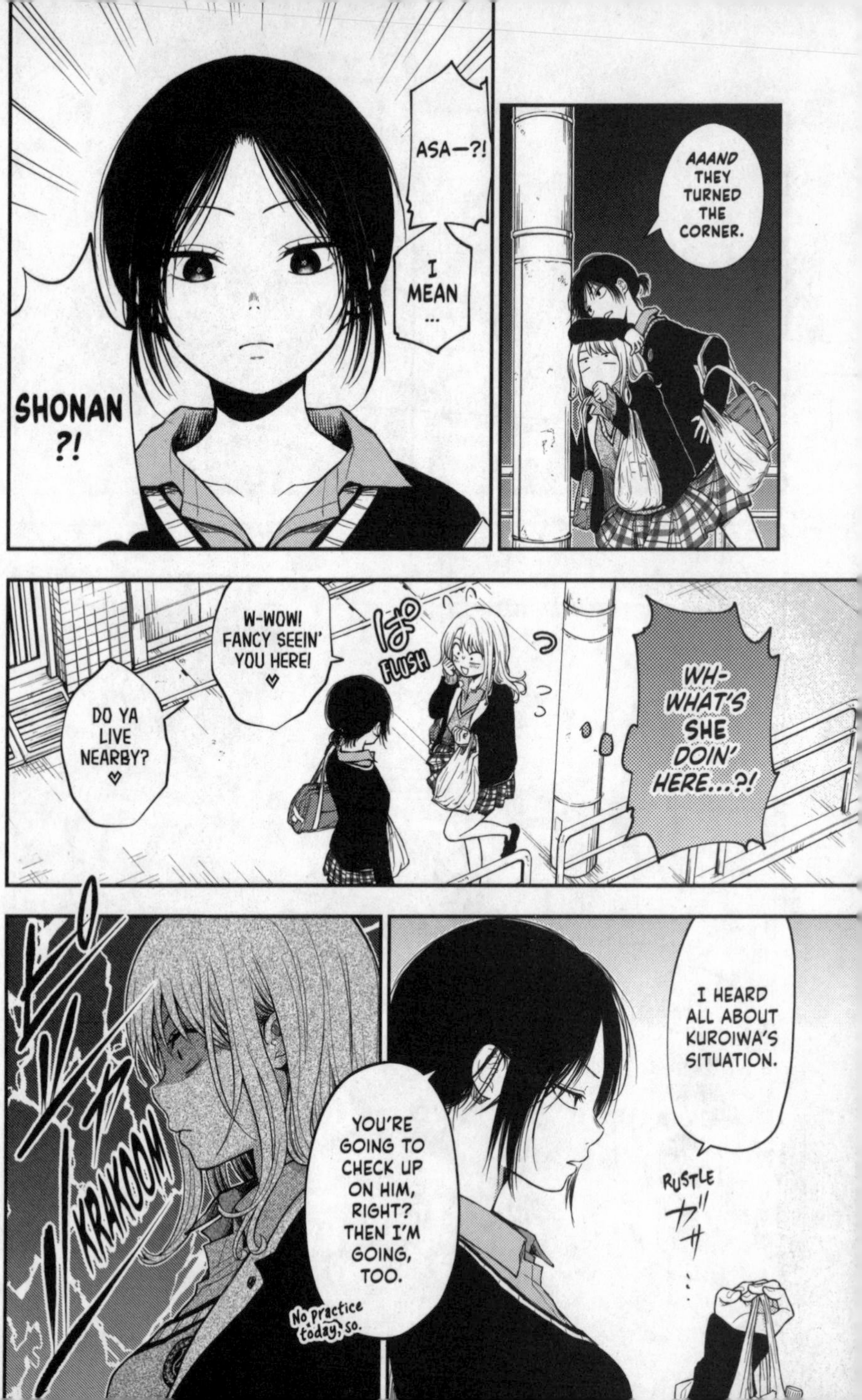
AAAND THEY TURNED THE CORNER.
ASA—?!
I MEAN...
SHONAN ?!
WH- WHAT'S SHE DOIN' HERE...?!
ぱ
FLUSH
W-WOW! FANCY SEEIN' YOU HERE! ♡
DO YA LIVE NEARBY? ♡
I HEARD ALL ABOUT KUROIWA'S SITUATION.
RUSTLE
ガサ
YOU'RE GOING TO CHECK UP ON HIM, RIGHT? THEN I'M GOING, TOO.
No practice today, so.
KRAKOOM

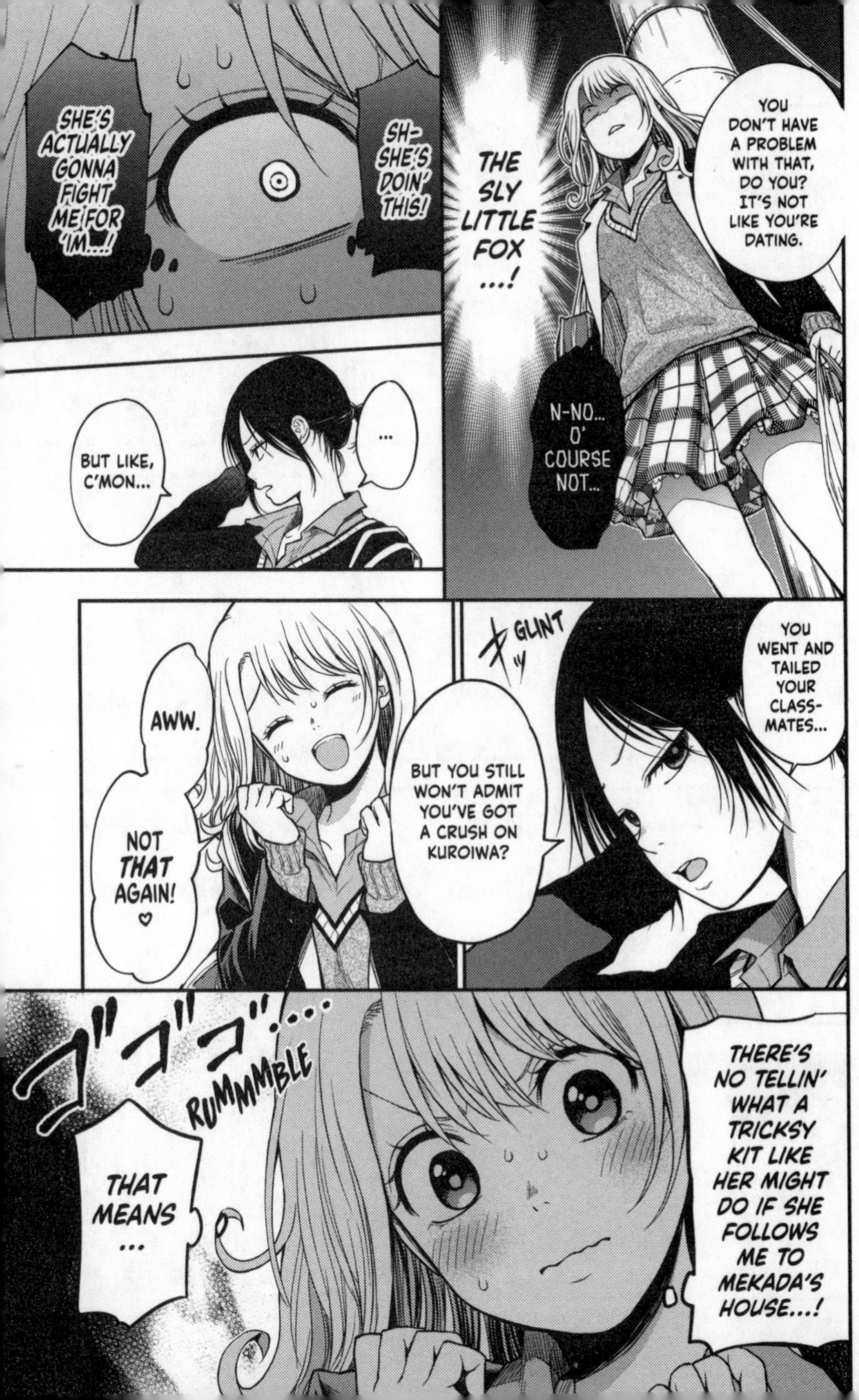
YOU DON'T HAVE A PROBLEM WITH THAT, DO YOU? IT'S NOT LIKE YOU'RE DATING.
THE SLY LITTLE FOX ...!
N-NO... O' COURSE NOT...
SH-SHE'S DOIN' THIS!
SHE'S ACTUALLY GONNA FIGHT ME FOR 'IM...!
...
BUT LIKE, C'MON...
GLINT
YOU WENT AND TAILED YOUR CLASS-MATES...
BUT YOU STILL WON'T ADMIT YOU'VE GOT A CRUSH ON KUROIWA?
AWW.
NOT THAT AGAIN! ♡
THERE'S NO TELLIN' WHAT A TRICKSY KIT LIKE HER MIGHT DO IF SHE FOLLOWS ME TO MEKADA'S HOUSE...!
ゴゴゴ...
RUMMMBLE
THAT MEANS ...

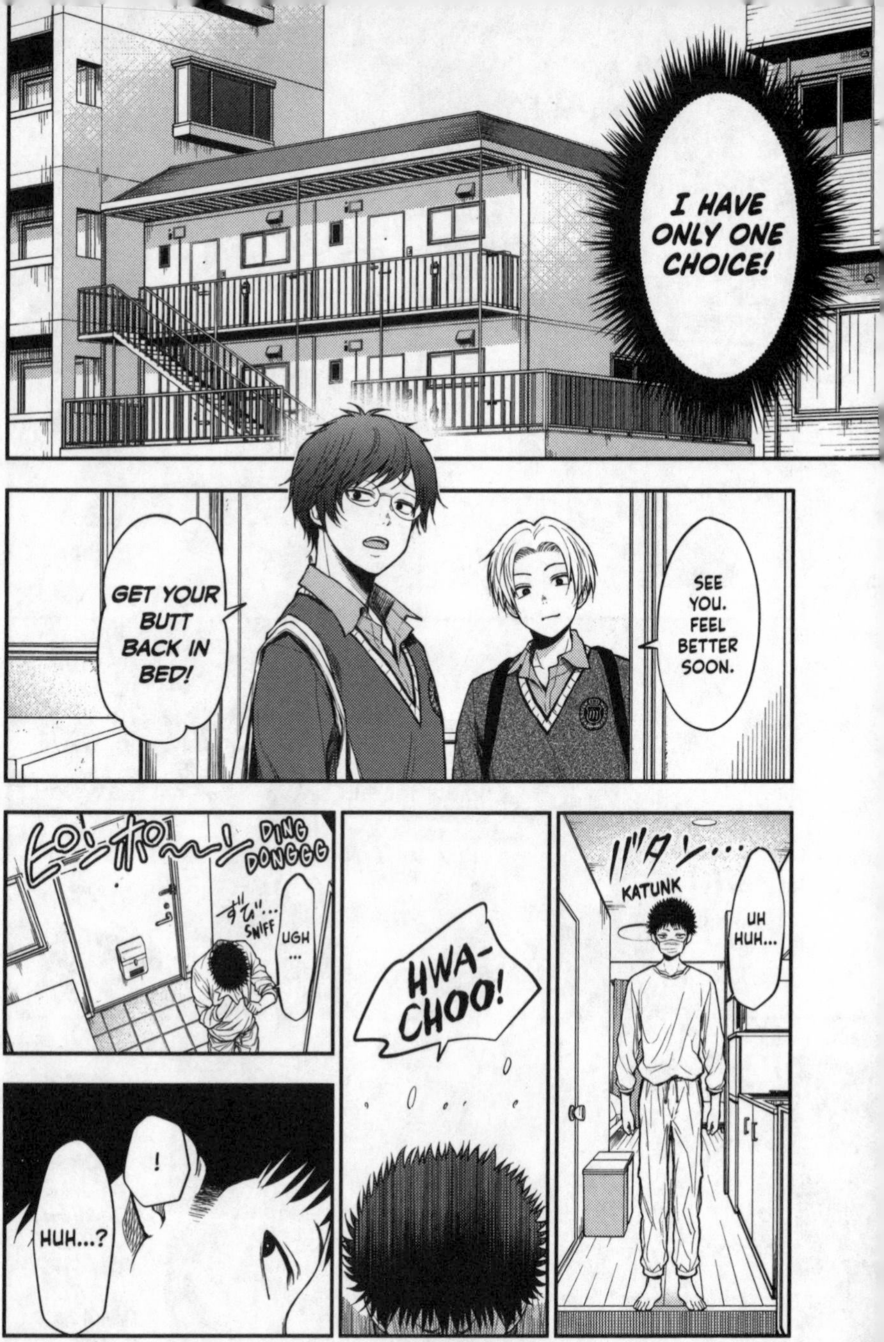
I HAVE ONLY ONE CHOICE!
SEE YOU. FEEL BETTER SOON.
GET YOUR BUTT BACK IN BED!
バタン…
KATUNK
UH HUH...
HWA-CHOO!
ピンポ〜ン
DING DONGGG
ずび…
SNIFF
UGH ...
!
HUH...?

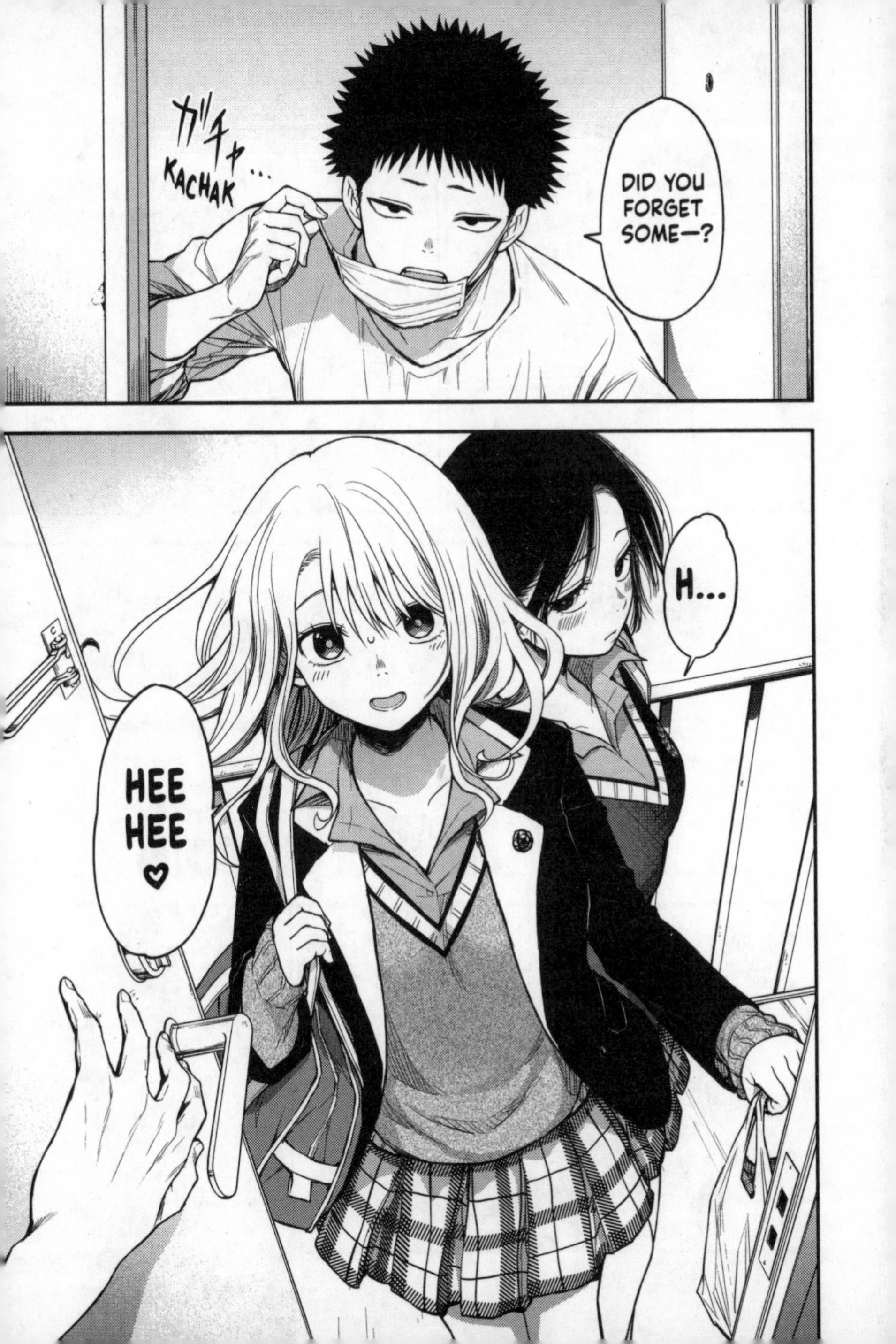
DID YOU FORGET SOME—?
ガチャ... KACHAK
H...
HEE HEE ♡

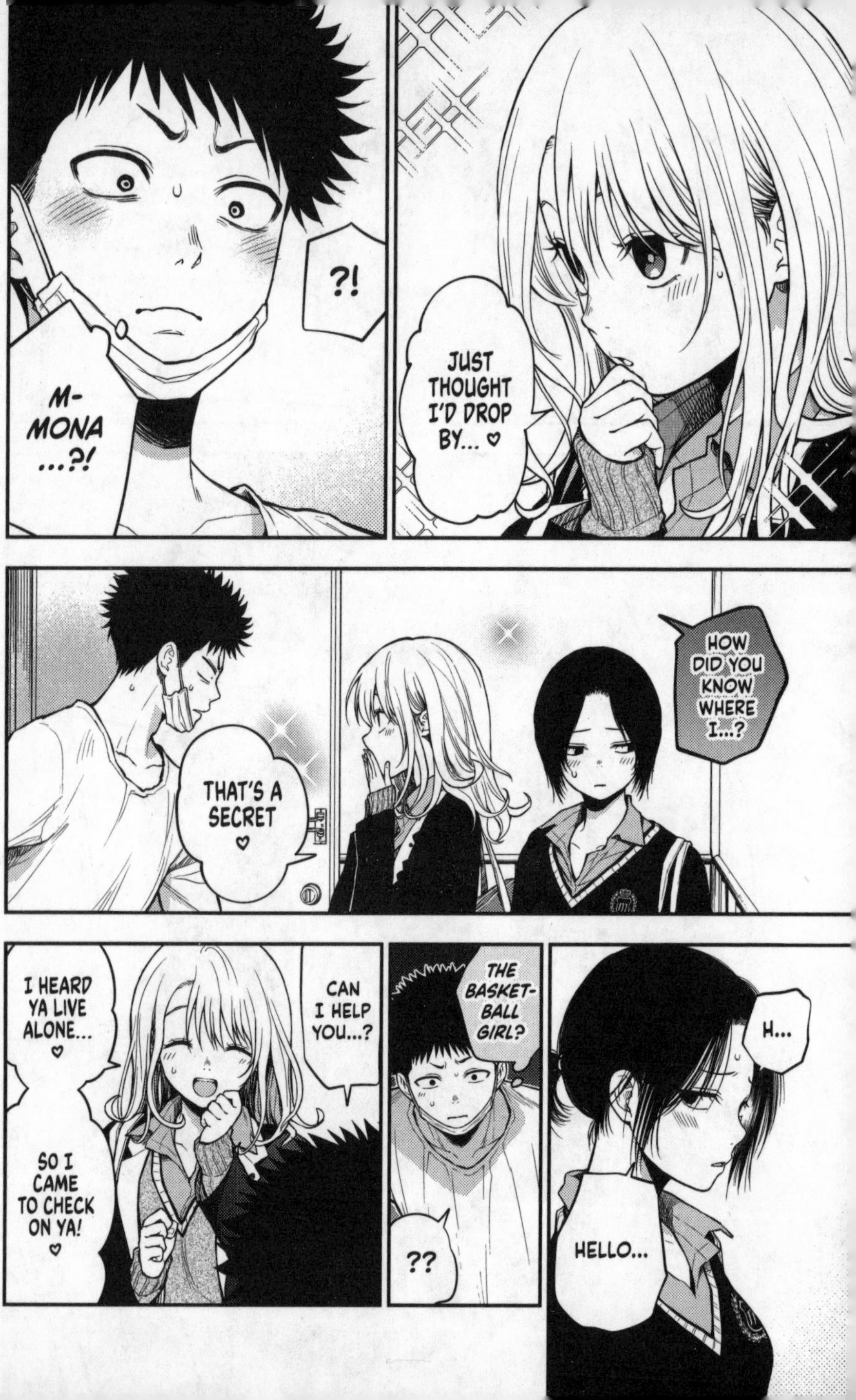
JUST THOUGHT I'D DROP BY... ♡
?!
M-MONA ...?!
HOW DID YOU KNOW WHERE I...?
THAT'S A SECRET ♡
H...
HELLO...
THE BASKET-BALL GIRL?
??
CAN I HELP YOU...?
I HEARD YA LIVE ALONE... ♡
SO I CAME TO CHECK ON YA! ♡

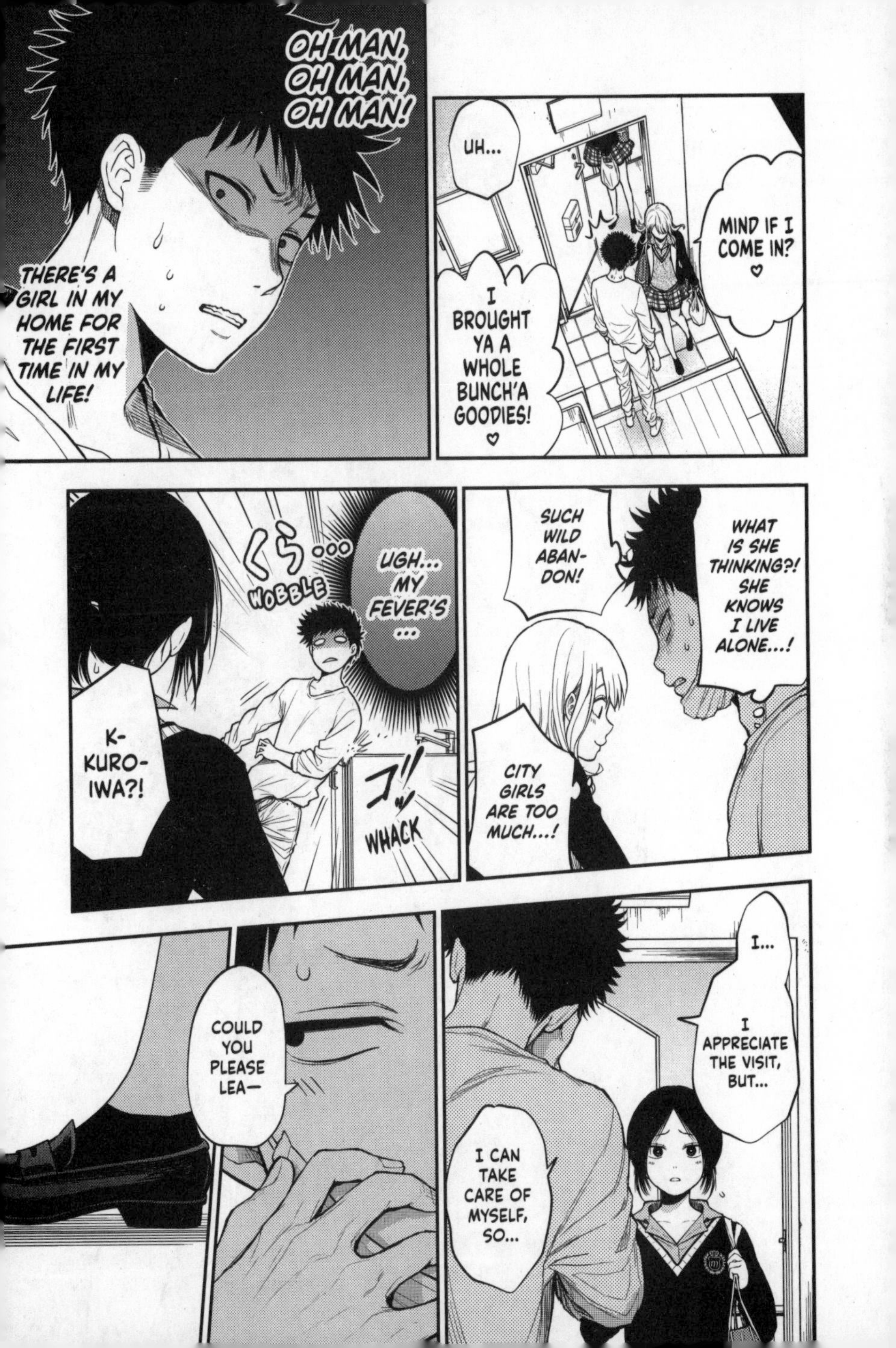
MIND IF I COME IN? ♡
UH...
I BROUGHT YA A WHOLE BUNCH'A GOODIES! ♡
OH MAN, OH MAN, OH MAN!
THERE'S A GIRL IN MY HOME FOR THE FIRST TIME IN MY LIFE!
WHAT IS SHE THINKING?! SHE KNOWS I LIVE ALONE...!
SUCH WILD ABAN-DON!
CITY GIRLS ARE TOO MUCH...!
UGH... MY FEVER'S ...
くら…
WOBBLE
ゴッ
WHACK
K-KURO-IWA?!
I...
I APPRECIATE THE VISIT, BUT...
I CAN TAKE CARE OF MYSELF, SO...
COULD YOU PLEASE LEA—

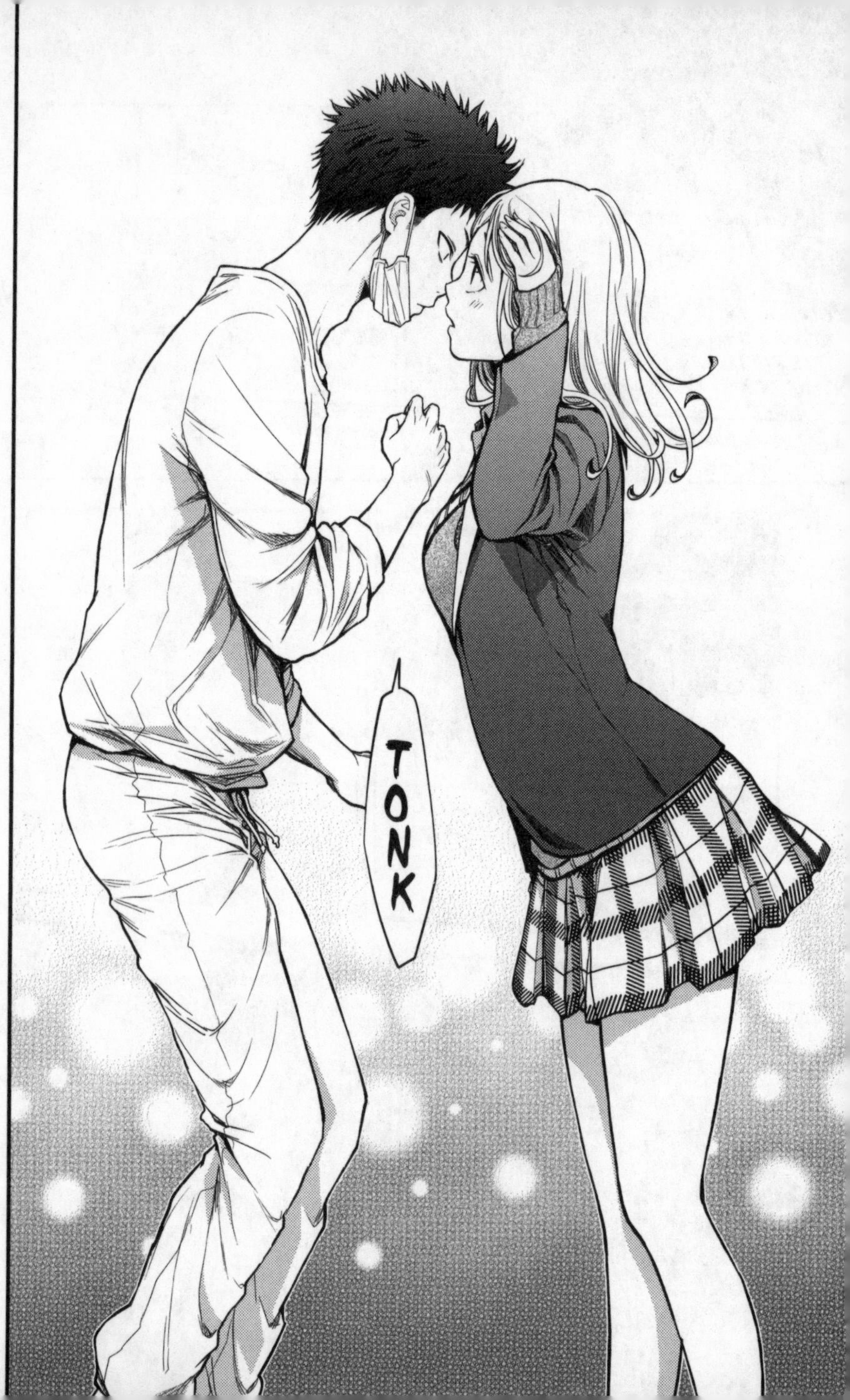
TONK

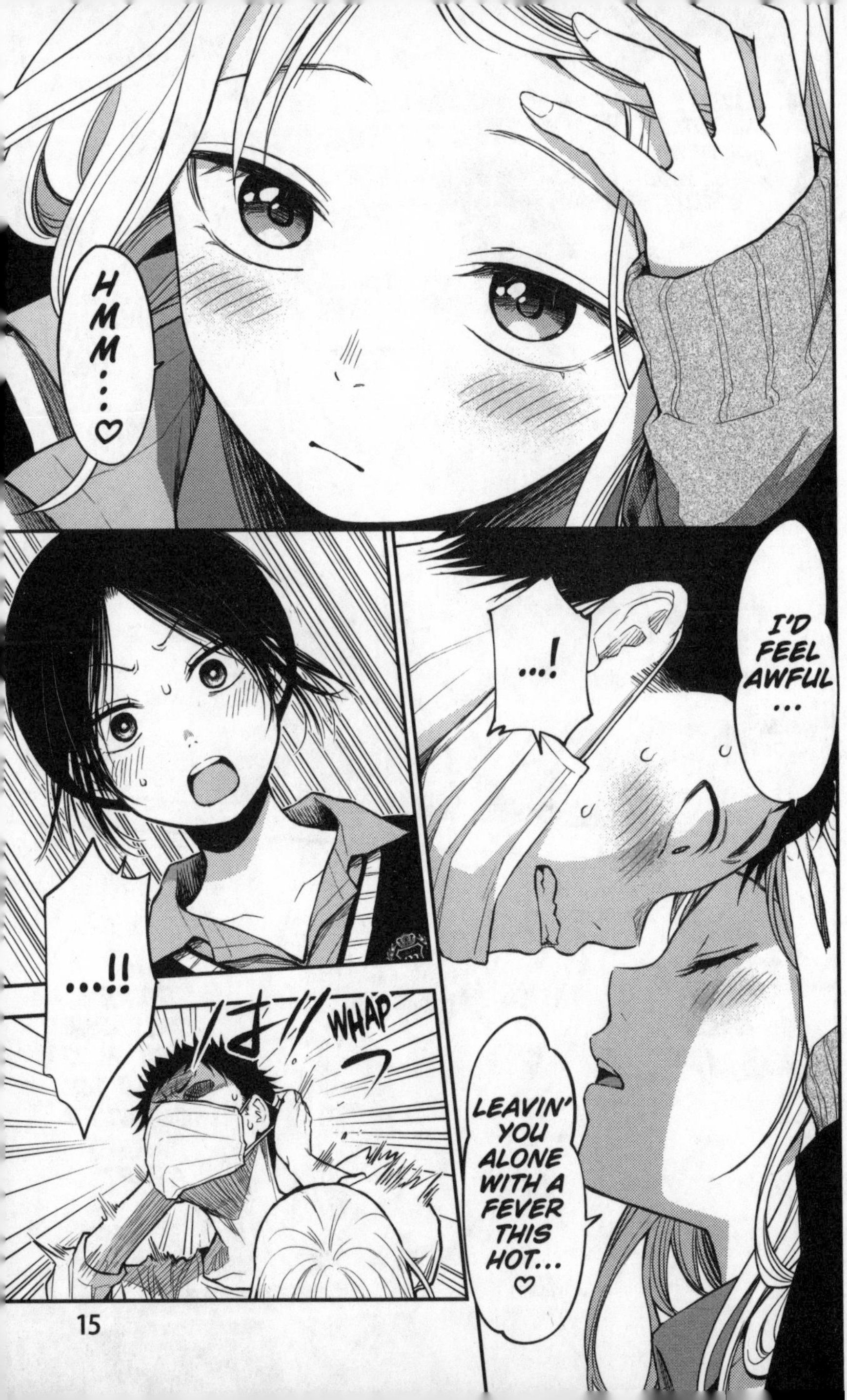
HMM...♡
I'D FEEL AWFUL...
...!
LEAVIN' YOU ALONE WITH A FEVER THIS HOT...♡
...!!
WHAP

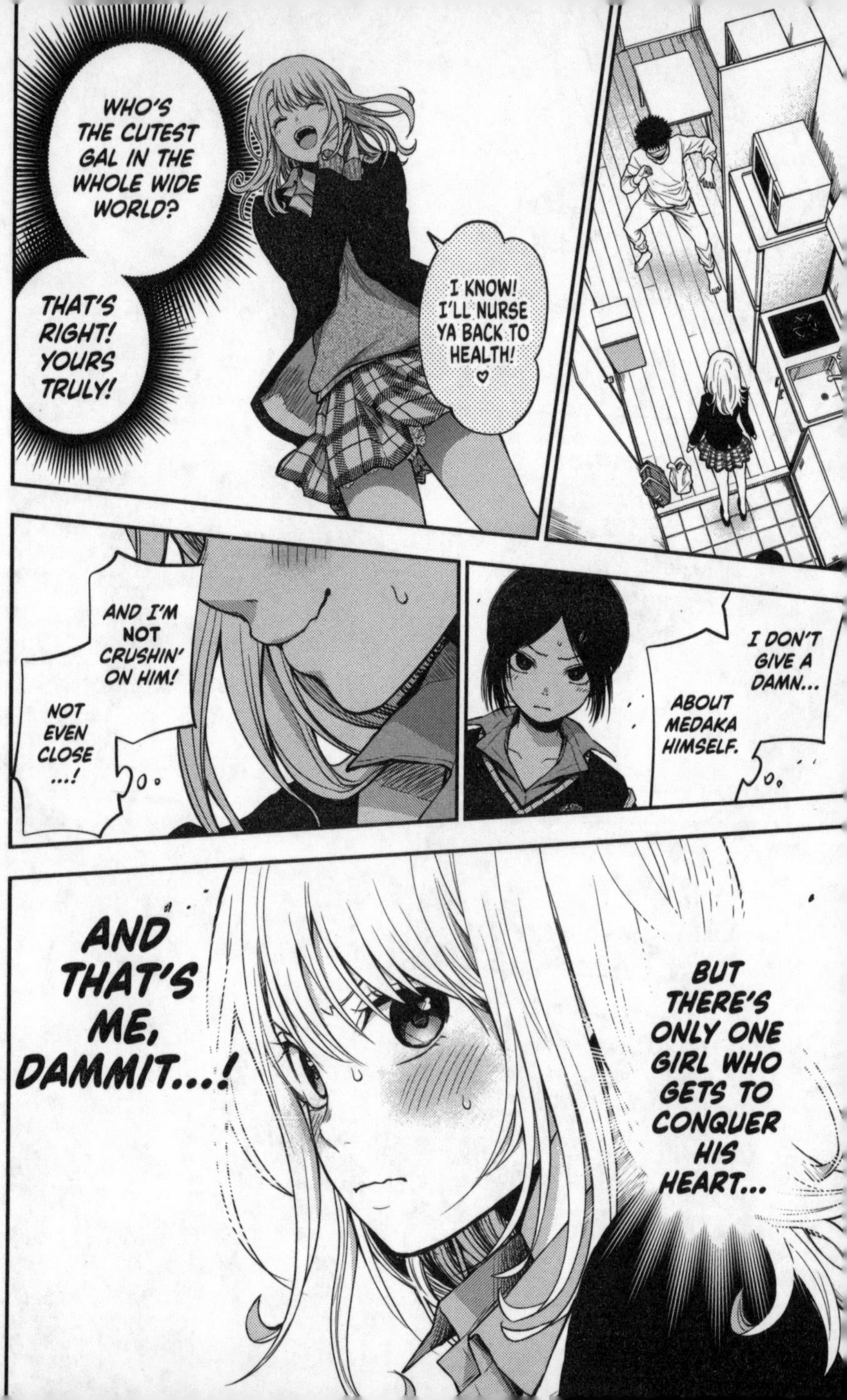
WHO'S THE CUTEST GAL IN THE WHOLE WIDE WORLD?
THAT'S RIGHT! YOURS TRULY!
I KNOW! I'LL NURSE YA BACK TO HEALTH! ♡
I DON'T GIVE A DAMN...
ABOUT MEDAKA HIMSELF.
AND I'M NOT CRUSHIN' ON HIM!
NOT EVEN CLOSE ...!
BUT THERE'S ONLY ONE GIRL WHO GETS TO CONQUER HIS HEART...
AND THAT'S ME, DAMMIT...!

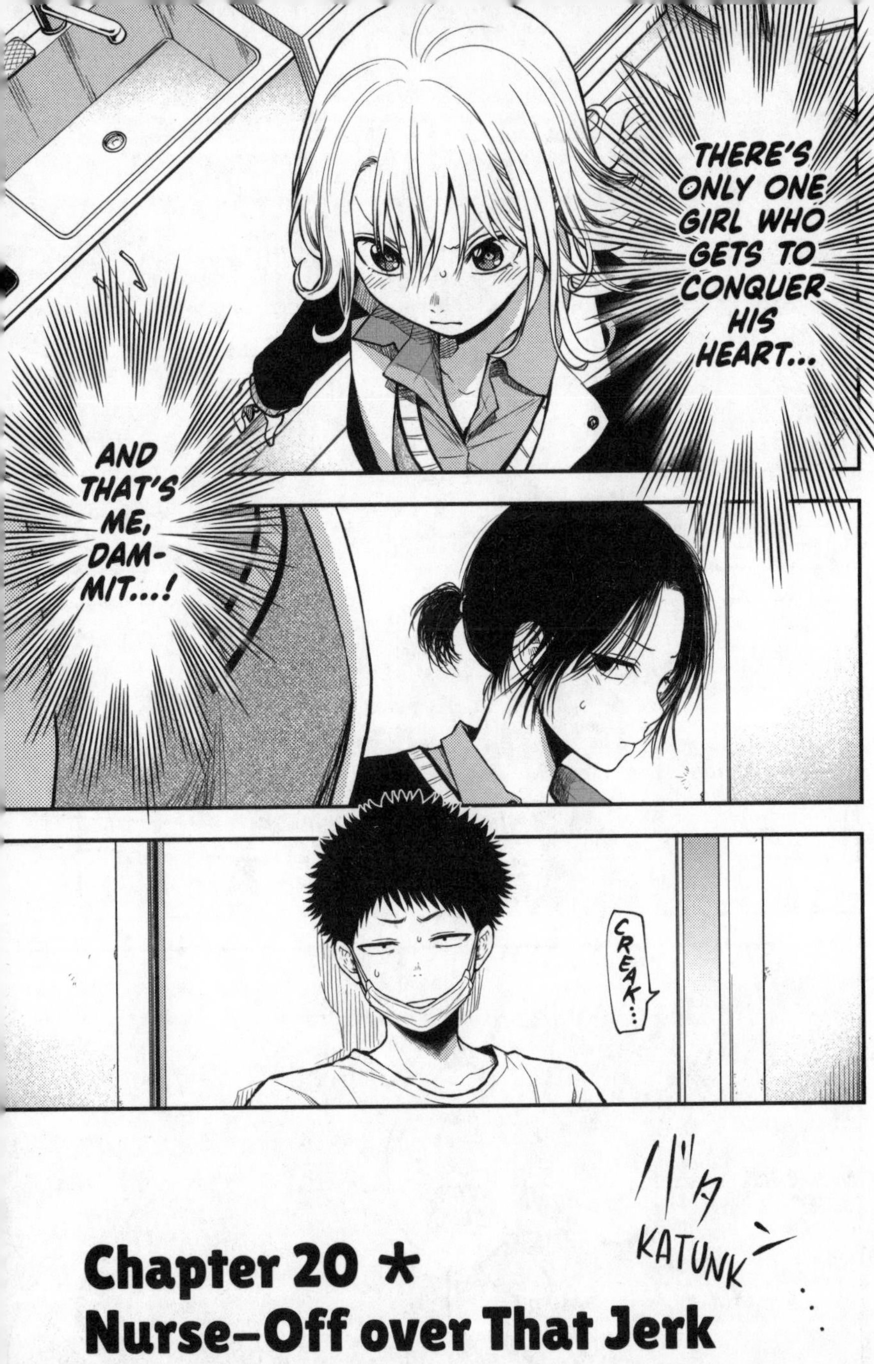
THERE'S ONLY ONE GIRL WHO GETS TO CONQUER HIS HEART...
AND THAT'S ME, DAM-MIT...!
CREAK...
バタ
KATUNK

Chapter 20 ★ Nurse-Off over That Jerk

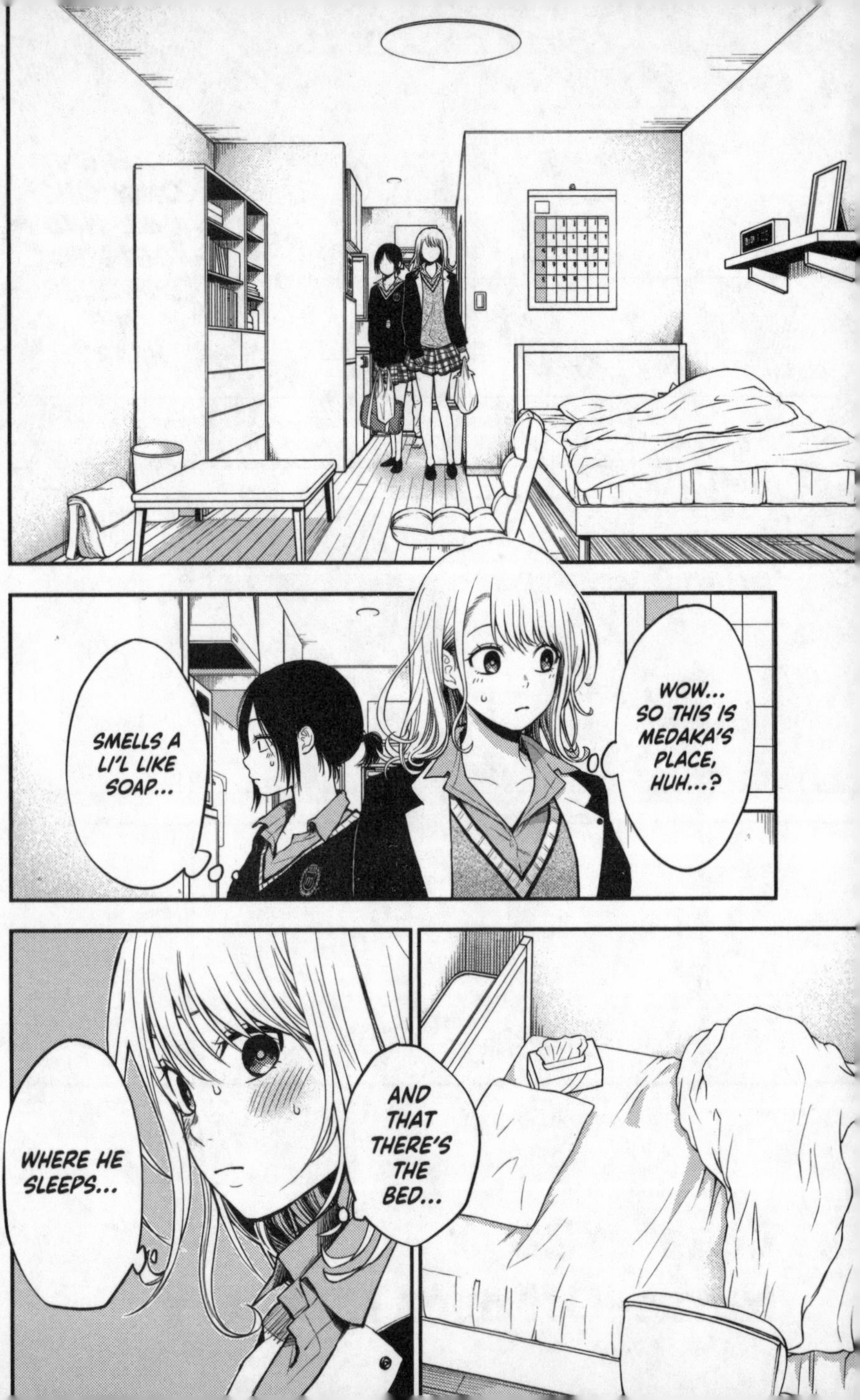
WOW... SO THIS IS MEDAKA'S PLACE, HUH...?
SMELLS A LI'L LIKE SOAP...
AND THAT THERE'S THE BED...
WHERE HE SLEEPS...

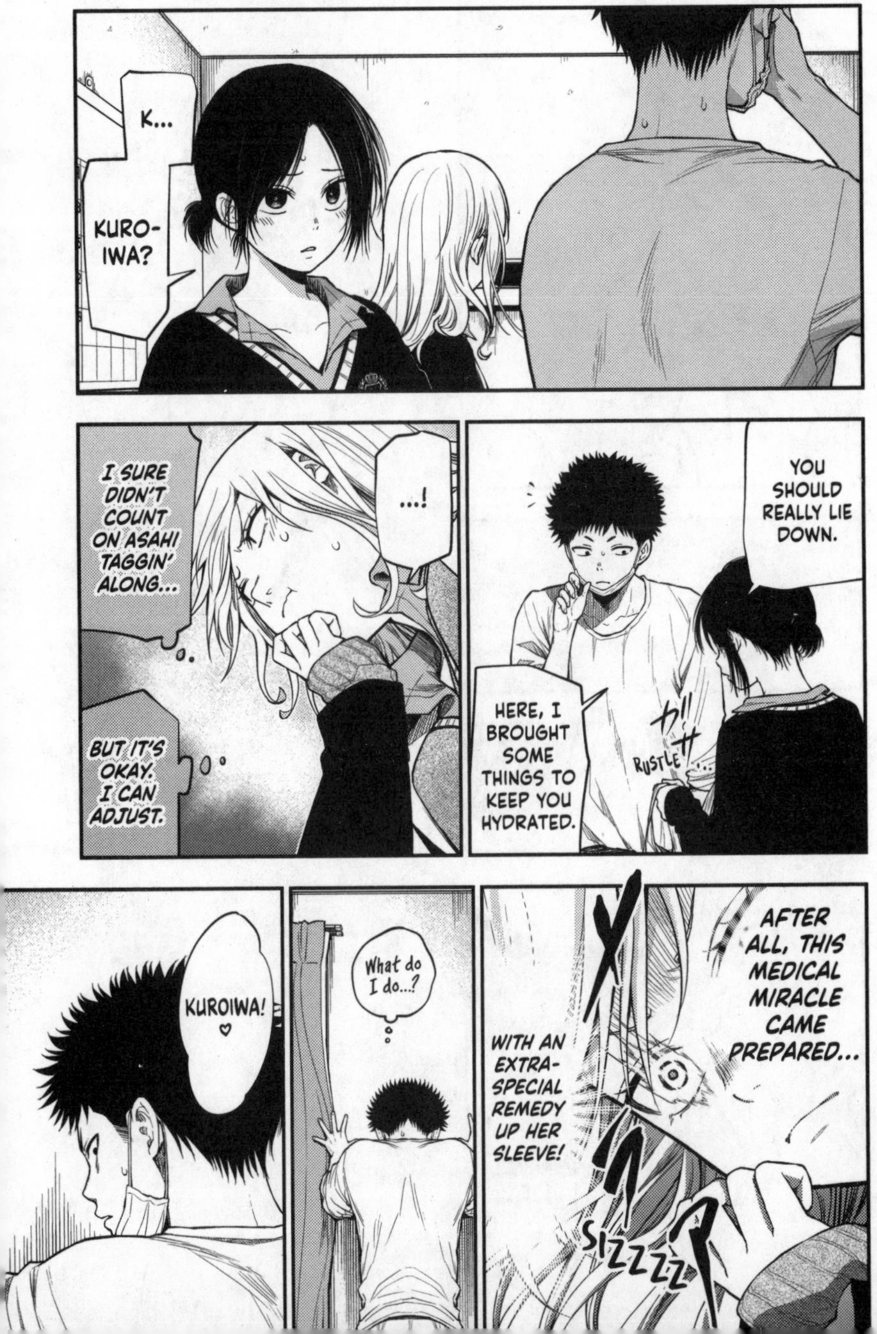
K...
KURO-IWA?
YOU SHOULD REALLY LIE DOWN.
HERE, I BROUGHT SOME THINGS TO KEEP YOU HYDRATED.
RUSTLE
...!
I SURE DIDN'T COUNT ON ASAHI TAGGIN' ALONG...
BUT IT'S OKAY. I CAN ADJUST.
AFTER ALL, THIS MEDICAL MIRACLE CAME PREPARED...
WITH AN EXTRA-SPECIAL REMEDY UP HER SLEEVE!
SIZZZZZ
What do I do...?
KUROIWA! ♡

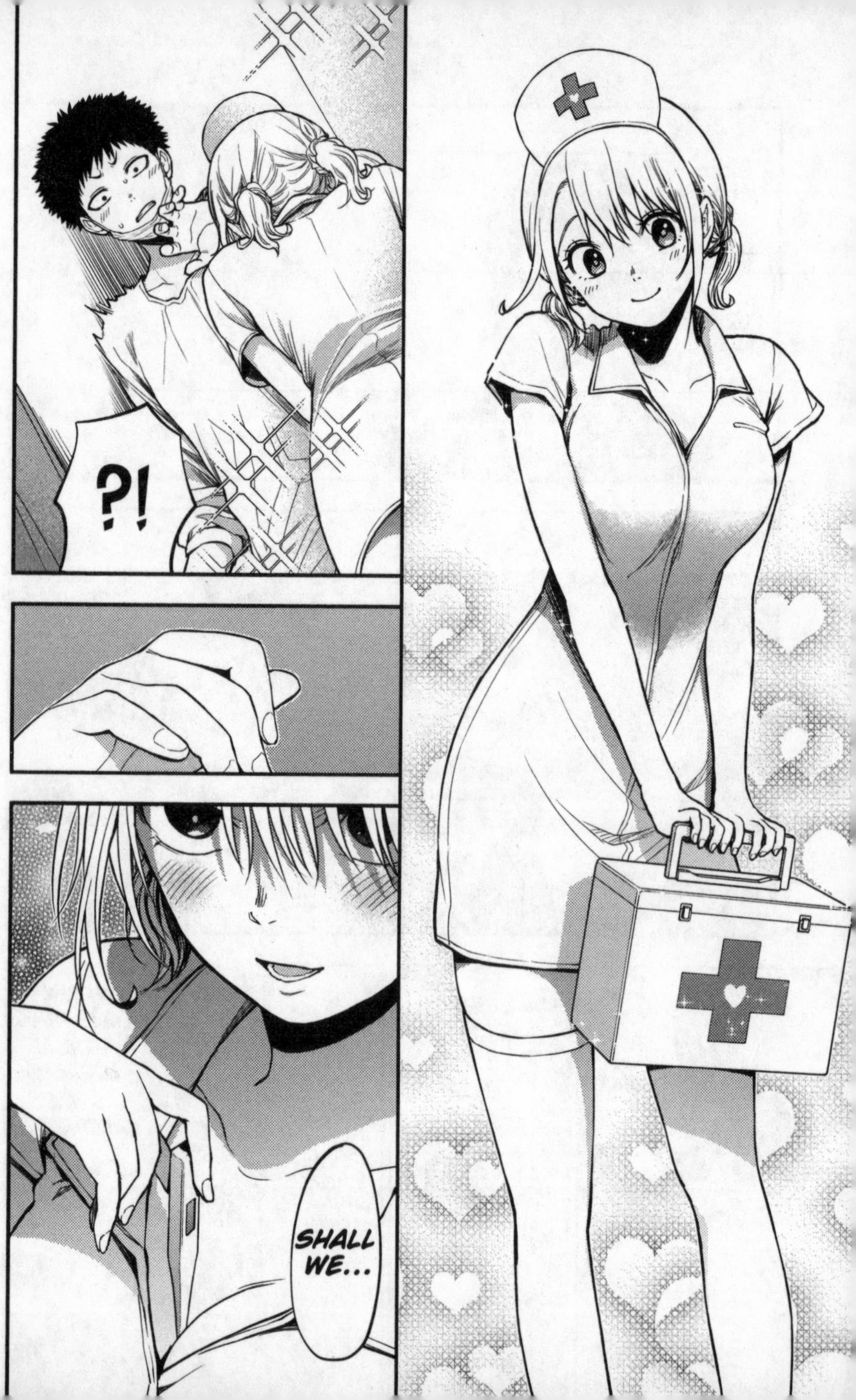
?!
SHALL WE...

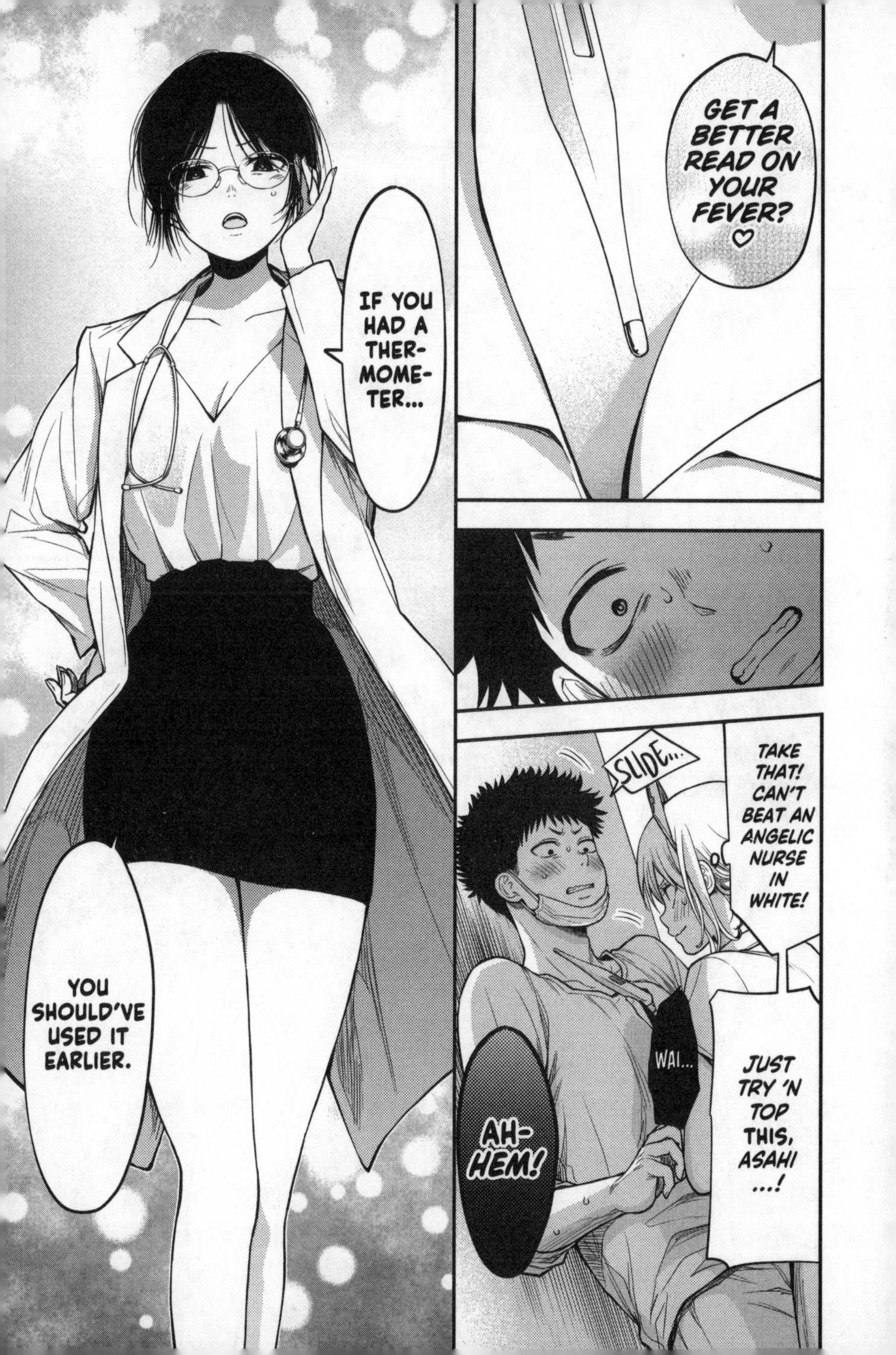
GET A BETTER READ ON YOUR FEVER? ♡
TAKE THAT! CAN'T BEAT AN ANGELIC NURSE IN WHITE!
SLIDE...
JUST TRY 'N TOP THIS, ASAHI...!
WAI...
AH-HEM!
IF YOU HAD A THER-MOME-TER...
YOU SHOULD'VE USED IT EARLIER.

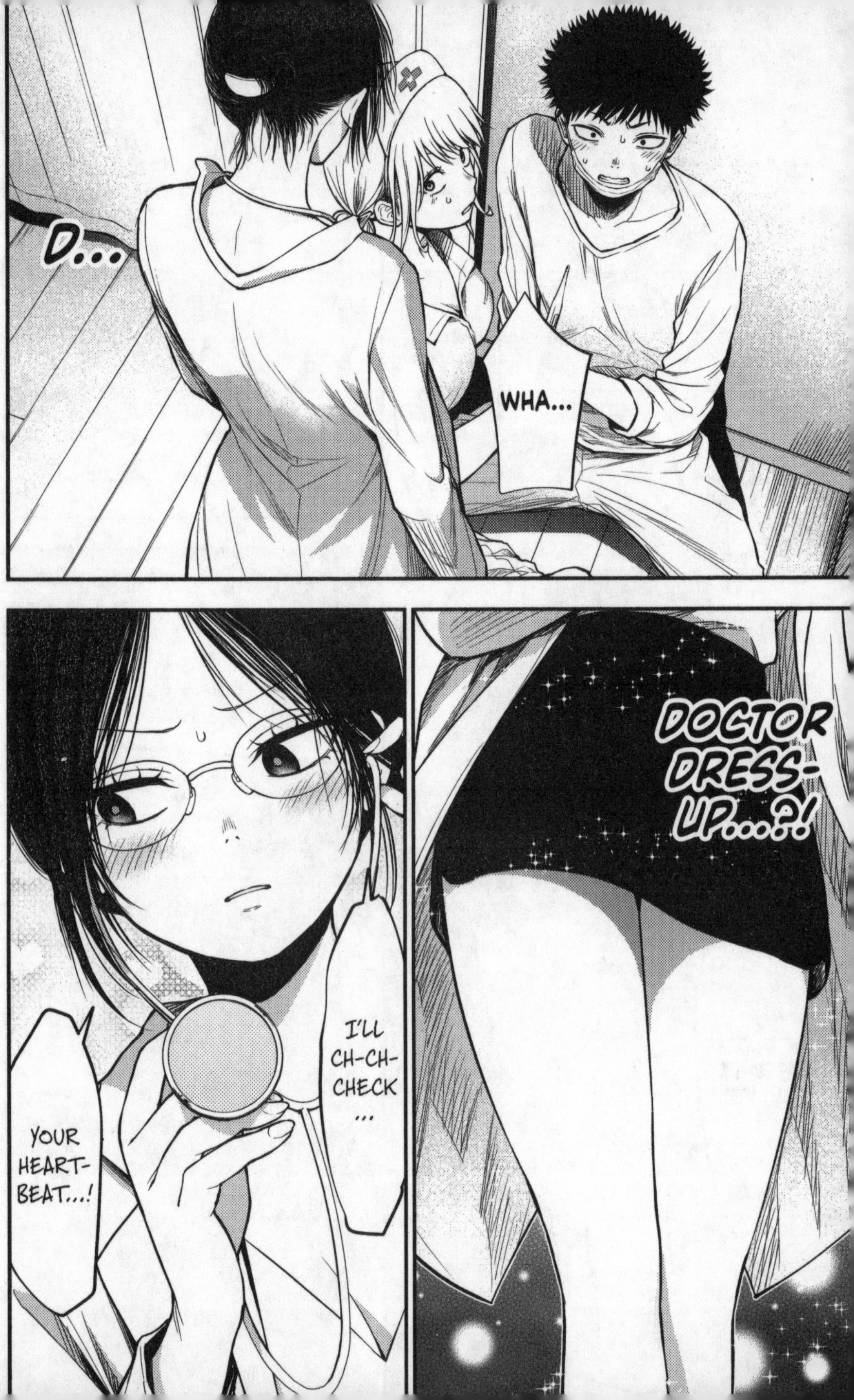
WHA...
D...
DOCTOR DRESS-UP...?!
I'LL CH-CH-CHECK ...
YOUR HEART-BEAT...!

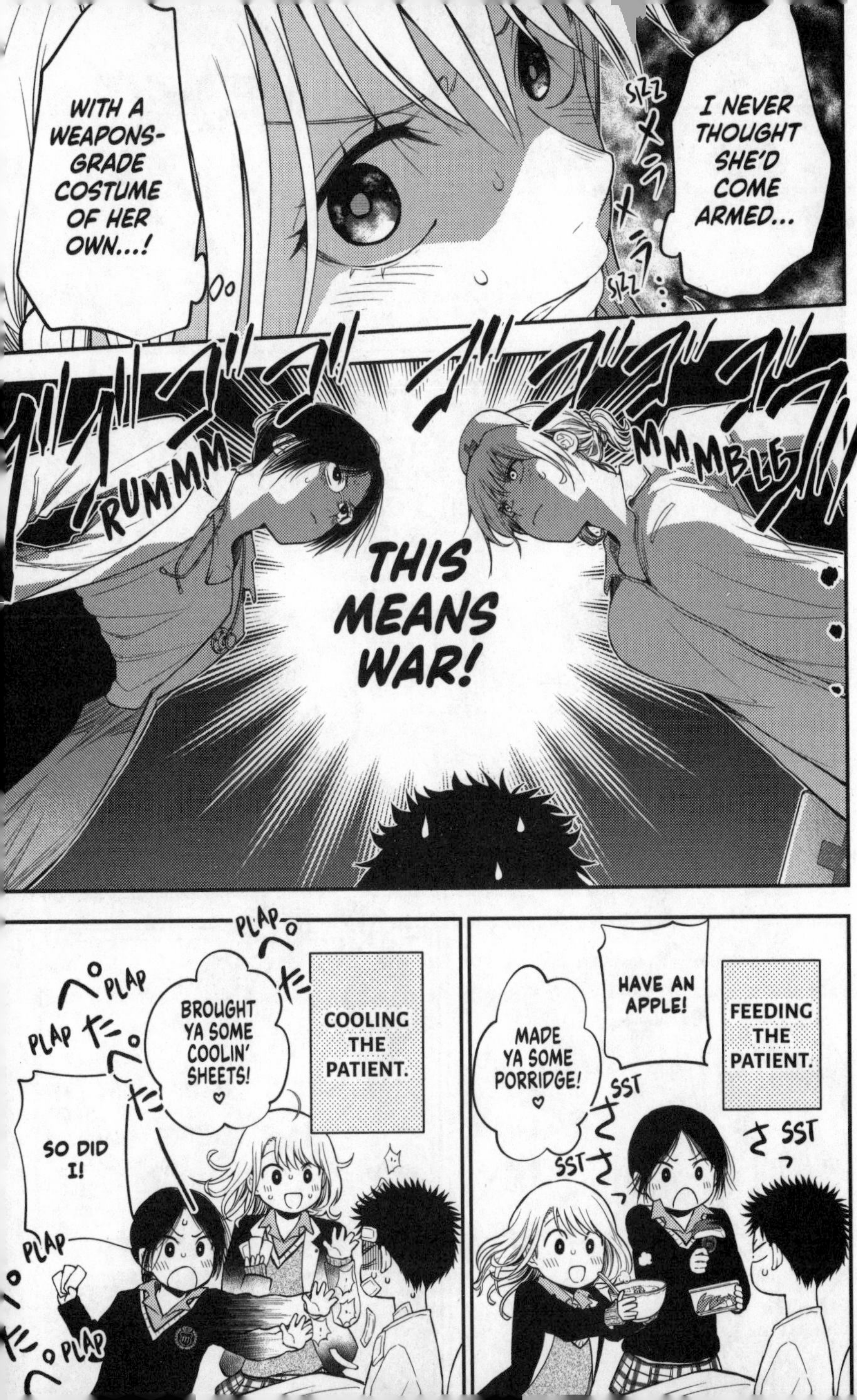
I NEVER THOUGHT SHE'D COME ARMED...
SIZZ
SIZZ
WITH A WEAPONS-GRADE COSTUME OF HER OWN...!
RUMMMMMBLE
THIS MEANS WAR!
FEEDING THE PATIENT.
SST
HAVE AN APPLE!
SST
MADE YA SOME PORRIDGE! ♡
SST
COOLING THE PATIENT.
PLAP
BROUGHT YA SOME COOLIN' SHEETS! ♡
PLAP
PLAP
SO DID I!
PLAP
PLAP

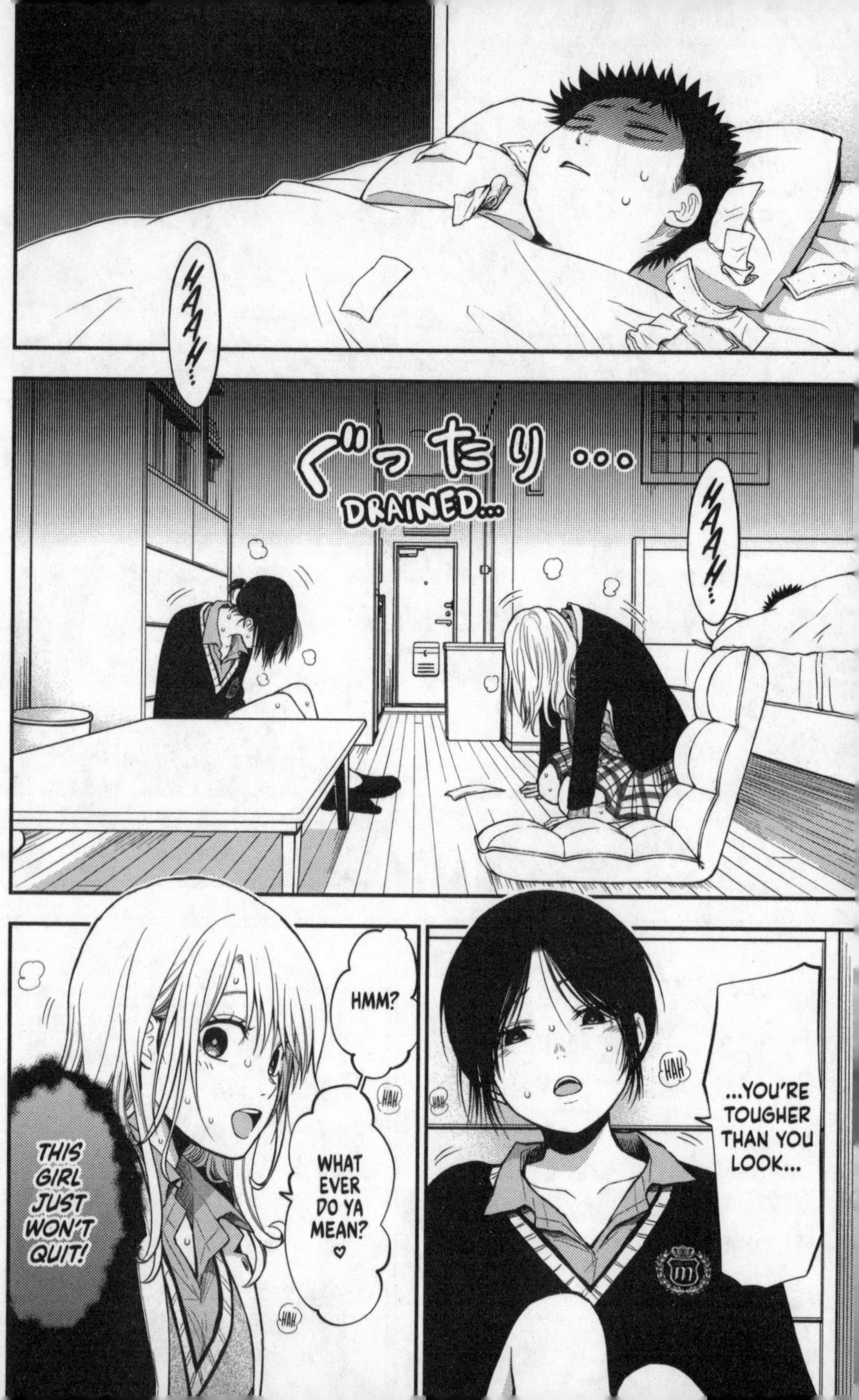

HAAAH...
HAAAH...
ぐったり...
DRAINED...
...YOU'RE TOUGHER THAN YOU LOOK...
HAH
HAH
HMM?
HAH
WHAT EVER DO YA MEAN? ♡
HAH
THIS GIRL JUST WON'T QUIT!

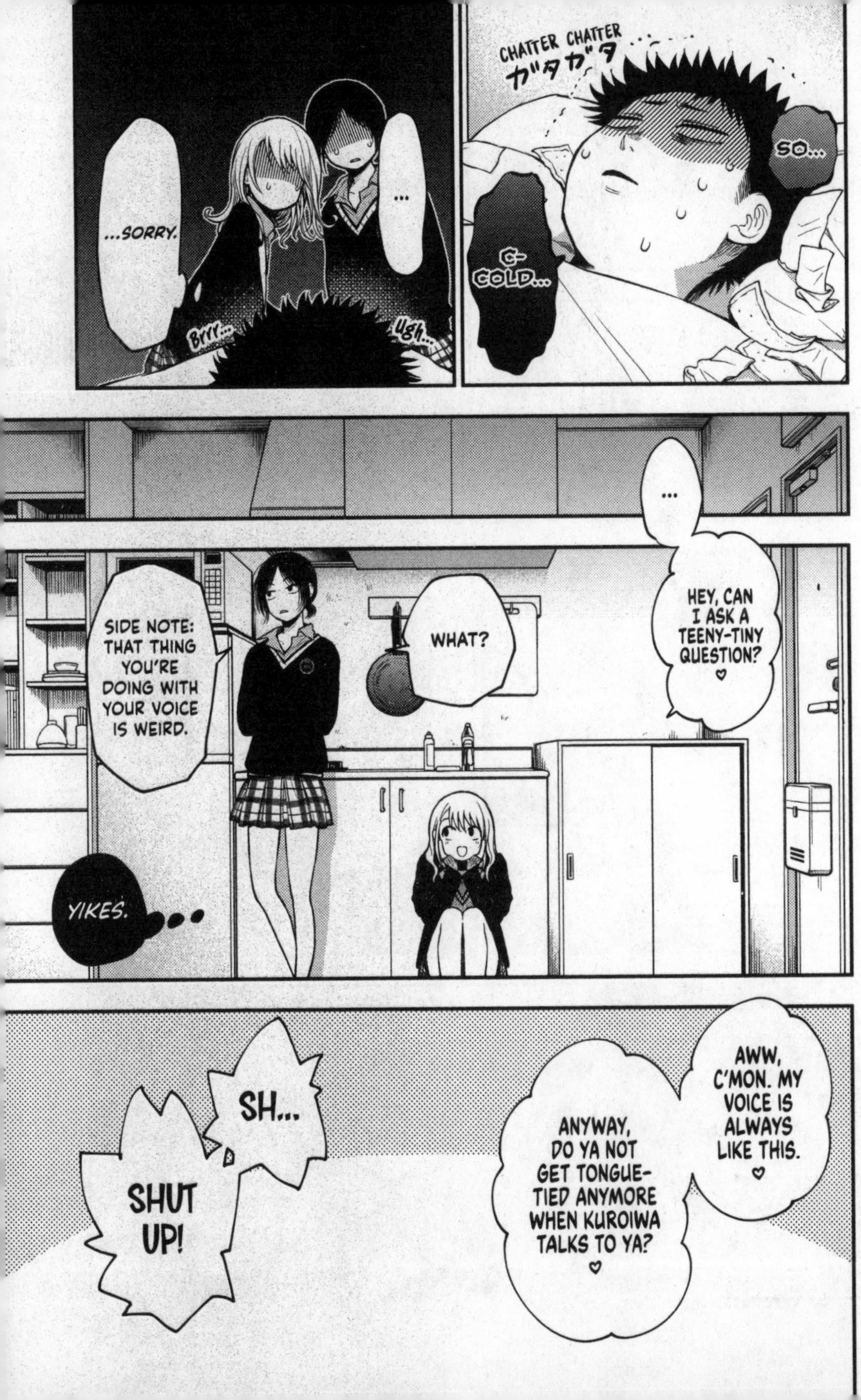
CHATTER CHATTER ガタガタ
SO...
C-COLD...
...
...SORRY.
Ugh...
Brrr...
...
HEY, CAN I ASK A TEENY-TINY QUESTION? ♡
WHAT?
SIDE NOTE: THAT THING YOU'RE DOING WITH YOUR VOICE IS WEIRD.
YIKES.
AWW, C'MON. MY VOICE IS ALWAYS LIKE THIS. ♡
ANYWAY, DO YA NOT GET TONGUE-TIED ANYMORE WHEN KUROIWA TALKS TO YA? ♡
SH...
SHUT UP!

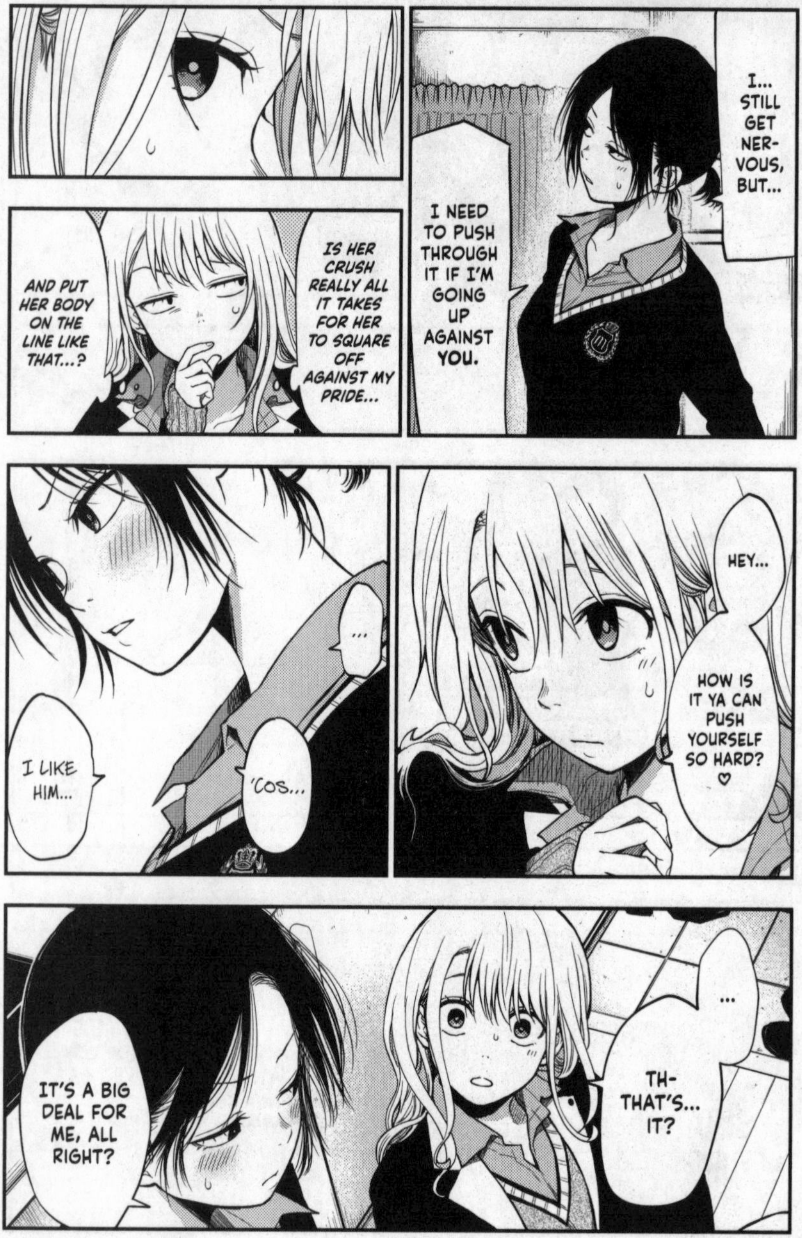
I... STILL GET NER-VOUS, BUT...
I NEED TO PUSH THROUGH IT IF I'M GOING UP AGAINST YOU.
IS HER CRUSH REALLY ALL IT TAKES FOR HER TO SQUARE OFF AGAINST MY PRIDE...
AND PUT HER BODY ON THE LINE LIKE THAT...?
HEY...
HOW IS IT YA CAN PUSH YOURSELF SO HARD? ♡
...
'COS...
I LIKE HIM...
...
TH-THAT'S... IT?
IT'S A BIG DEAL FOR ME, ALL RIGHT?

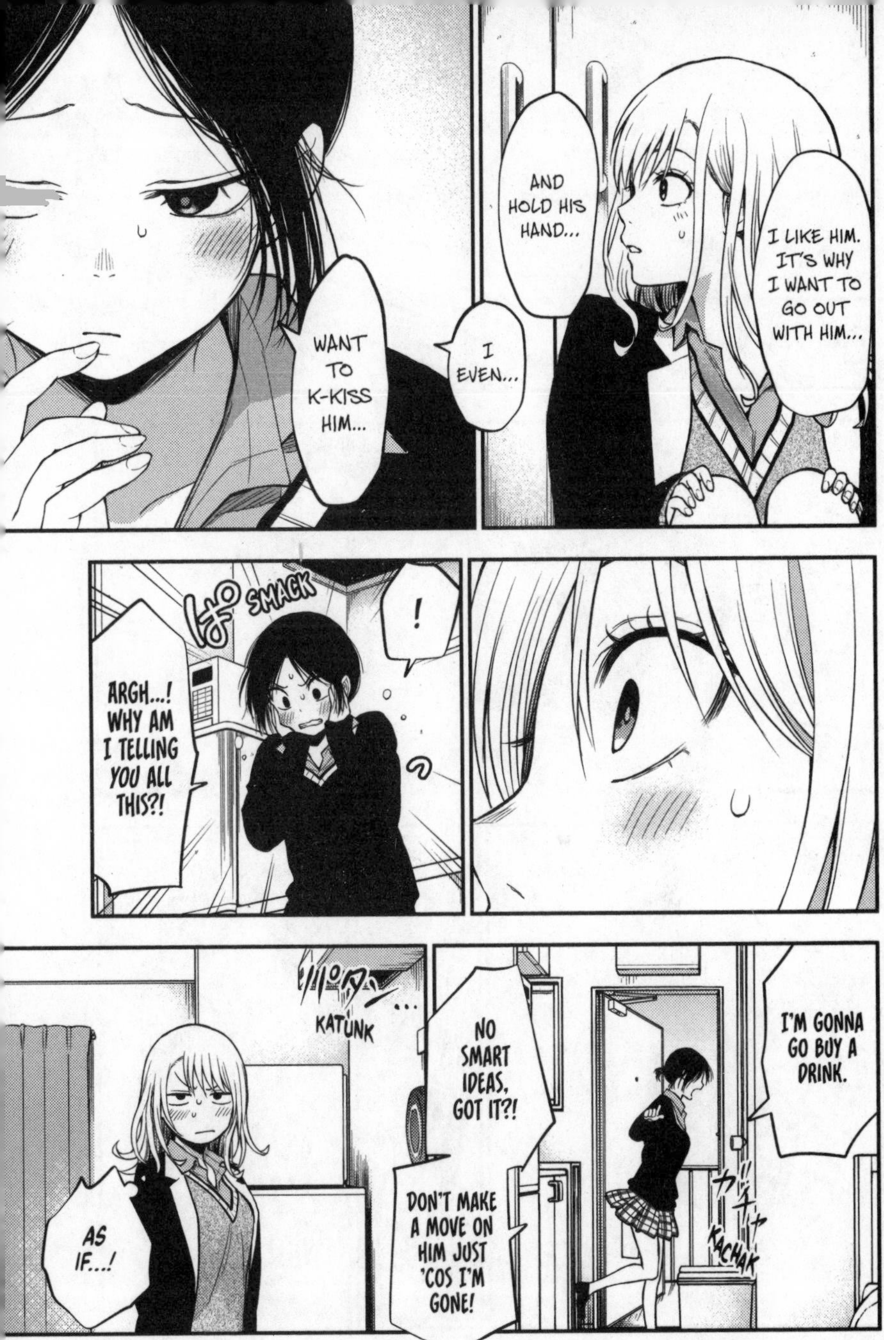
I LIKE HIM. IT'S WHY I WANT TO GO OUT WITH HIM...
AND HOLD HIS HAND...
I EVEN...
WANT TO K-KISS HIM...
!
SMACK
ARGH...! WHY AM I TELLING YOU ALL THIS?!
I'M GONNA GO BUY A DRINK.
KACHAK
NO SMART IDEAS, GOT IT?!
DON'T MAKE A MOVE ON HIM JUST 'COS I'M GONE!
KATUNK
AS IF...!

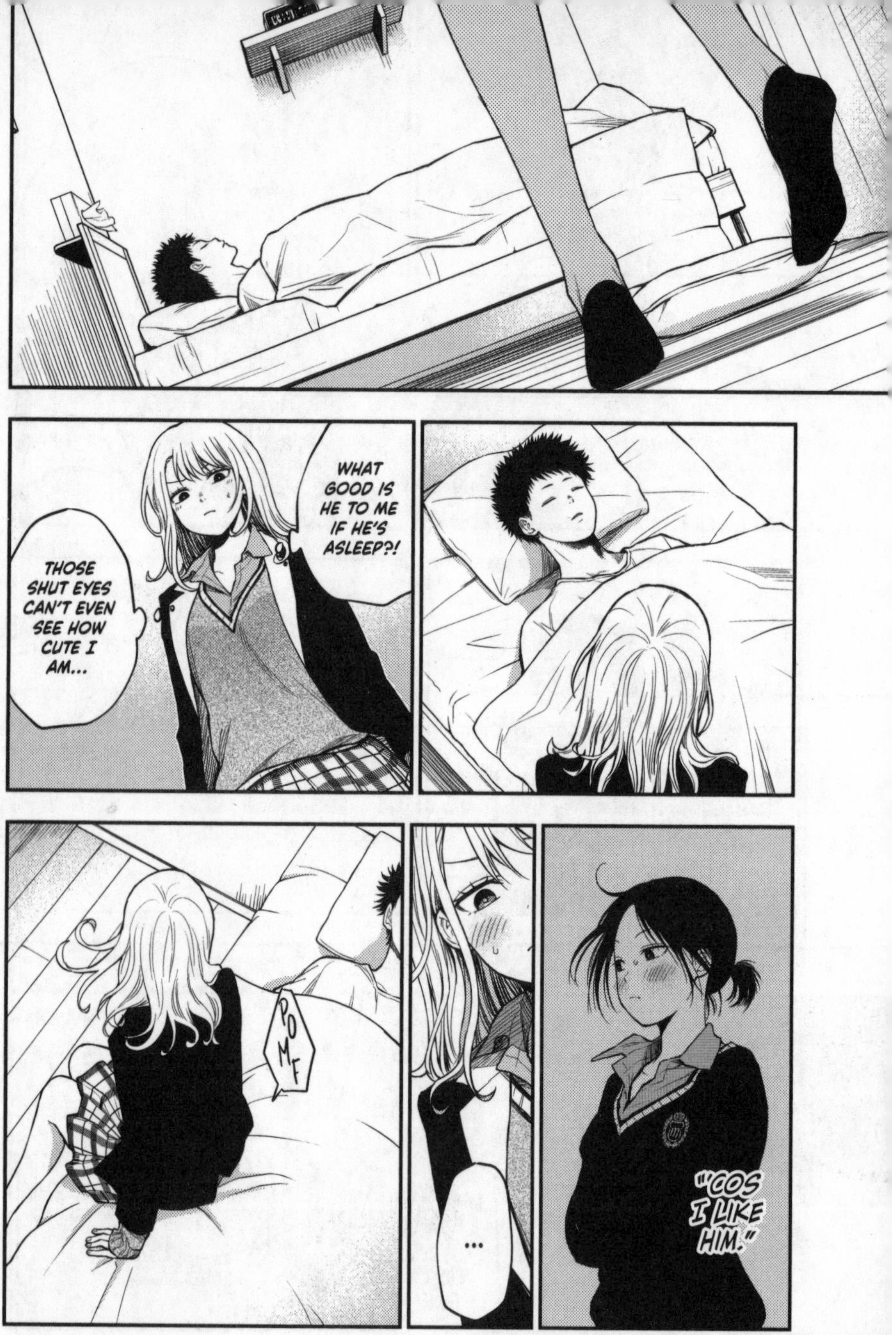
WHAT GOOD IS HE TO ME IF HE'S ASLEEP?!
THOSE SHUT EYES CAN'T EVEN SEE HOW CUTE I AM...
"COS I LIKE HIM."
...
POMF

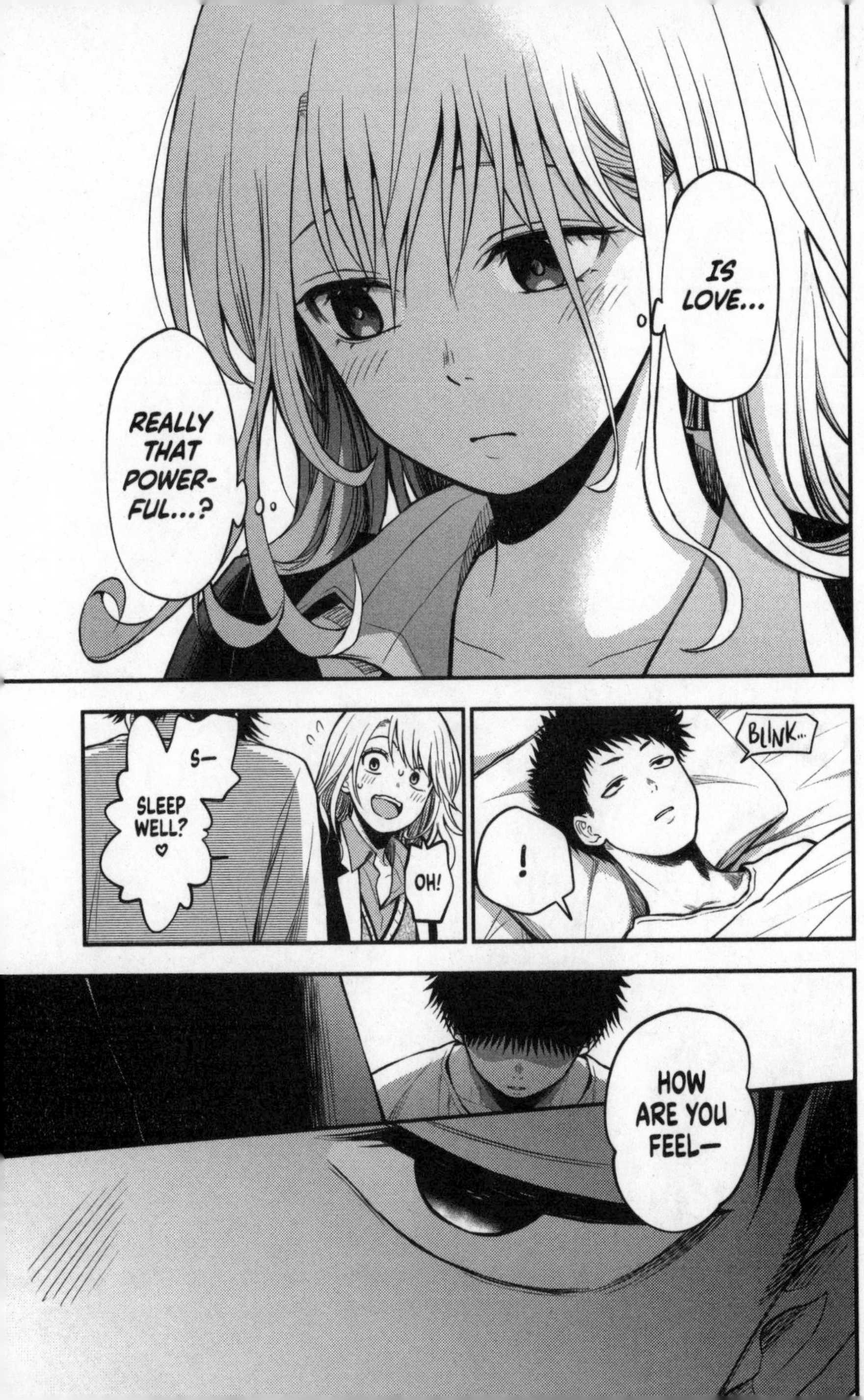
IS LOVE...
REALLY THAT POWER-FUL...?
BLINK...
!
OH!
S— SLEEP WELL? ♡
HOW ARE YOU FEEL—

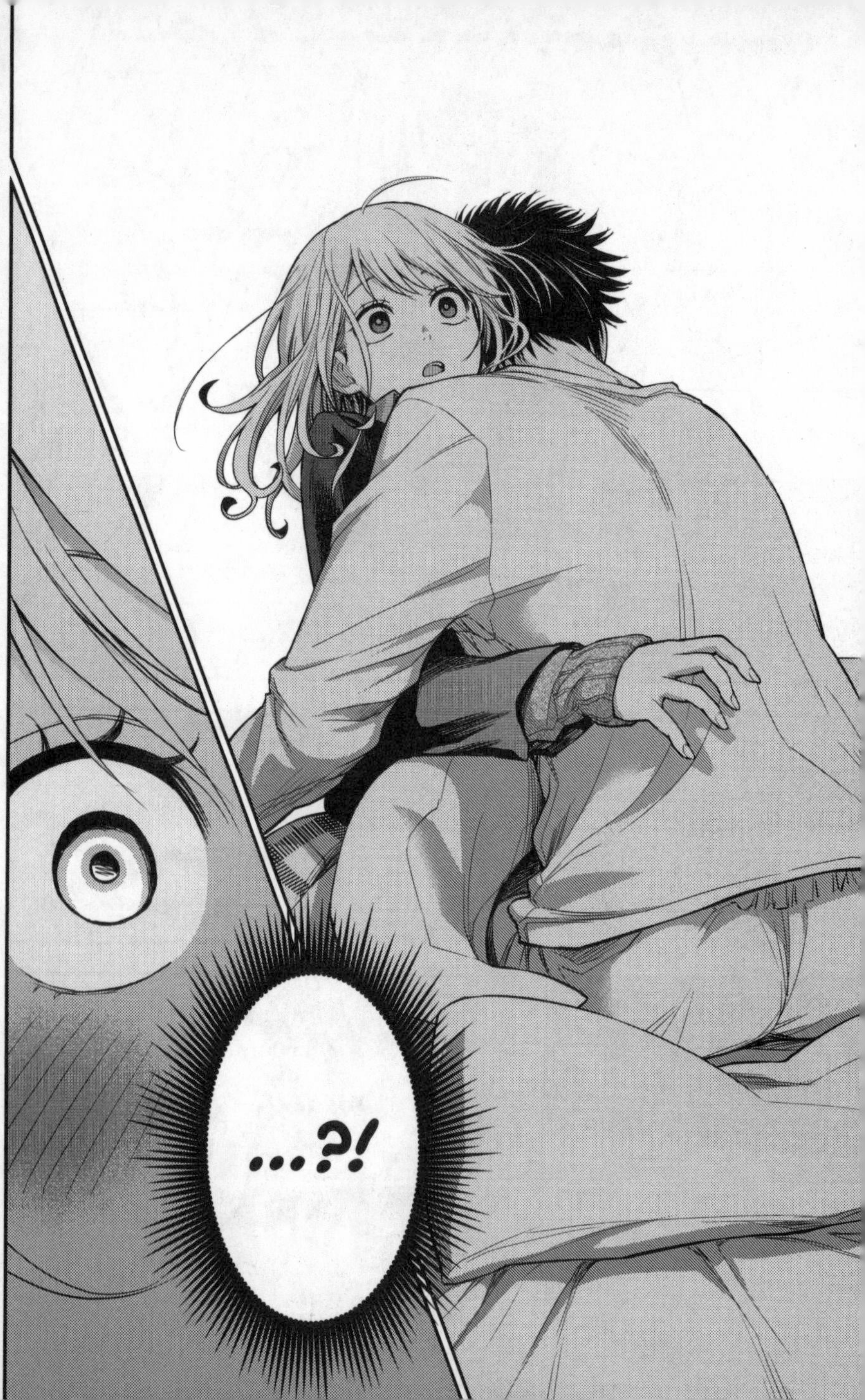
...?!

Chapter 21 ★ A K*** with That Jerk

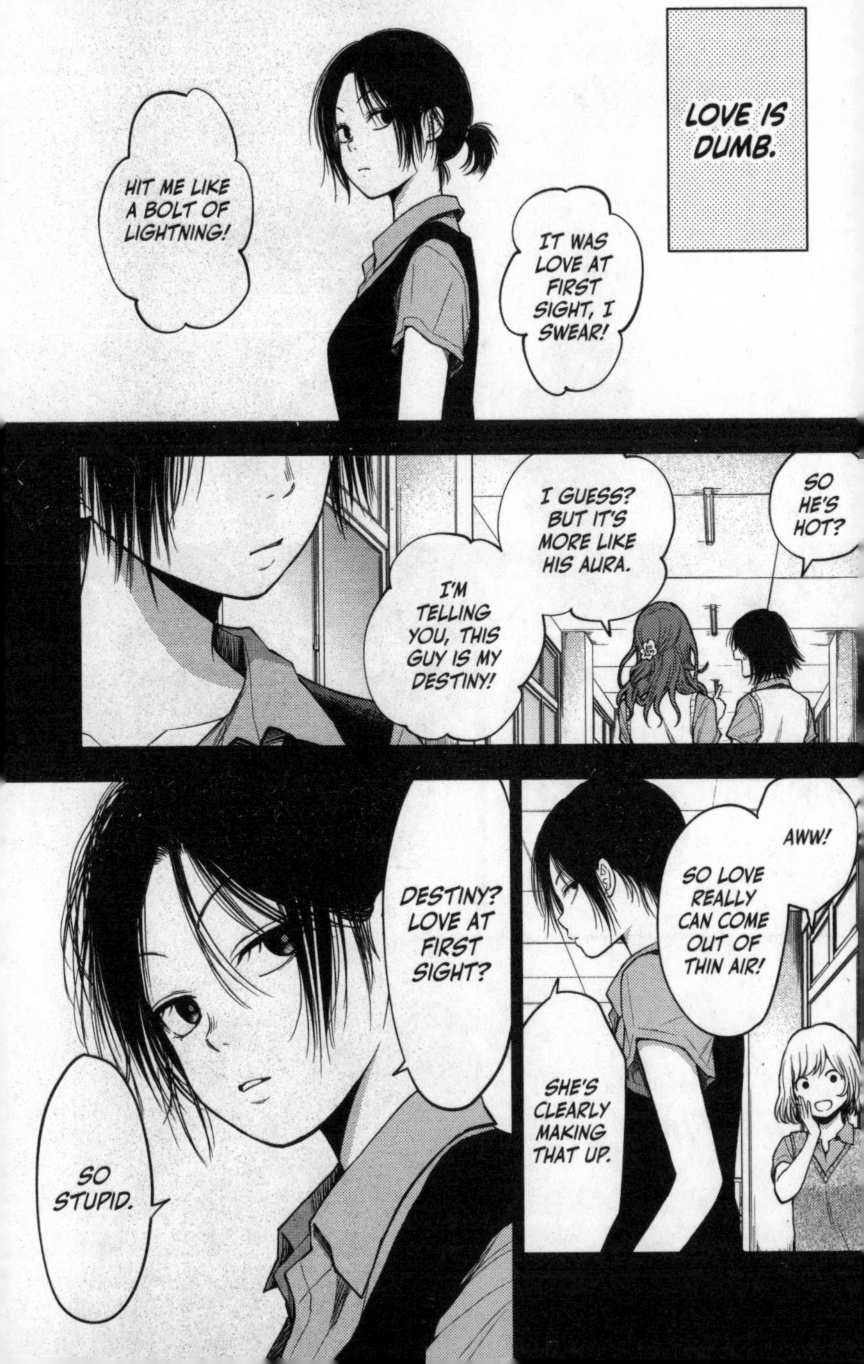
LOVE IS DUMB.
IT WAS LOVE AT FIRST SIGHT, I SWEAR!
HIT ME LIKE A BOLT OF LIGHTNING!
SO HE'S HOT?
I GUESS? BUT IT'S MORE LIKE HIS AURA.
I'M TELLING YOU, THIS GUY IS MY DESTINY!
AWW!
SO LOVE REALLY CAN COME OUT OF THIN AIR!
SHE'S CLEARLY MAKING THAT UP.
DESTINY? LOVE AT FIRST SIGHT?
SO STUPID.

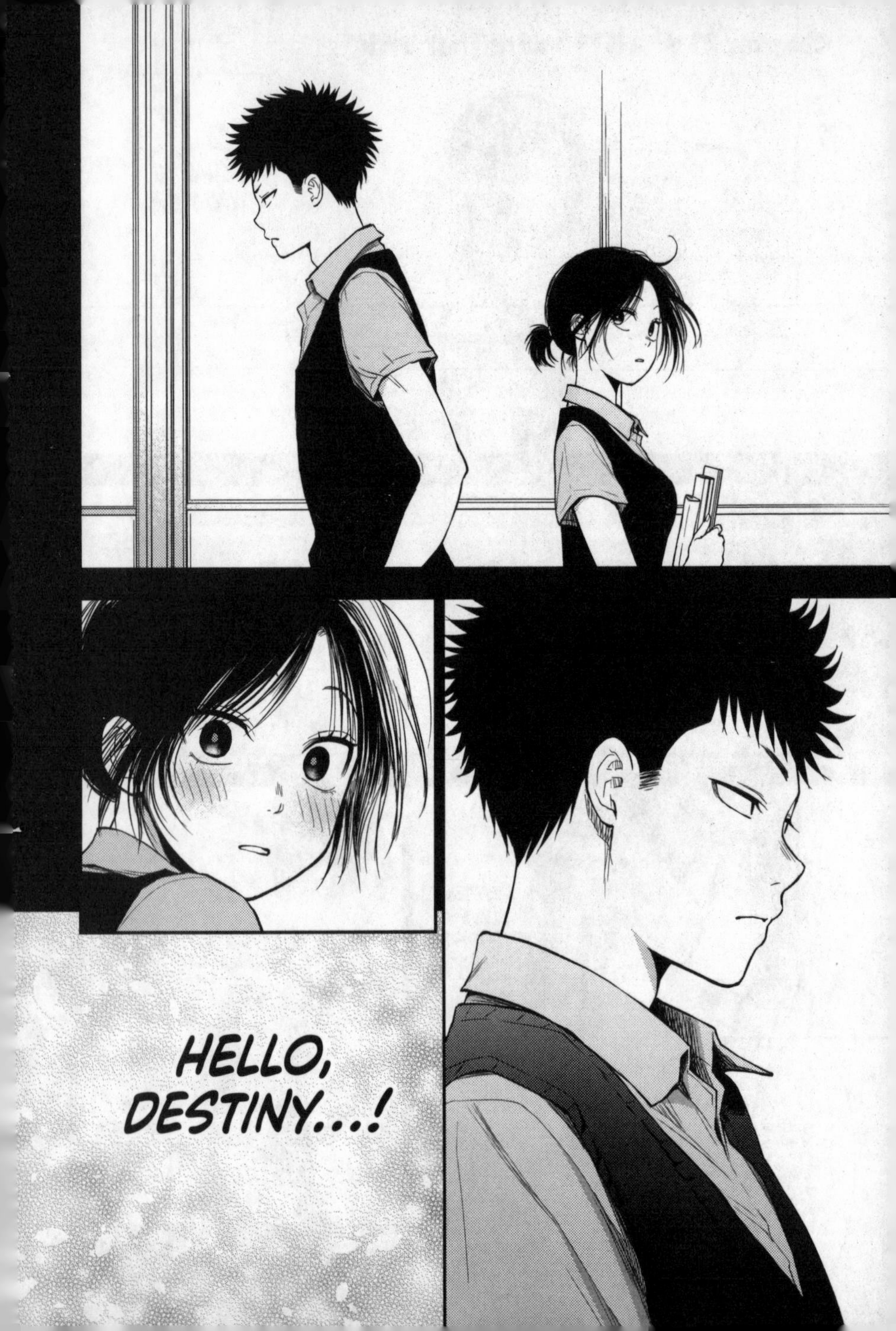
HELLO, DESTINY...!

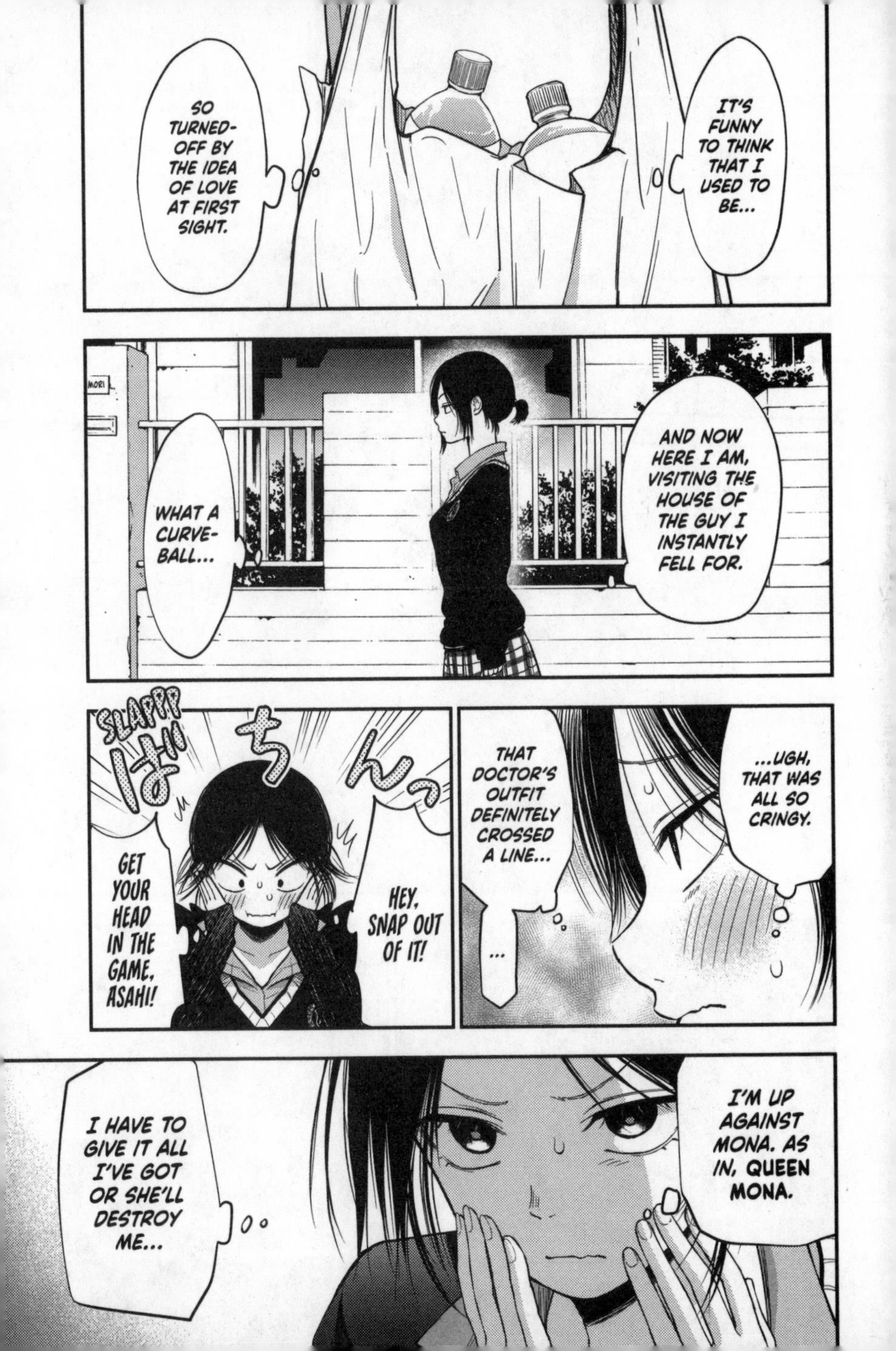
IT'S FUNNY TO THINK THAT I USED TO BE...
SO TURNED-OFF BY THE IDEA OF LOVE AT FIRST SIGHT.
MORI
AND NOW HERE I AM, VISITING THE HOUSE OF THE GUY I INSTANTLY FELL FOR.
WHAT A CURVE-BALL...
...UGH, THAT WAS ALL SO CRINGY.
THAT DOCTOR'S OUTFIT DEFINITELY CROSSED A LINE...
...
SLAPPP
ぱちんっ
HEY, SNAP OUT OF IT!
GET YOUR HEAD IN THE GAME, ASAHI!
I'M UP AGAINST MONA. AS IN, QUEEN MONA.
I HAVE TO GIVE IT ALL I'VE GOT OR SHE'LL DESTROY ME...

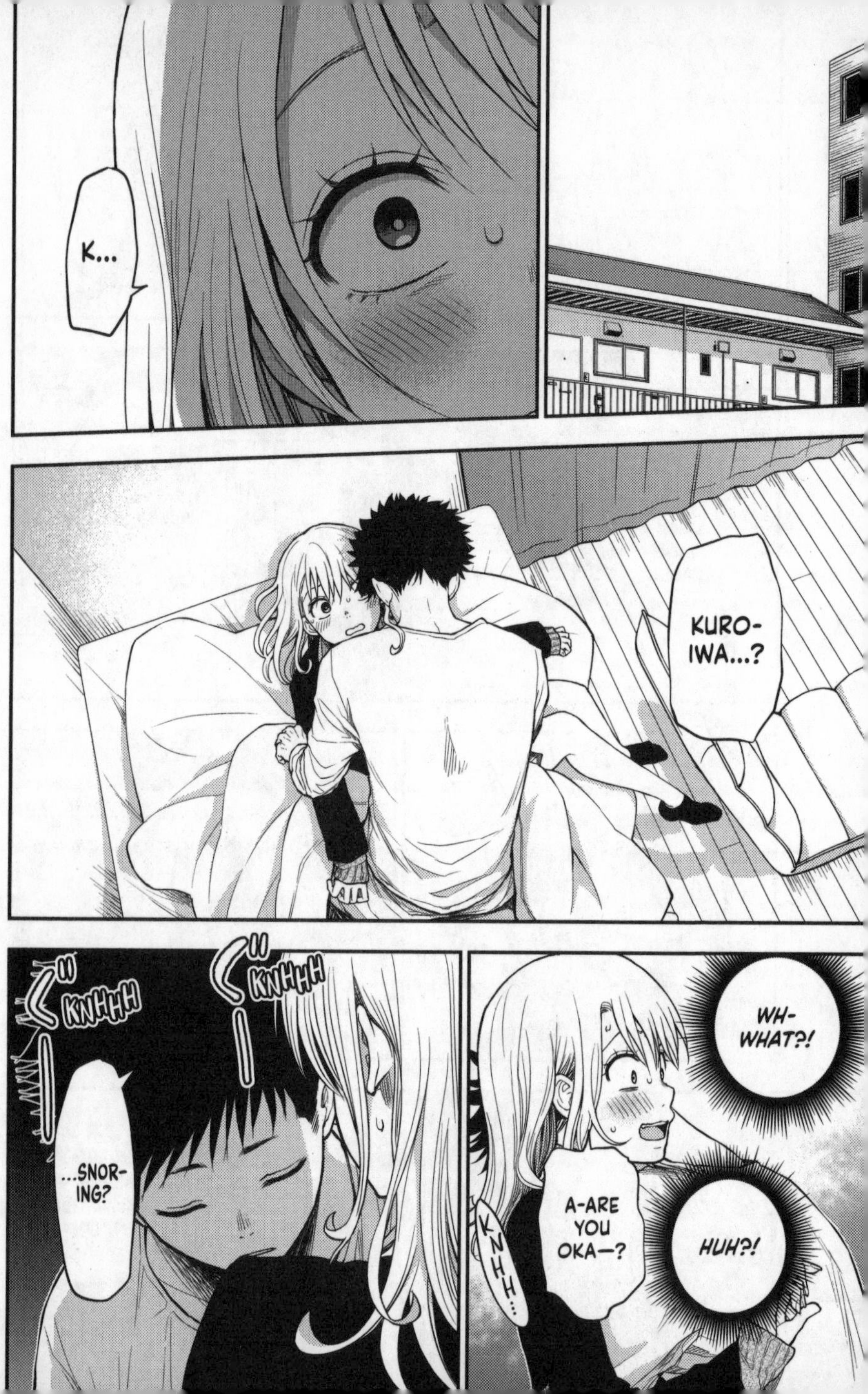
K...
KURO-
IWA...?
WH-
WHAT?!
A-ARE
YOU
OKA—?
HUH?!
KNHH...
KNHHH
KNHHH
...SNOR-
ING?

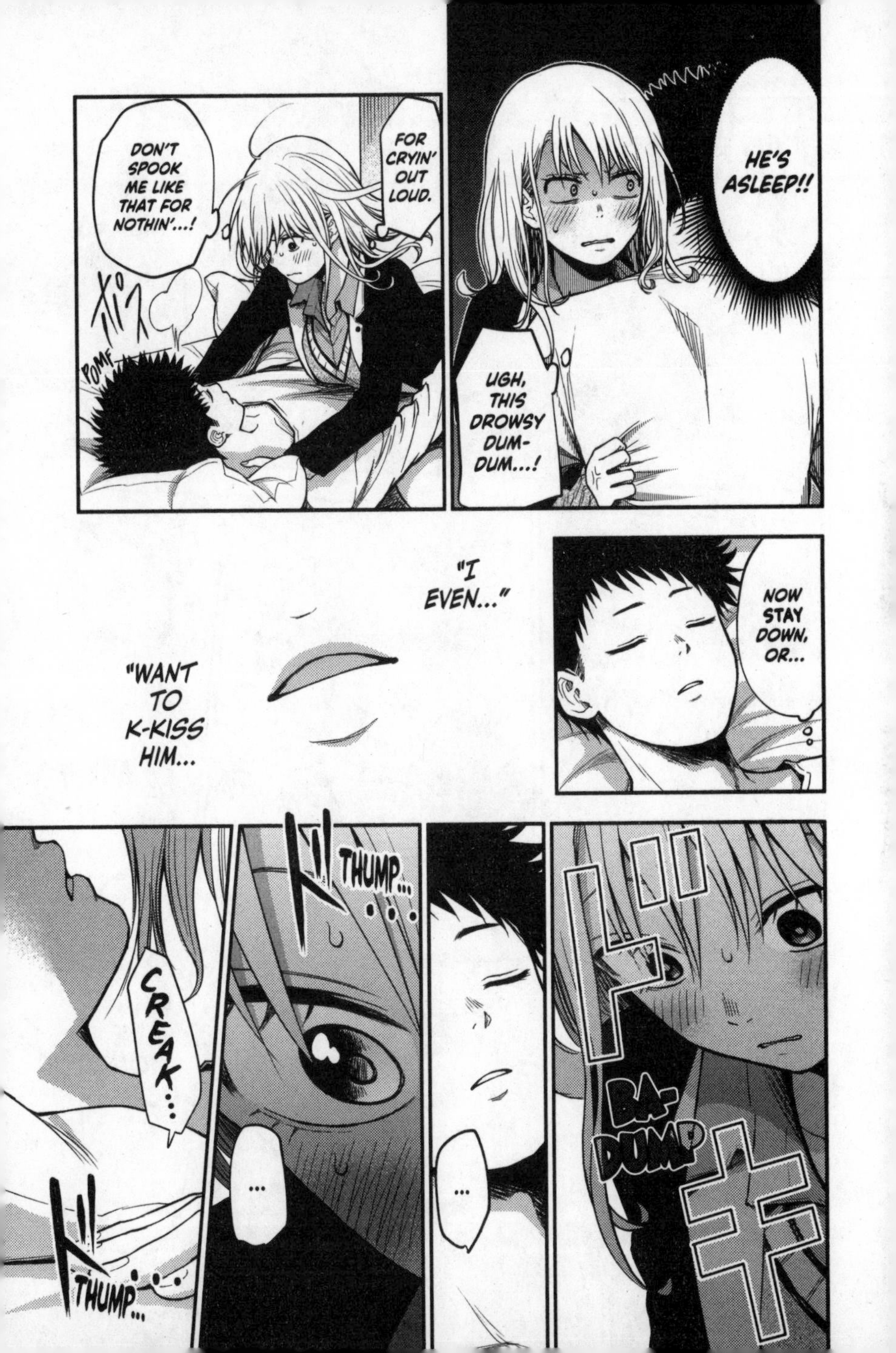
HE'S ASLEEP!!
UGH, THIS DROWSY DUM-DUM...!
FOR CRYIN' OUT LOUD.
DON'T SPOOK ME LIKE THAT FOR NOTHIN'...!
POMF
NOW STAY DOWN, OR...
"I EVEN..."
"WANT TO K-KISS HIM...
BA-DUMP
...
THUMP...
...
CREAK...
THUMP...

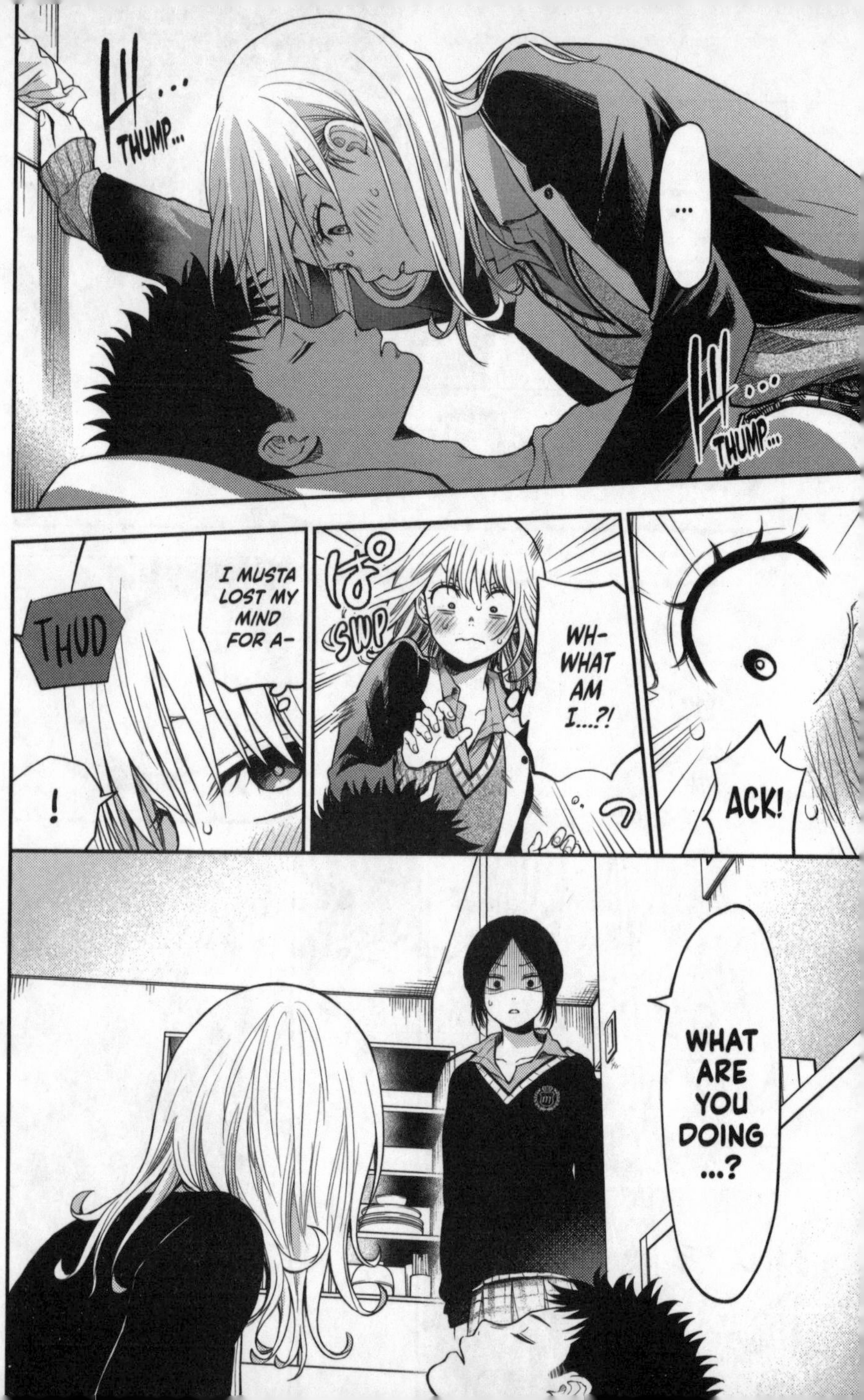
...
THUMP...
THUMP...
ACK!
ぱ
SWP
WH- WHAT AM I...?!
I MUSTA LOST MY MIND FOR A-
THUD
!
WHAT ARE YOU DOING ...?

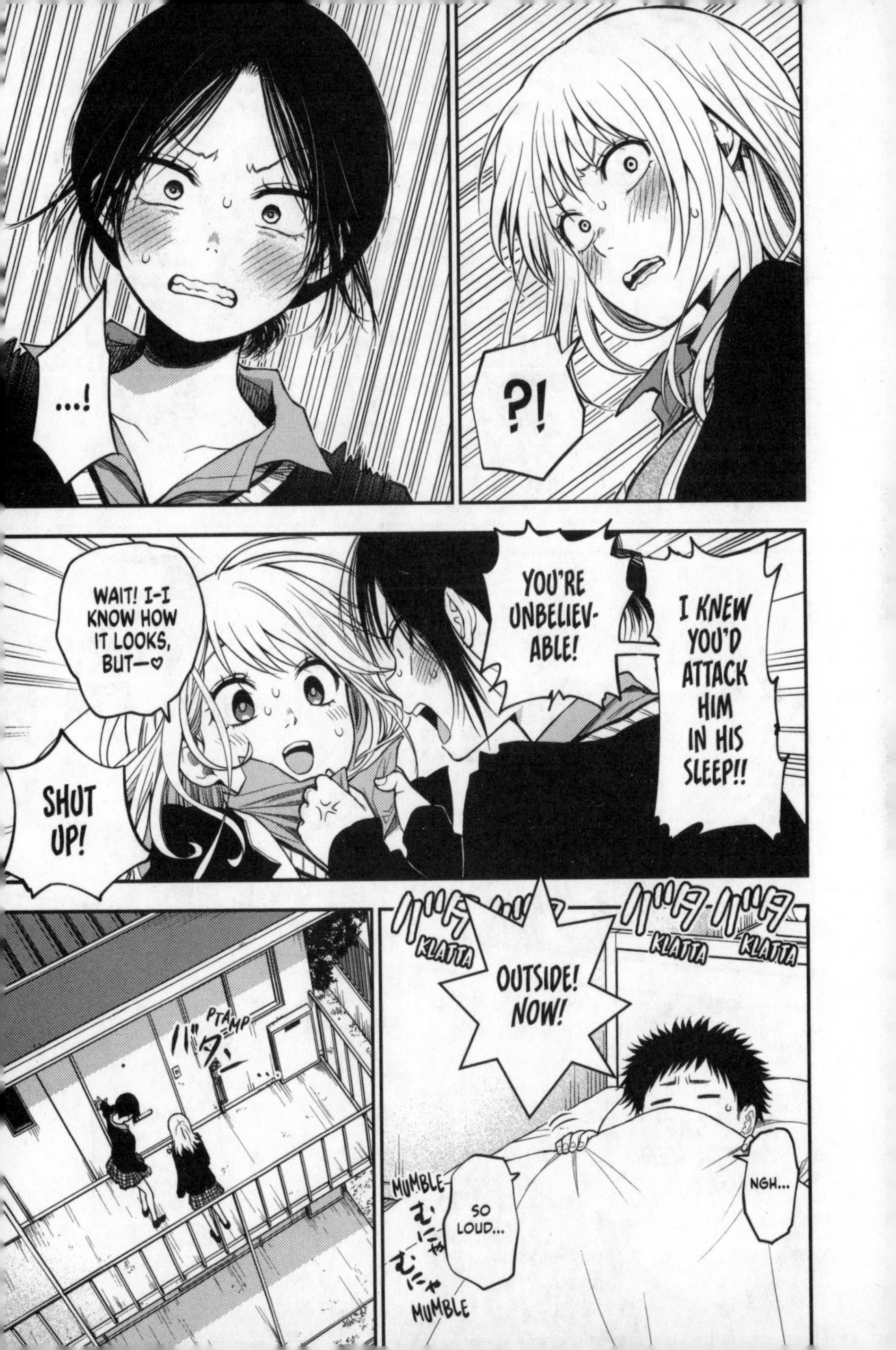
?!
...!
I KNEW YOU'D ATTACK HIM IN HIS SLEEP!!
YOU'RE UNBELIEV-ABLE!
WAIT! I-I KNOW HOW IT LOOKS, BUT—♡
SHUT UP!
バタバタ
KLATTA KLATTA
KLATTA
OUTSIDE! NOW!
NGH...
MUMBLE むにゃむにゃ MUMBLE
SO LOUD...
バタン
PTAMP
...

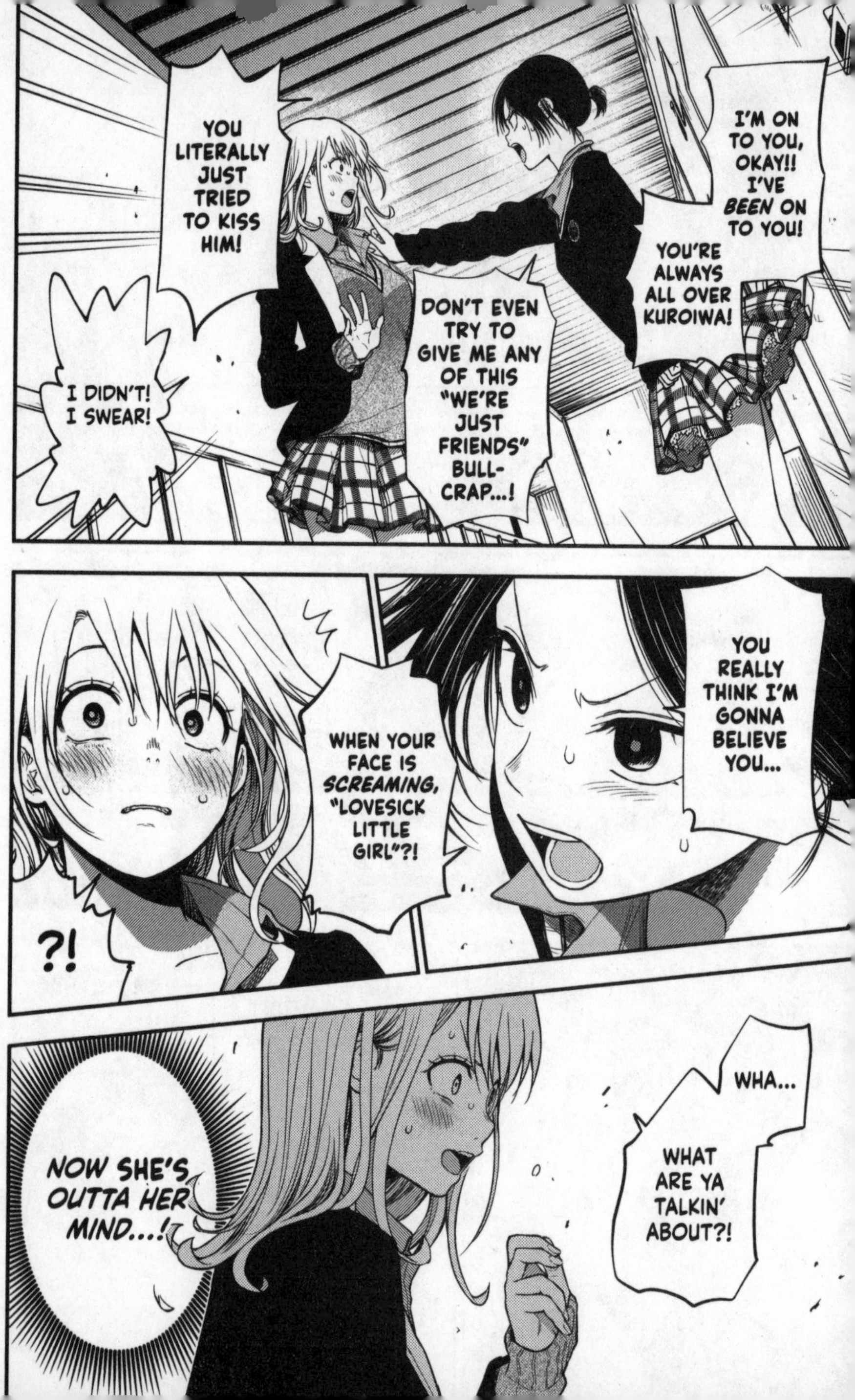
I'M ON TO YOU, OKAY!! I'VE *BEEN* ON TO YOU!
YOU'RE ALWAYS ALL OVER KUROIWA!
DON'T EVEN TRY TO GIVE ME ANY OF THIS "WE'RE JUST FRIENDS" BULL-CRAP...!
YOU LITERALLY JUST TRIED TO KISS HIM!
I DIDN'T! I SWEAR!
YOU REALLY THINK I'M GONNA BELIEVE YOU...
WHEN YOUR FACE IS *SCREAMING*, "LOVESICK LITTLE GIRL"?!
?!
WHA...
WHAT ARE YA TALKIN' ABOUT?!
NOW SHE'S OUTTA HER MIND...!

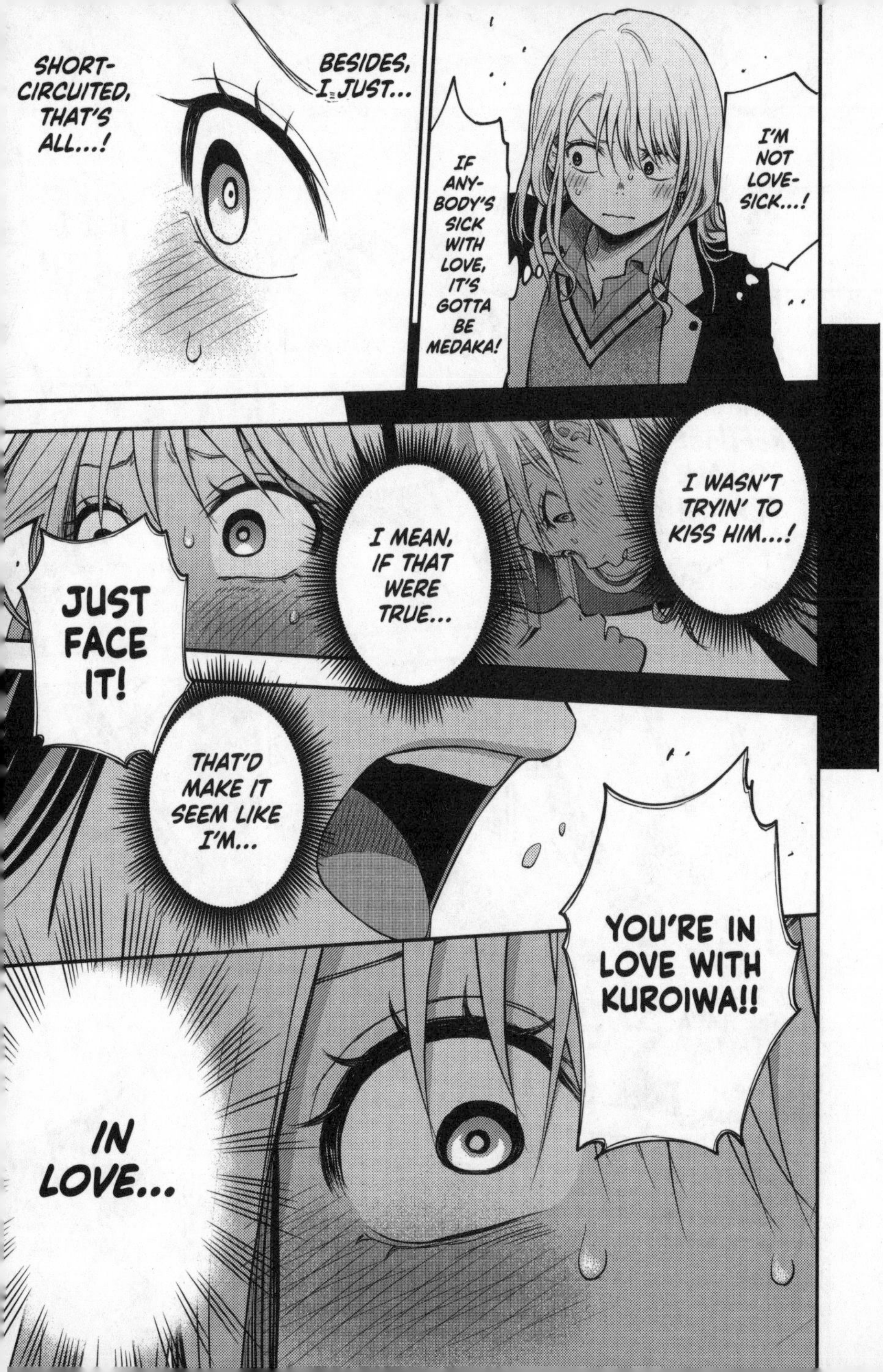

I'M NOT LOVE-SICK...!
IF ANYBODY'S SICK WITH LOVE, IT'S GOTTA BE MEDAKA!
BESIDES, I JUST...
SHORT-CIRCUITED, THAT'S ALL...!
I WASN'T TRYIN' TO KISS HIM...!
I MEAN, IF THAT WERE TRUE...
THAT'D MAKE IT SEEM LIKE I'M...
JUST FACE IT!
YOU'RE IN LOVE WITH KUROIWA!!
IN LOVE...

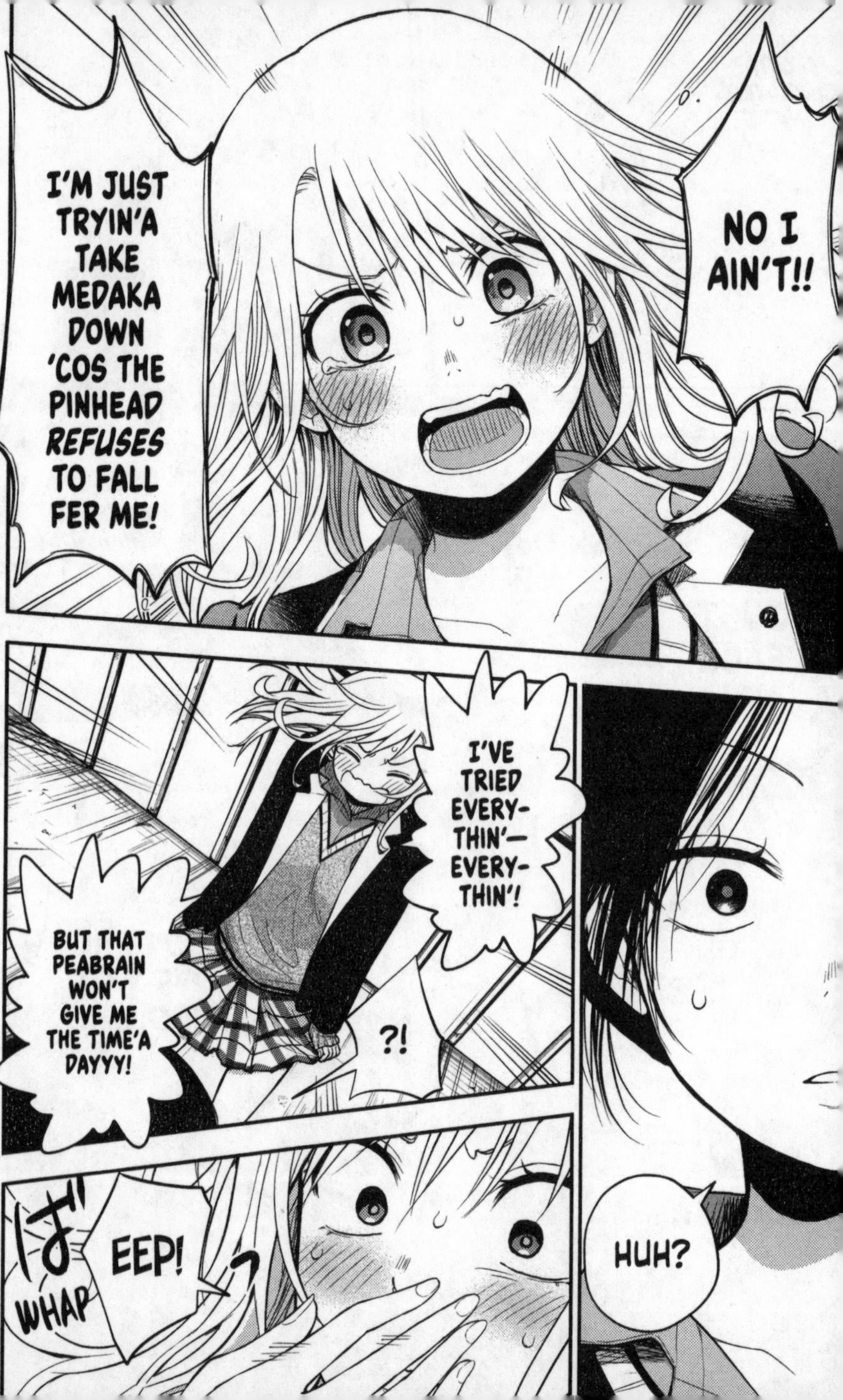

NO I AIN'T!!
I'M JUST TRYIN'A TAKE MEDAKA DOWN 'COS THE PINHEAD *REFUSES* TO FALL FER ME!
I'VE TRIED EVERY-THIN'— EVERY-THIN'!
BUT THAT PEABRAIN WON'T GIVE ME THE TIME'A DAYYY!
?!
HUH?
EEP!
ぱ
WHAP

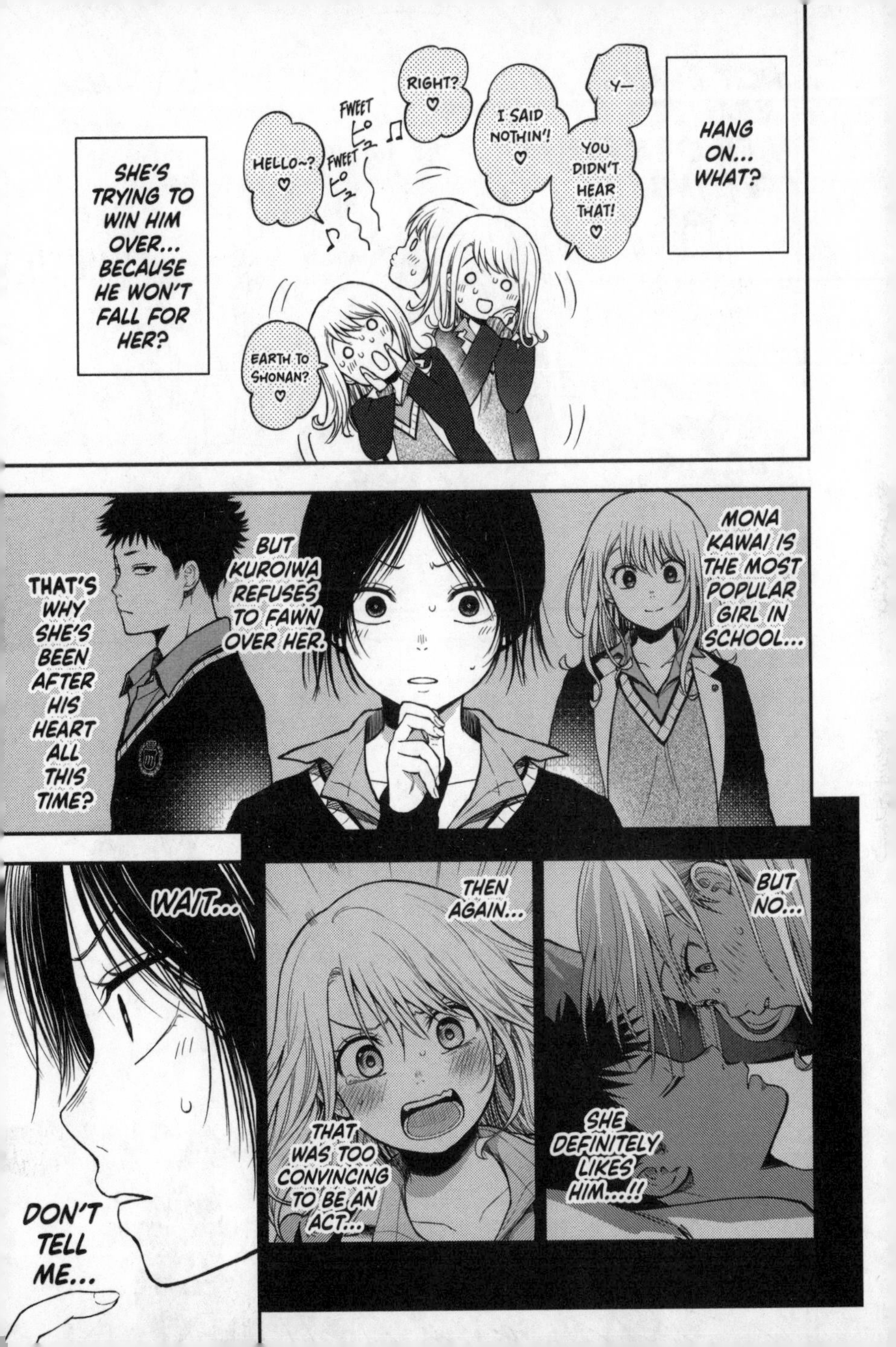
HANG ON... WHAT?
Y—
YOU DIDN'T HEAR THAT! ♡
I SAID NOTHIN'! ♡
RIGHT? ♡
FWEET
FWEET
HELLO~? ♡
SHE'S TRYING TO WIN HIM OVER... BECAUSE HE WON'T FALL FOR HER?
EARTH TO SHONAN? ♡
MONA KAWAI IS THE MOST POPULAR GIRL IN SCHOOL...
BUT KUROIWA REFUSES TO FAWN OVER HER.
THAT'S WHY SHE'S BEEN AFTER HIS HEART ALL THIS TIME?
BUT NO...
SHE DEFINITELY LIKES HIM...!!
THEN AGAIN...
THAT WAS TOO CONVINCING TO BE AN ACT...
WAIT...
DON'T TELL ME...

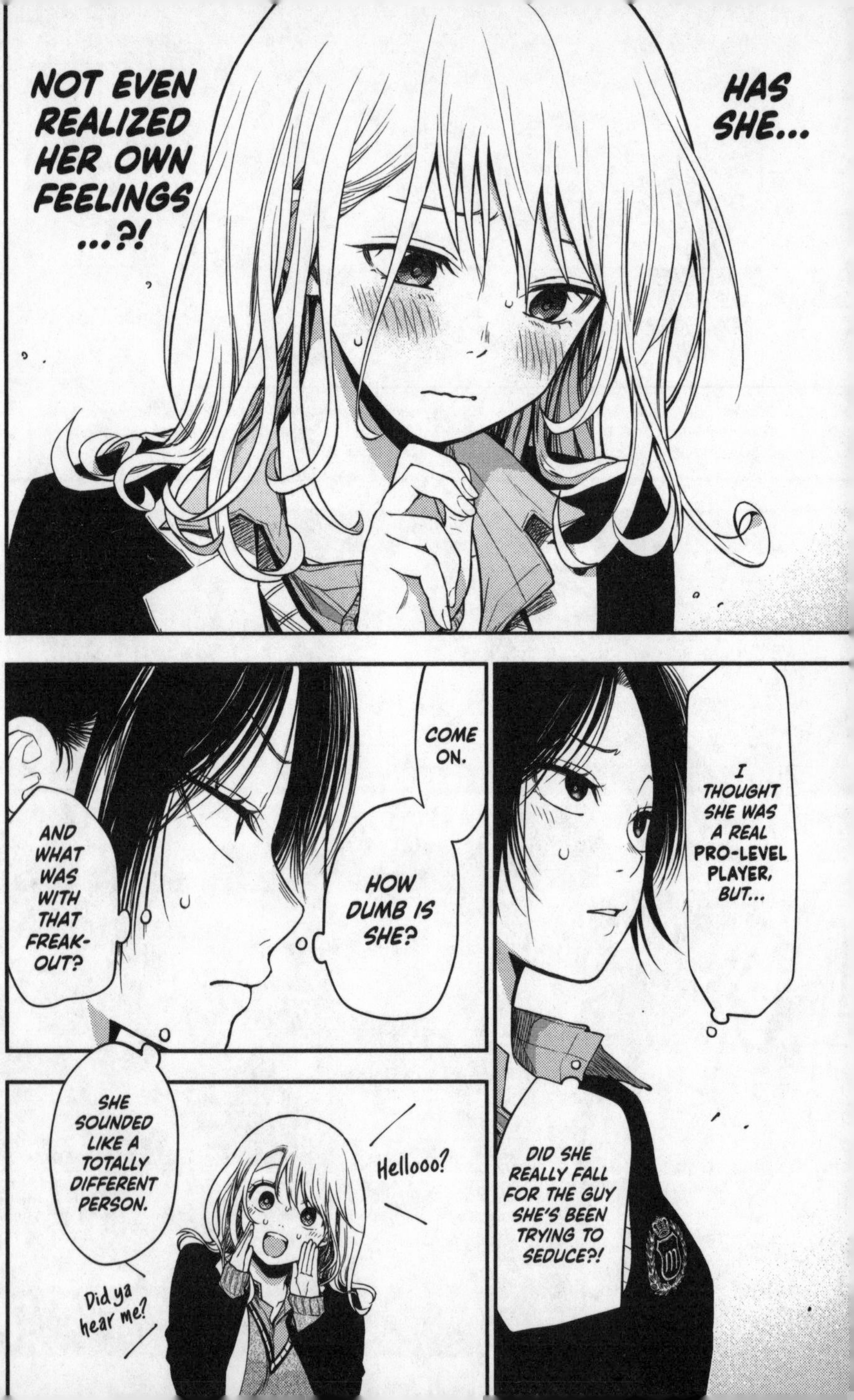
HAS SHE...
NOT EVEN REALIZED HER OWN FEELINGS ...?!
I THOUGHT SHE WAS A REAL PRO-LEVEL PLAYER, BUT...
DID SHE REALLY FALL FOR THE GUY SHE'S BEEN TRYING TO SEDUCE?!
COME ON.
HOW DUMB IS SHE?
AND WHAT WAS WITH THAT FREAK-OUT?
Hellooo?
SHE SOUNDED LIKE A TOTALLY DIFFERENT PERSON.
Did ya hear me?

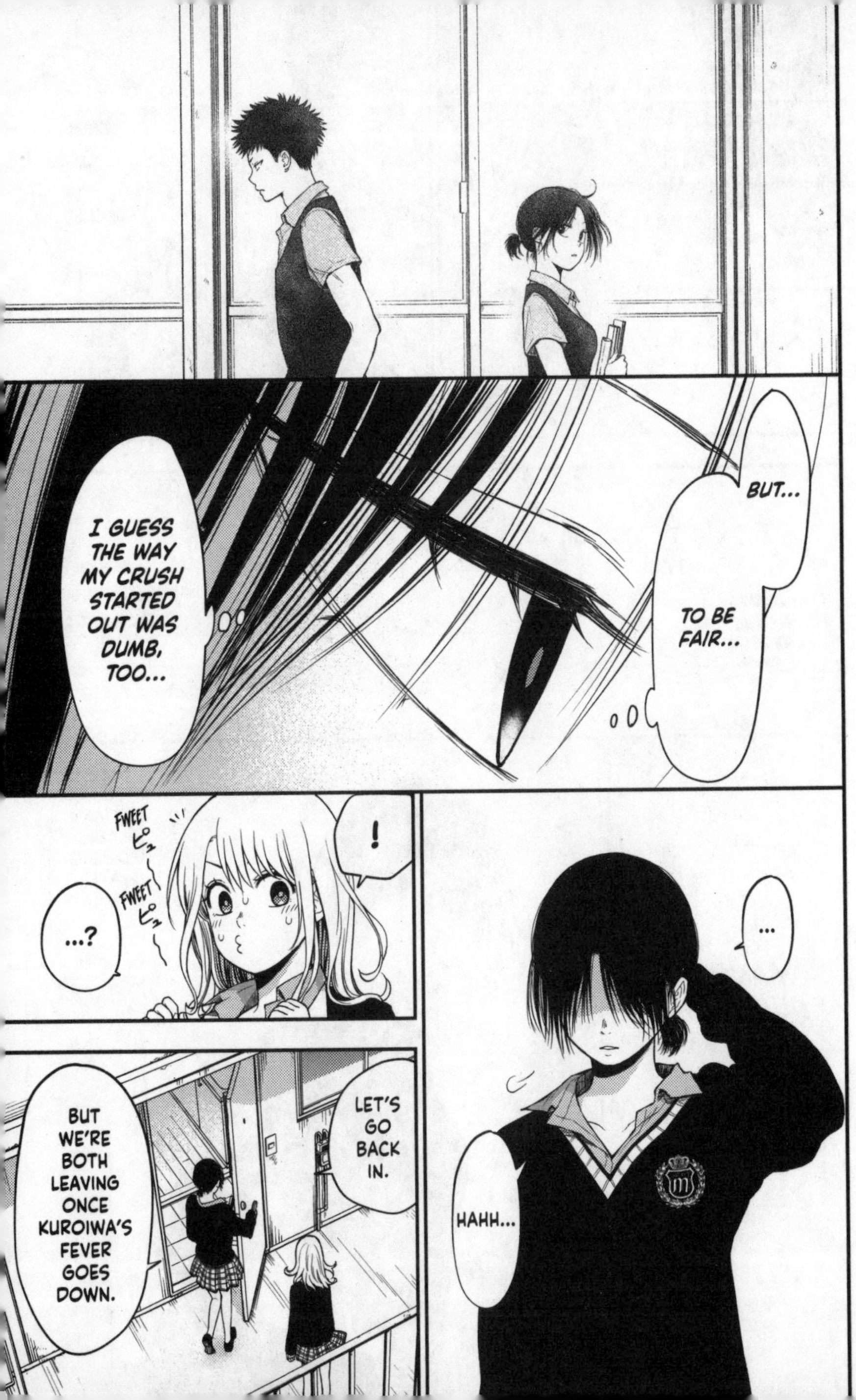
BUT...
TO BE FAIR...
I GUESS THE WAY MY CRUSH STARTED OUT WAS DUMB, TOO...
...
HAHH...
!
FWEET ピュ
FWEET ピュ
...?
LET'S GO BACK IN.
BUT WE'RE BOTH LEAVING ONCE KUROIWA'S FEVER GOES DOWN.

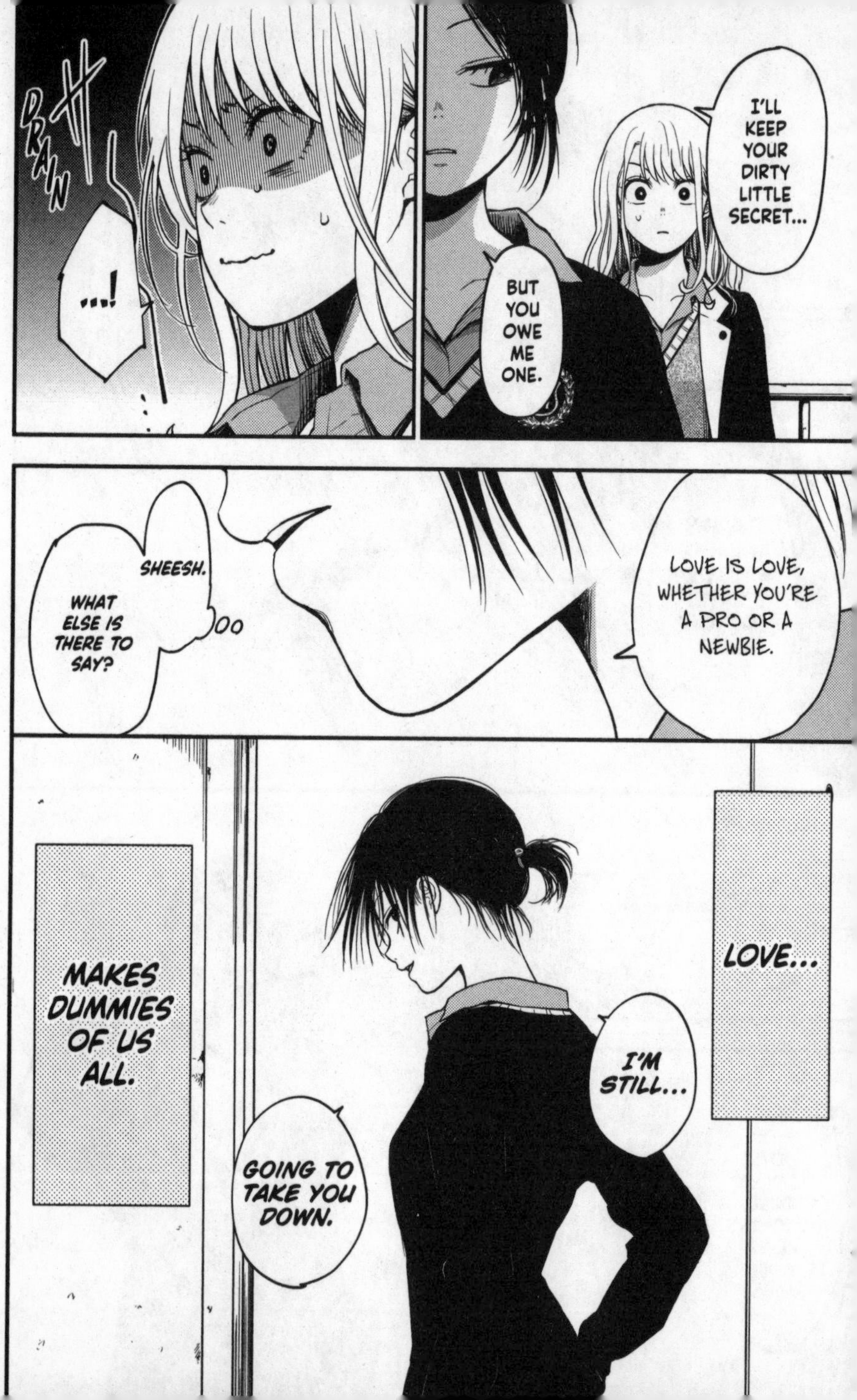
I'LL KEEP YOUR DIRTY LITTLE SECRET...
BUT YOU OWE ME ONE.
DRAIN
...!
LOVE IS LOVE, WHETHER YOU'RE A PRO OR A NEWBIE.
SHEESH.
WHAT ELSE IS THERE TO SAY?
LOVE...
I'M STILL...
GOING TO TAKE YOU DOWN.
MAKES DUMMIES OF US ALL.

Chapter 22 ★ In Rough Shape with That Jerk

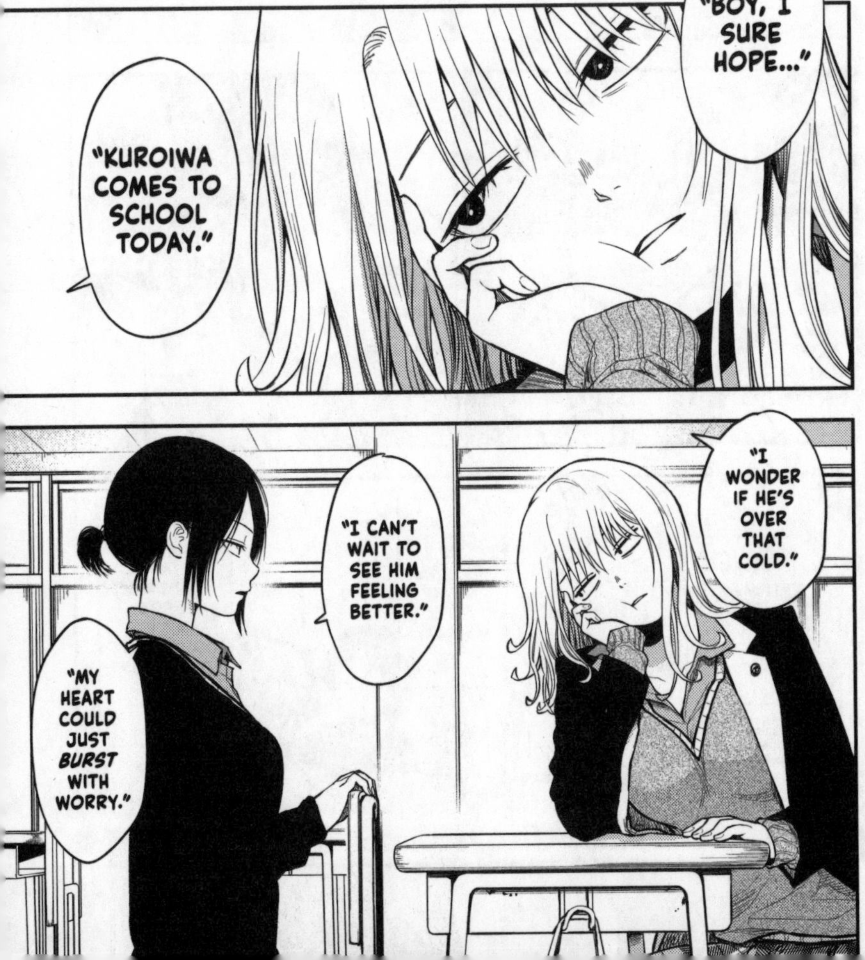
"BOY, I SURE HOPE..."
"KUROIWA COMES TO SCHOOL TODAY."
"I WONDER IF HE'S OVER THAT COLD."
"I CAN'T WAIT TO SEE HIM FEELING BETTER."
"MY HEART COULD JUST *BURST* WITH WORRY."

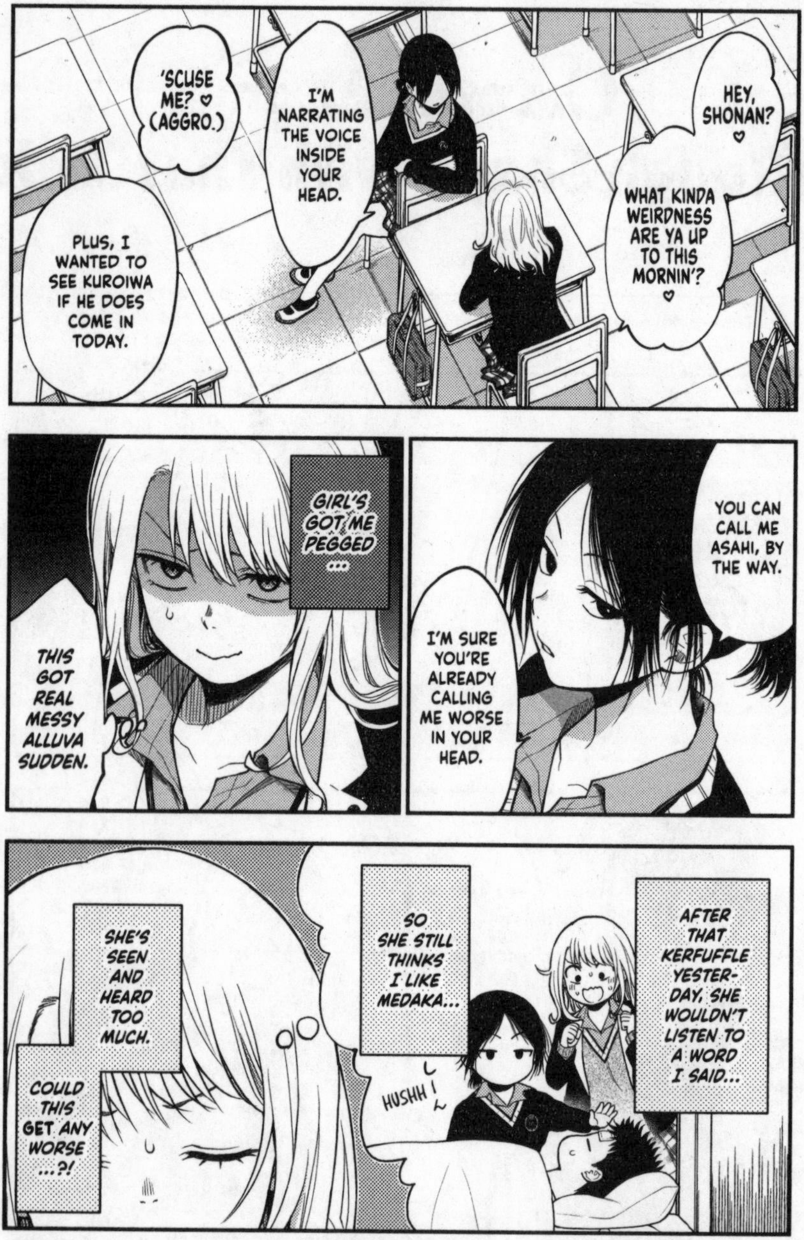
HEY, SHONAN? ♡
WHAT KINDA WEIRDNESS ARE YA UP TO THIS MORNIN'? ♡
I'M NARRATING THE VOICE INSIDE YOUR HEAD.
'SCUSE ME? ♡ (AGGRO.)
PLUS, I WANTED TO SEE KUROIWA IF HE DOES COME IN TODAY.
YOU CAN CALL ME ASAHI, BY THE WAY.
I'M SURE YOU'RE ALREADY CALLING ME WORSE IN YOUR HEAD.
GIRL'S GOT ME PEGGED ...
THIS GOT REAL MESSY ALLUVA SUDDEN.
AFTER THAT KERFUFFLE YESTER-DAY, SHE WOULDN'T LISTEN TO A WORD I SAID...
SO SHE STILL THINKS I LIKE MEDAKA...
HUSHH!
SHE'S SEEN AND HEARD TOO MUCH.
COULD THIS GET ANY WORSE ...?!

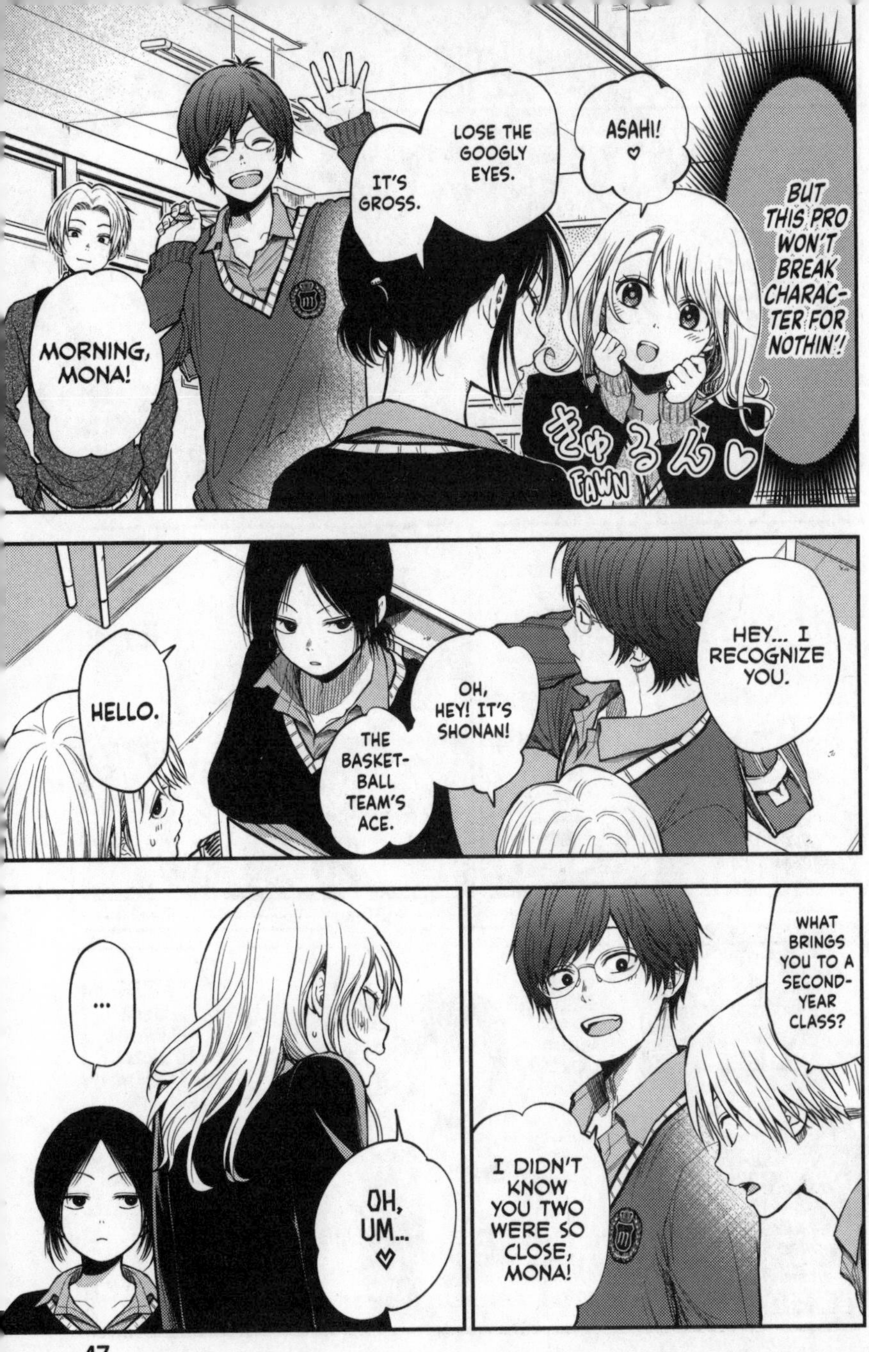
BUT THIS PRO WON'T BREAK CHARAC-TER FOR NOTHIN'!
ASAHI! ♡
LOSE THE GOOGLY EYES.
IT'S GROSS.
MORNING, MONA!
きゅるん♡
FAWN
HEY... I RECOGNIZE YOU.
OH, HEY! IT'S SHONAN!
THE BASKET-BALL TEAM'S ACE.
HELLO.
WHAT BRINGS YOU TO A SECOND-YEAR CLASS?
I DIDN'T KNOW YOU TWO WERE SO CLOSE, MONA!
...
OH, UM... ♡

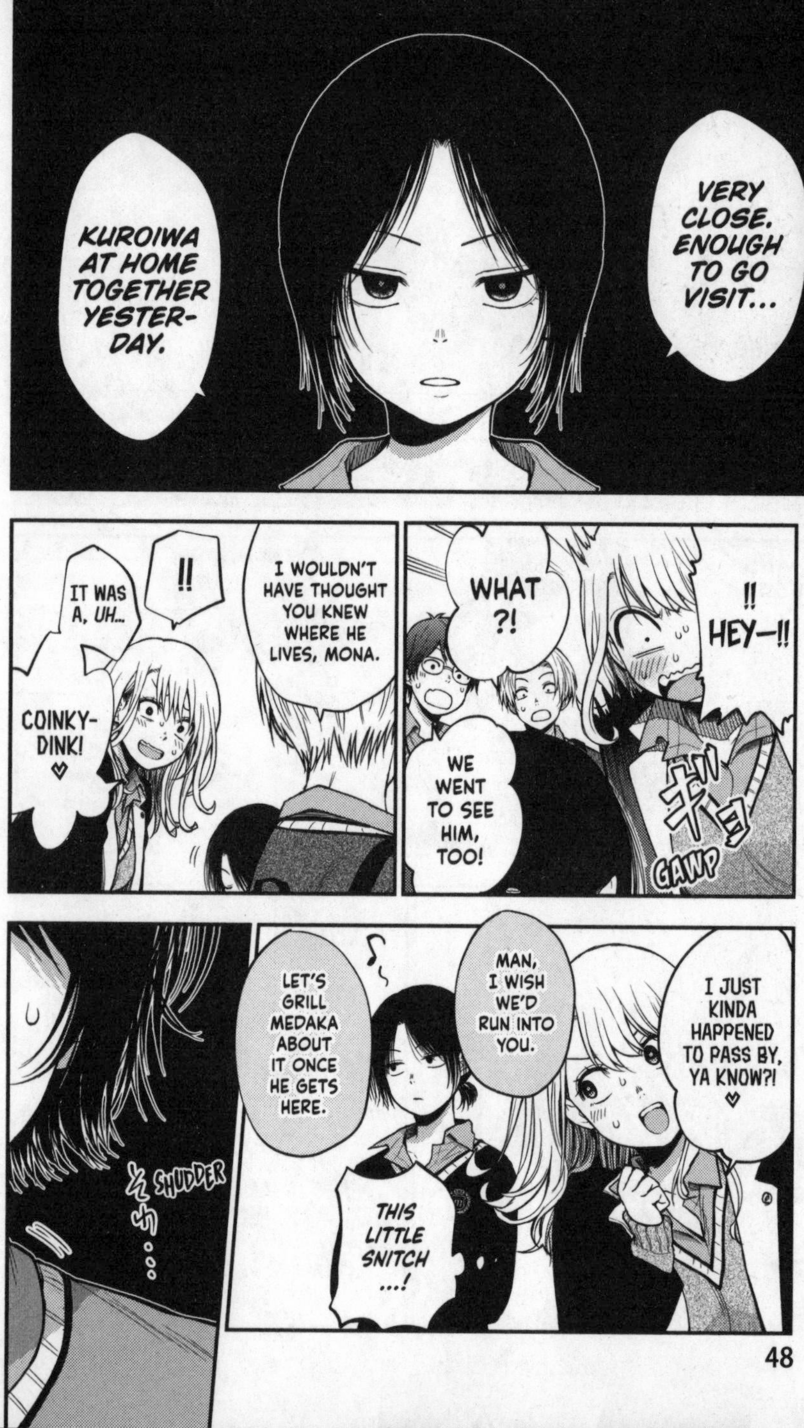
VERY CLOSE. ENOUGH TO GO VISIT...
KUROIWA AT HOME TOGETHER YESTER-DAY.
!! HEY—!!
WHAT?!
WE WENT TO SEE HIM, TOO!
GAWP
I WOULDN'T HAVE THOUGHT YOU KNEW WHERE HE LIVES, MONA.
!!
IT WAS A, UH...
COINKY-DINK! ♥
I JUST KINDA HAPPENED TO PASS BY, YA KNOW?! ♥
MAN, I WISH WE'D RUN INTO YOU.
LET'S GRILL MEDAKA ABOUT IT ONCE HE GETS HERE.
THIS LITTLE SNITCH...!
SHUDDER

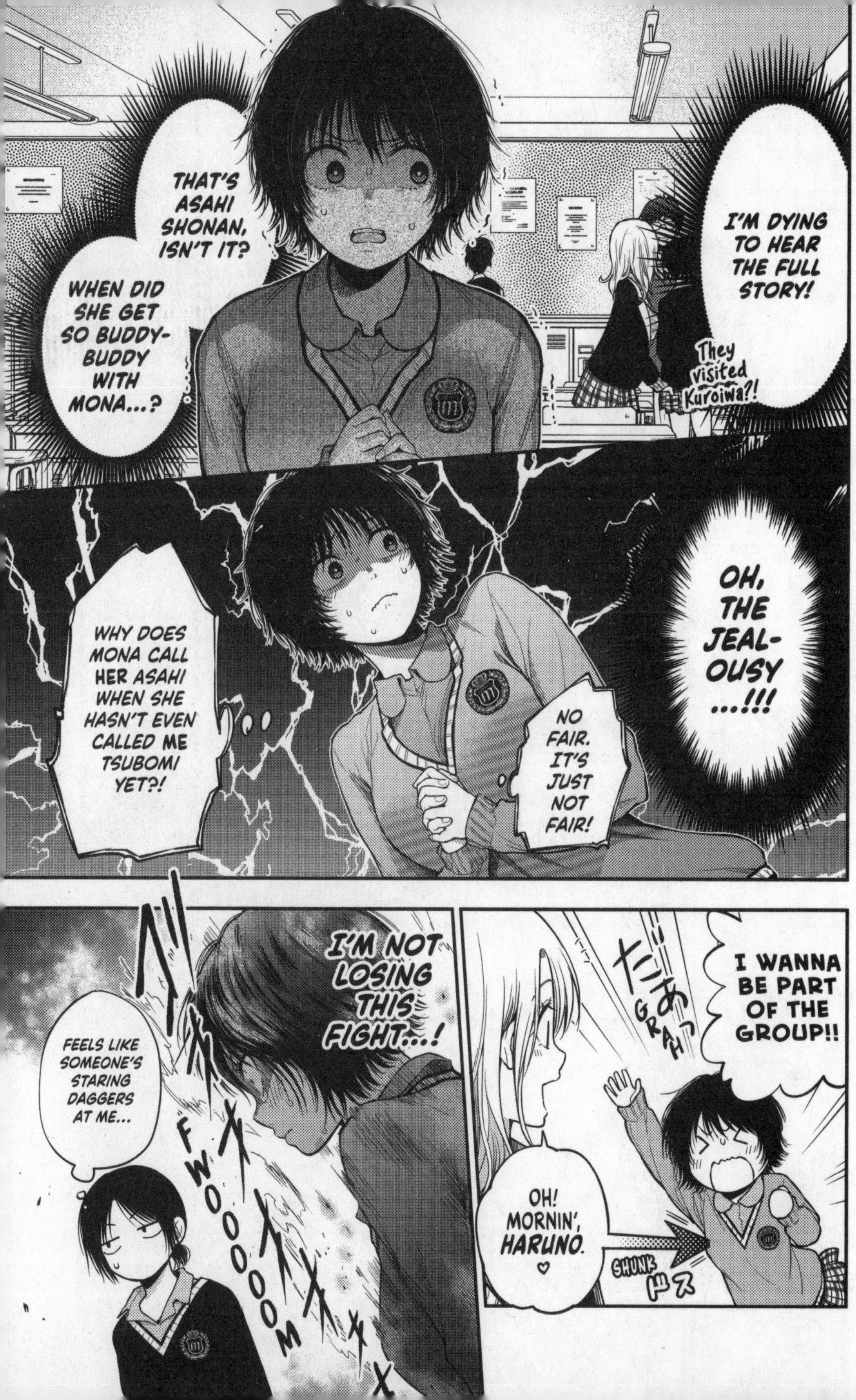
I'M DYING TO HEAR THE FULL STORY!
They visited Kuroiwa?!
THAT'S ASAHI SHONAN, ISN'T IT?
WHEN DID SHE GET SO BUDDY-BUDDY WITH MONA...?
OH, THE JEAL-OUSY ...!!!
NO FAIR. IT'S JUST NOT FAIR!
WHY DOES MONA CALL HER ASAHI WHEN SHE HASN'T EVEN CALLED ME TSUBOMI YET?!
I WANNA BE PART OF THE GROUP!!
GRAH
OH! MORNIN', HARUNO. ♡
SHUNK
I'M NOT LOSING THIS FIGHT...!
FWOOOOOOM
FEELS LIKE SOMEONE'S STARING DAGGERS AT ME...

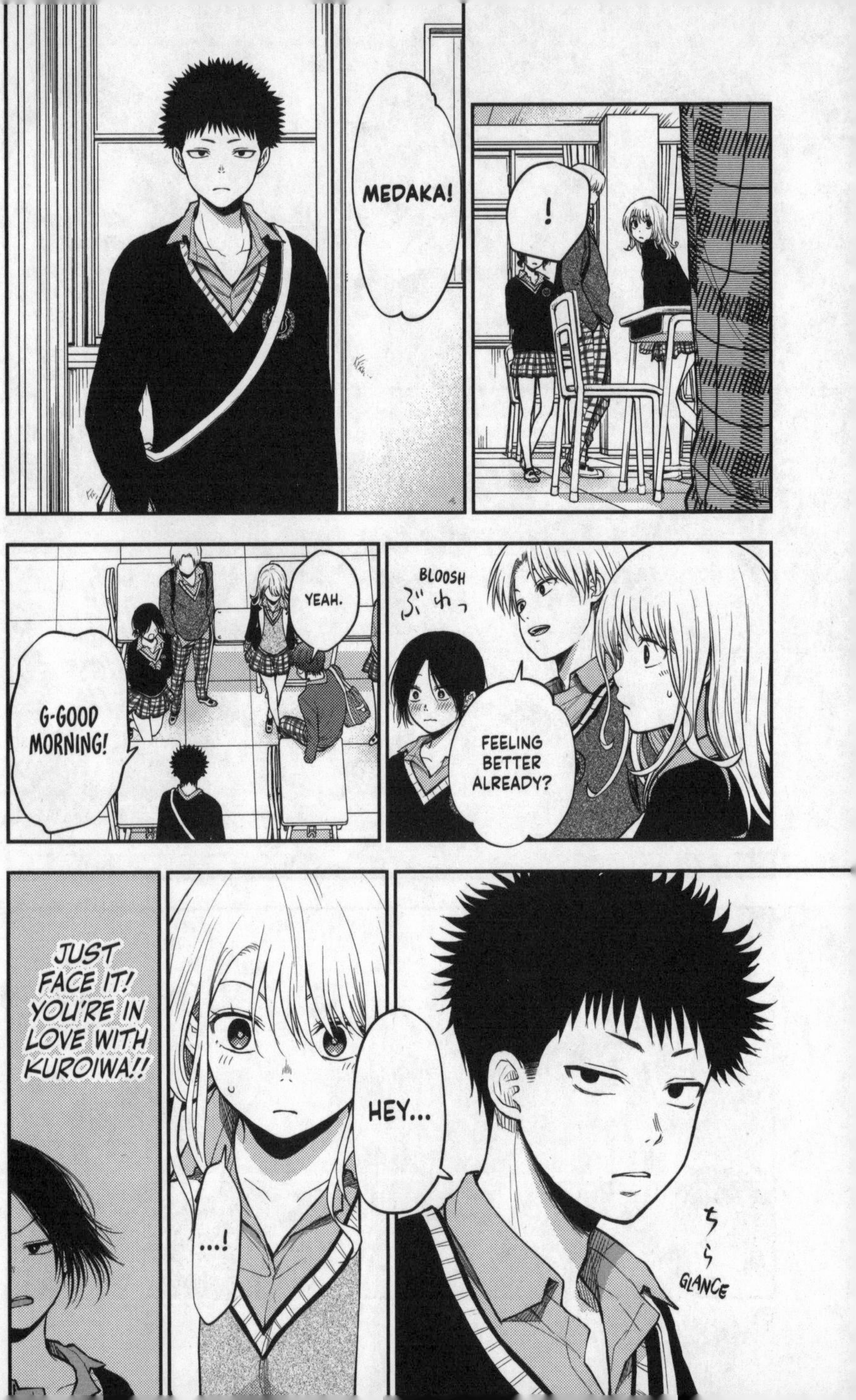
!
MEDAKA!
BLOOSH
ぶわっ
FEELING BETTER ALREADY?
YEAH.
G-GOOD MORNING!
ちら
GLANCE
HEY...
...!
JUST FACE IT! YOU'RE IN LOVE WITH KUROIWA!!

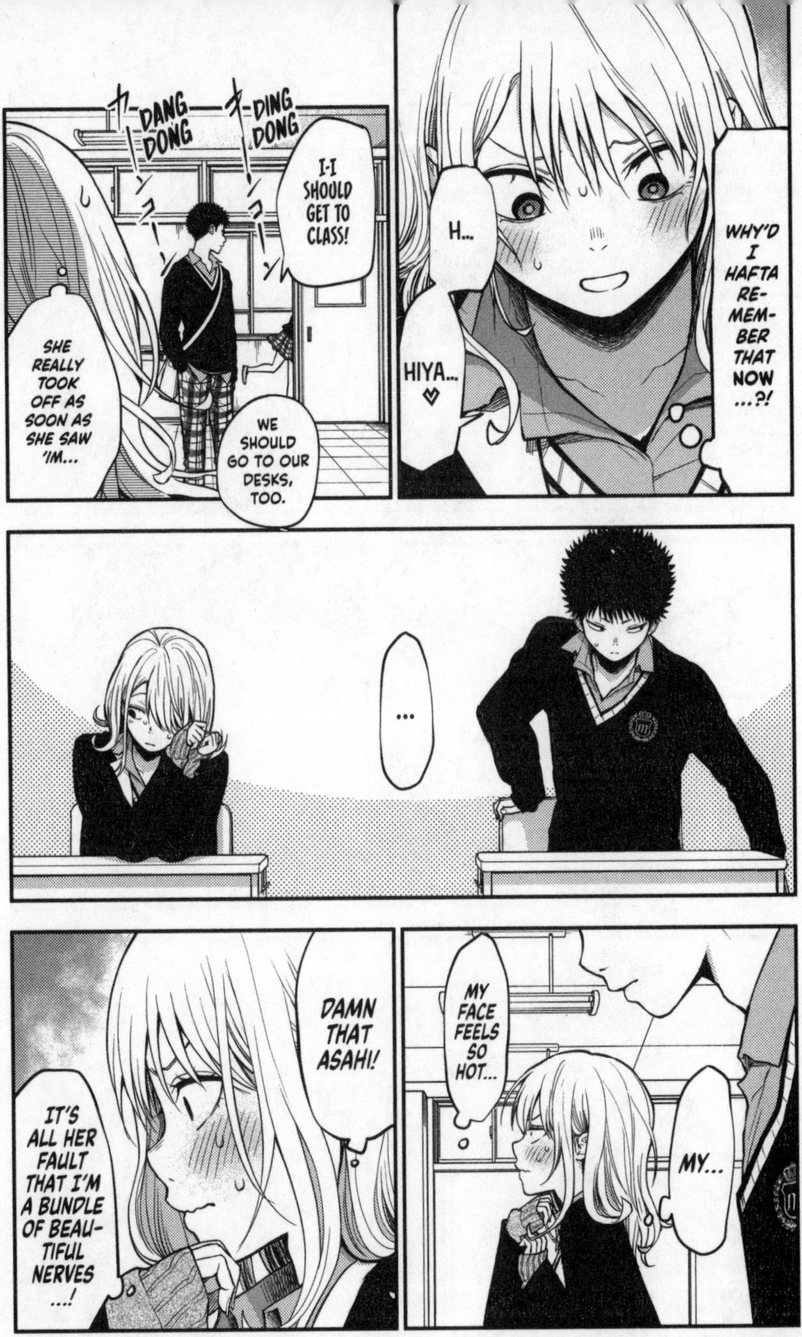
H...
HIYA...
WHY'D I HAFTA RE-MEM-BER THAT NOW ...?!
DING DONG
DANG DONG
I-I SHOULD GET TO CLASS!
SHE REALLY TOOK OFF AS SOON AS SHE SAW 'IM...
WE SHOULD GO TO OUR DESKS, TOO.
...
MY FACE FEELS SO HOT...
MY...
DAMN THAT ASAHI!
IT'S ALL HER FAULT THAT I'M A BUNDLE OF BEAU-TIFUL NERVES ...!

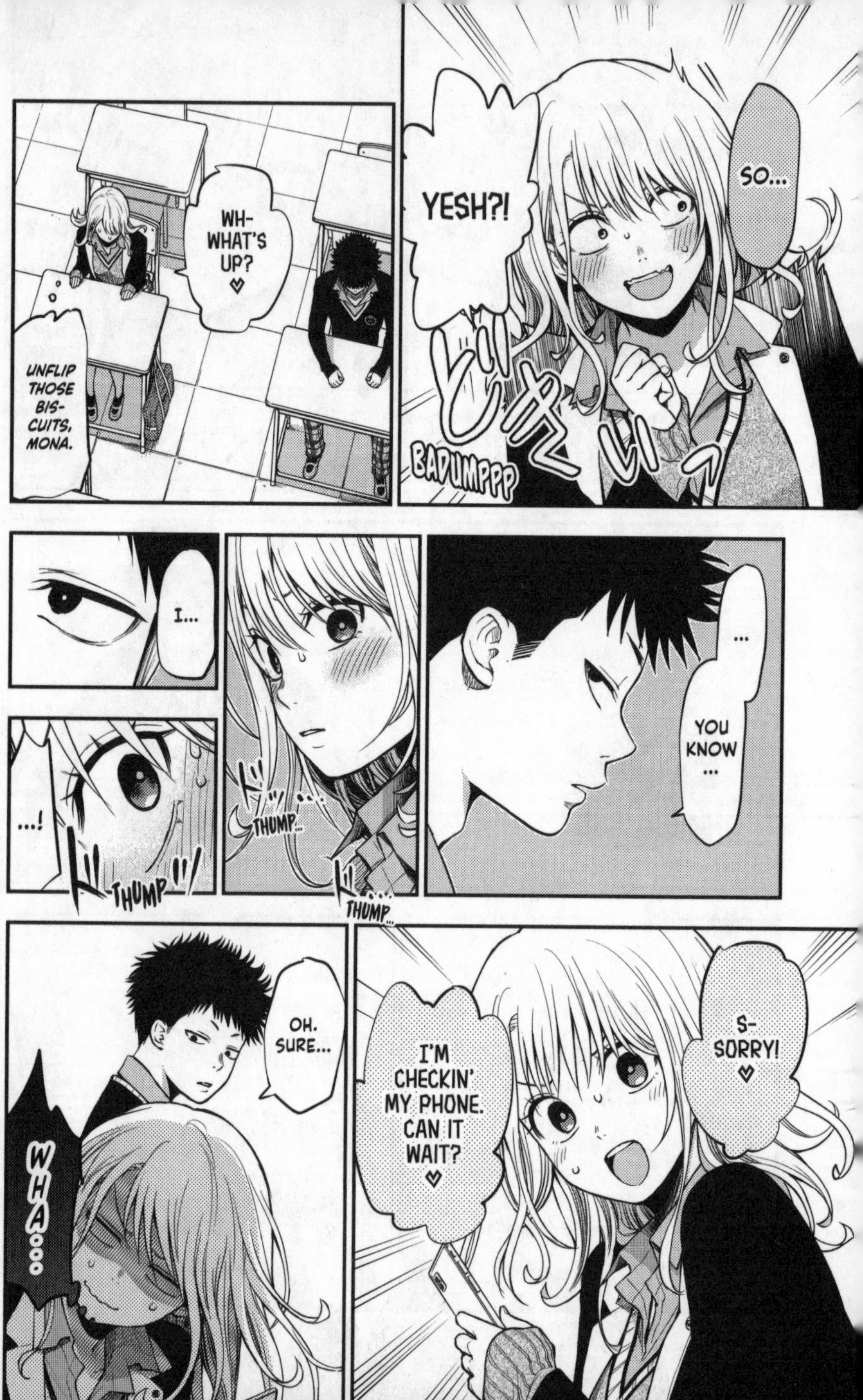

SO...
YESH?!
BADUMPPP
WH-WHAT'S UP? ♡
UNFLIP THOSE BIS-CUITS, MONA.
...
YOU KNOW ...
THUMP...
I...
...!
THUMP
THUMP...
S-SORRY! ♡
I'M CHECKIN' MY PHONE. CAN IT WAIT? ♡
OH. SURE...
WHAooo

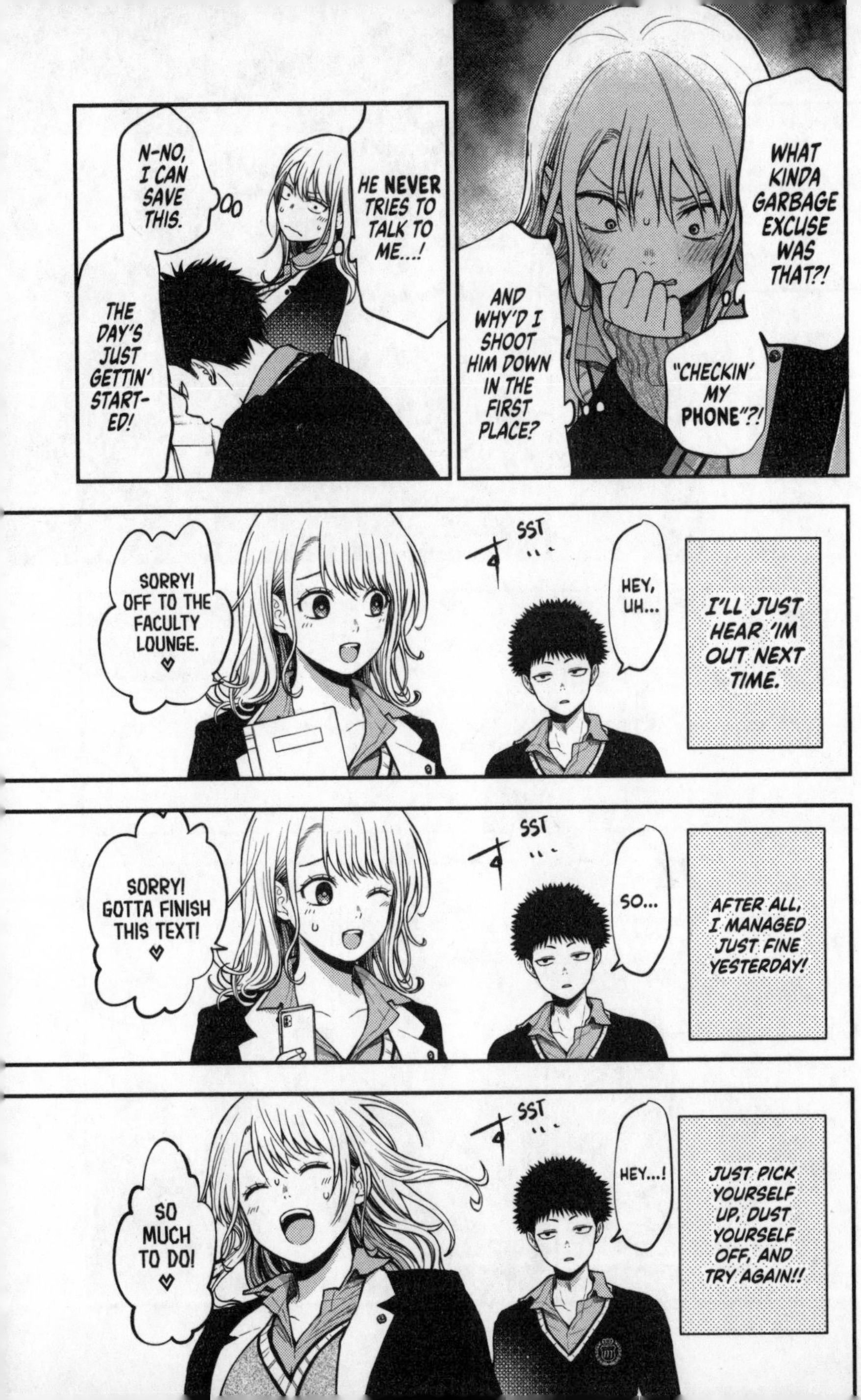
WHAT KINDA GARBAGE EXCUSE WAS THAT?!
"CHECKIN' MY PHONE"?!
AND WHY'D I SHOOT HIM DOWN IN THE FIRST PLACE?
HE NEVER TRIES TO TALK TO ME...!
N-NO, I CAN SAVE THIS.
THE DAY'S JUST GETTIN' START-ED!
I'LL JUST HEAR 'IM OUT NEXT TIME.
HEY, UH...
SST
SORRY! OFF TO THE FACULTY LOUNGE.
AFTER ALL, I MANAGED JUST FINE YESTERDAY!
SO...
SST
SORRY! GOTTA FINISH THIS TEXT!
JUST PICK YOURSELF UP, DUST YOURSELF OFF, AND TRY AGAIN!!
HEY...!
SST
SO MUCH TO DO!

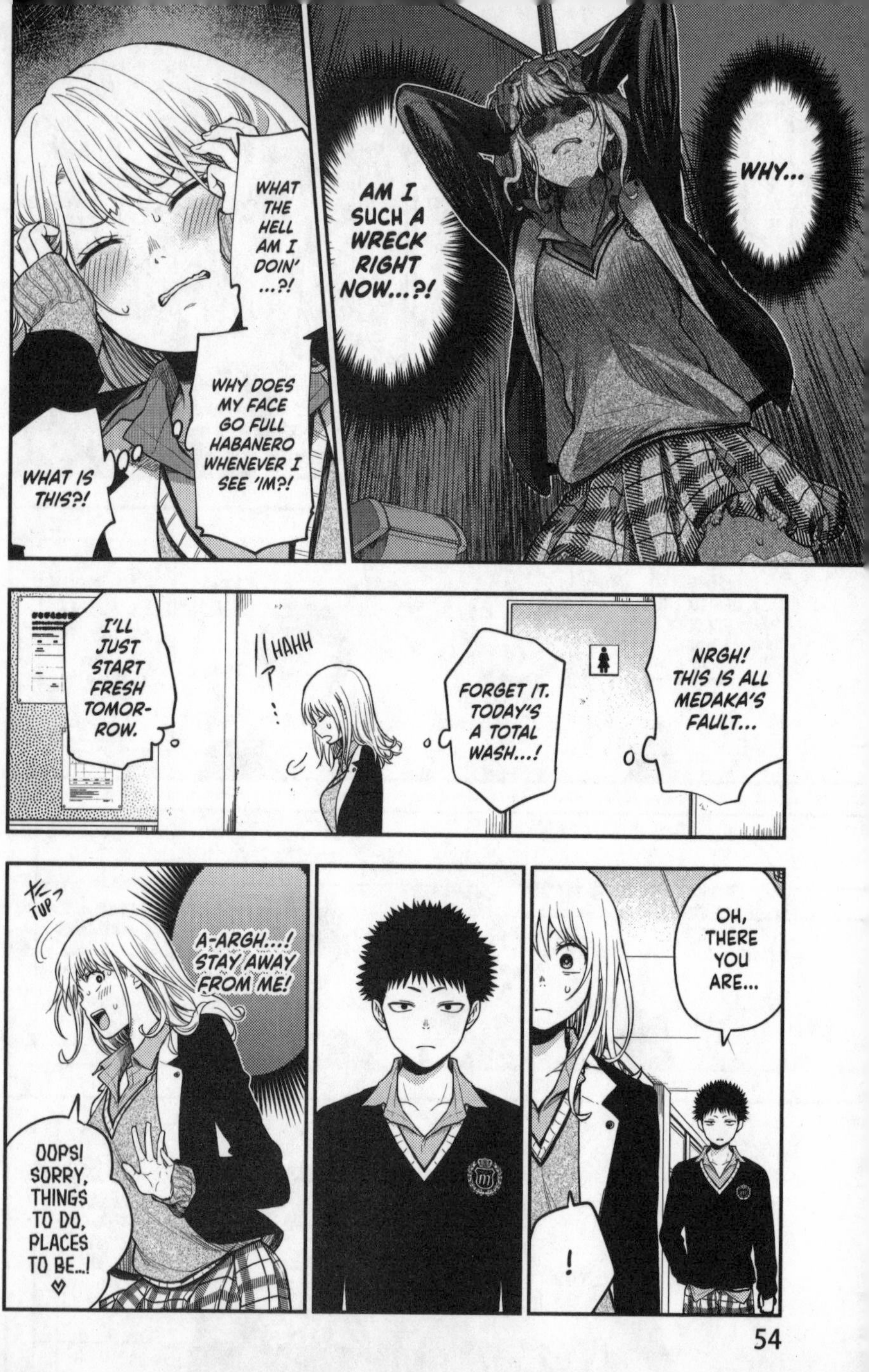
WHY...
AM I SUCH A WRECK RIGHT NOW...?!
WHAT THE HELL AM I DOIN' ...?!
WHY DOES MY FACE GO FULL HABANERO WHENEVER I SEE 'IM?!
WHAT IS THIS?!
NRGH! THIS IS ALL MEDAKA'S FAULT...
FORGET IT. TODAY'S A TOTAL WASH...!
HAHH
I'LL JUST START FRESH TOMORROW.
OH, THERE YOU ARE...
!
TUP
A-ARGH...! STAY AWAY FROM ME!
OOPS! SORRY, THINGS TO DO, PLACES TO BE...! ♥

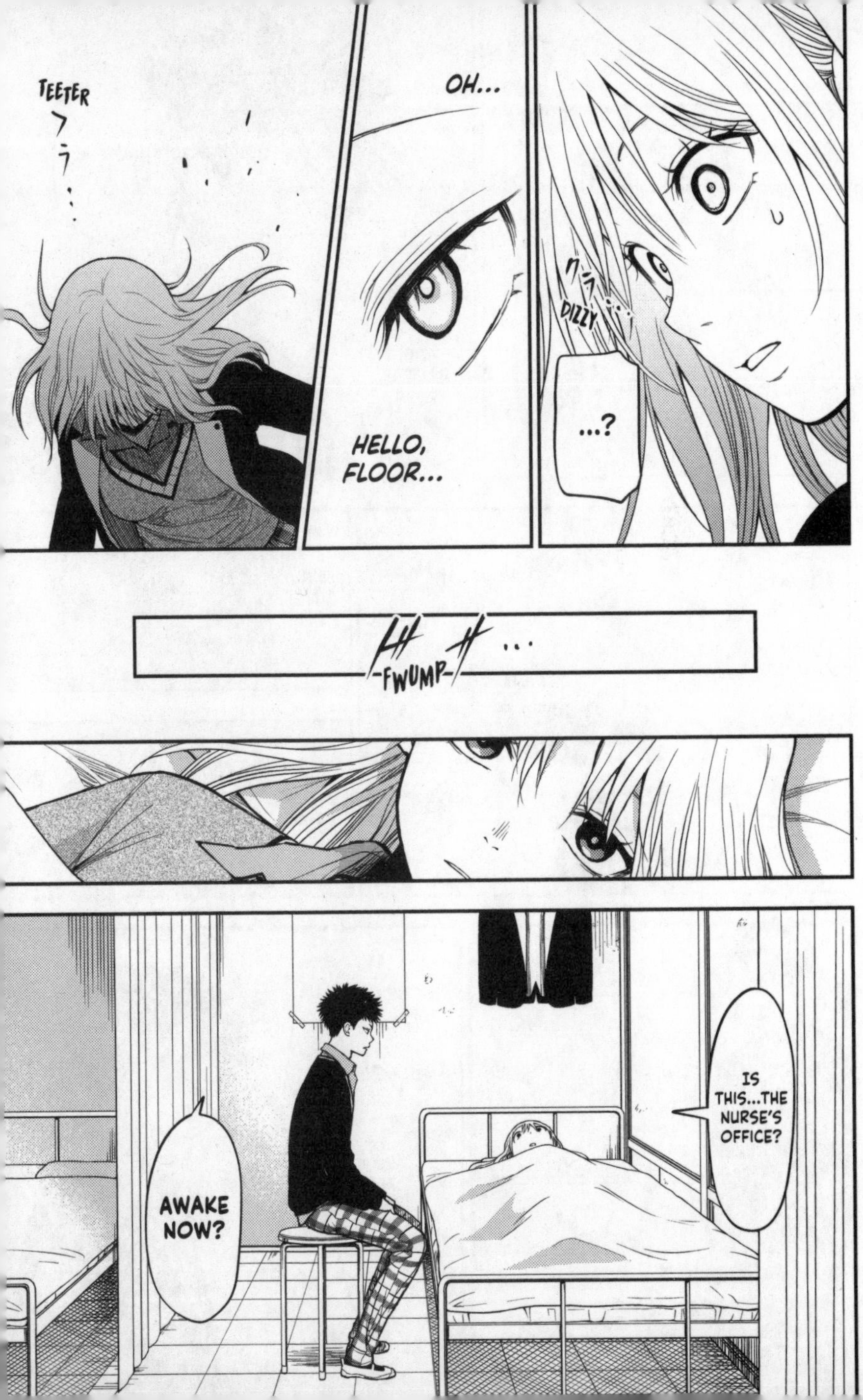

グラ
DIZZY
...?
OH...
HELLO, FLOOR...
TEETER
フラ
FWUMP
IS THIS...THE NURSE'S OFFICE?
AWAKE NOW?

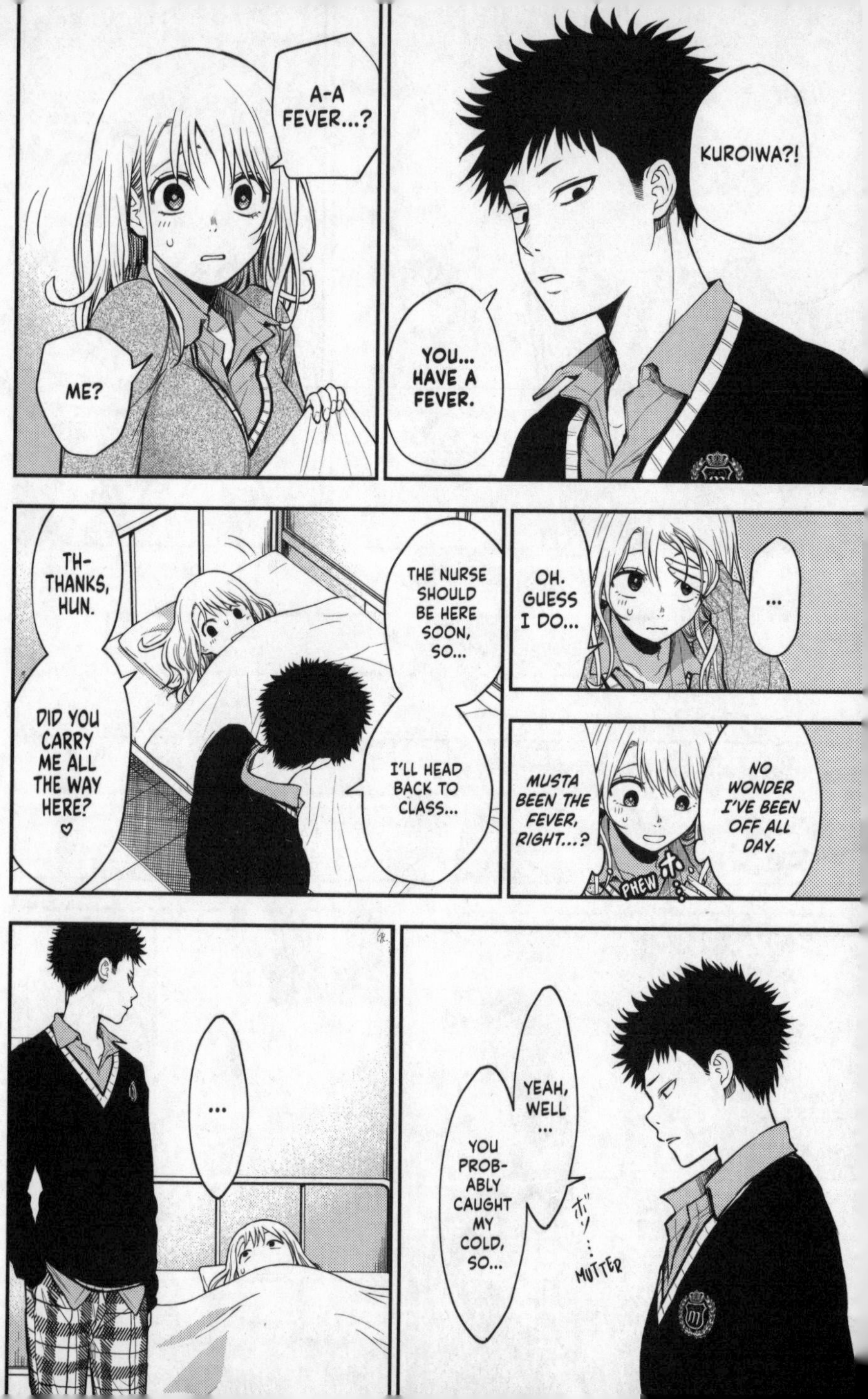
KUROIWA?!
YOU... HAVE A FEVER.
A-A FEVER...?
ME?
...
OH. GUESS I DO...
NO WONDER I'VE BEEN OFF ALL DAY.
MUSTA BEEN THE FEVER, RIGHT...?
PHEW
THE NURSE SHOULD BE HERE SOON, SO...
I'LL HEAD BACK TO CLASS...
TH-THANKS, HUN.
DID YOU CARRY ME ALL THE WAY HERE? ♡
YEAH, WELL ...
YOU PROB-ABLY CAUGHT MY COLD, SO...
MUTTER
...

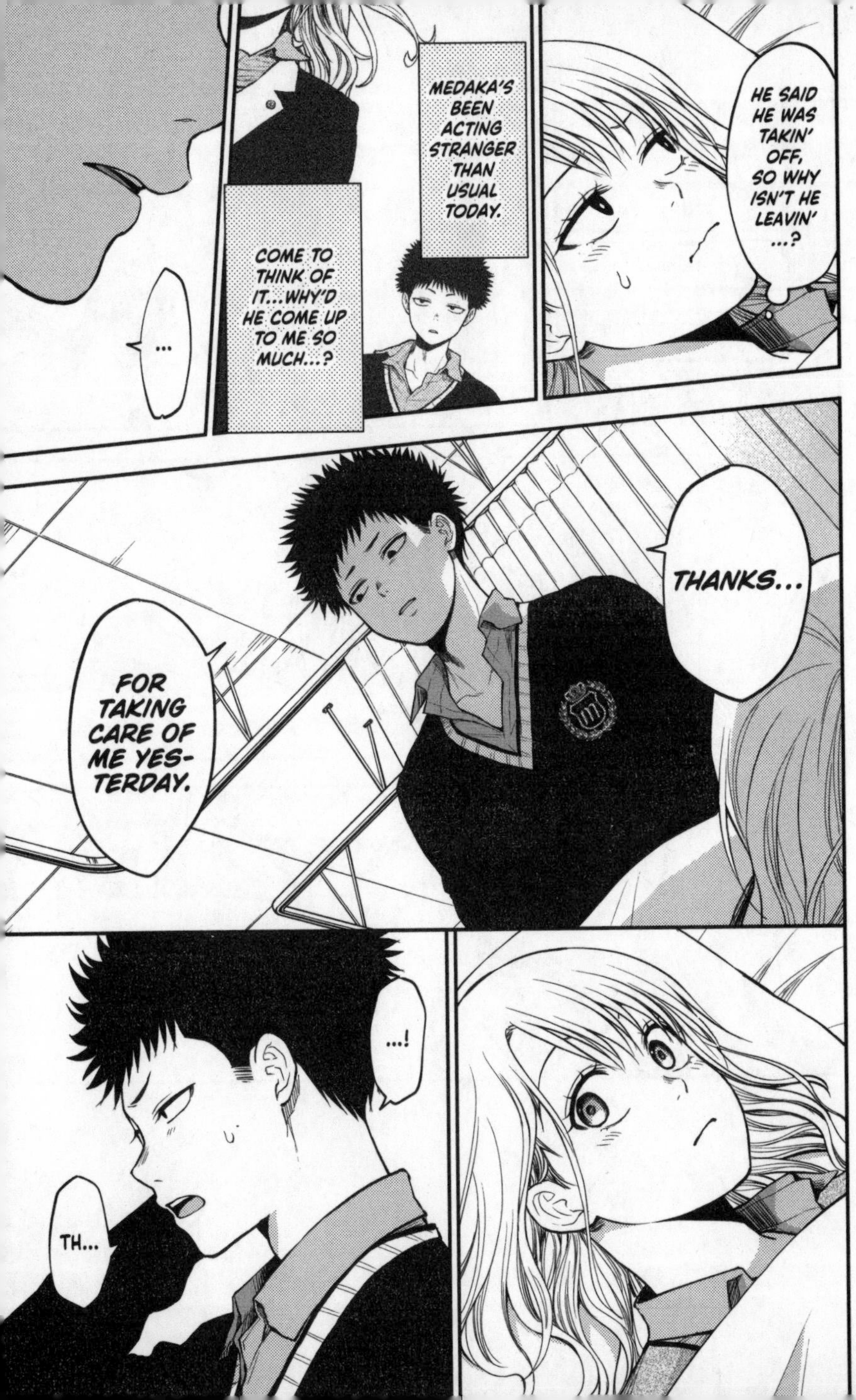
HE SAID HE WAS TAKIN' OFF, SO WHY ISN'T HE LEAVIN' ...?
MEDAKA'S BEEN ACTING STRANGER THAN USUAL TODAY.
COME TO THINK OF IT...WHY'D HE COME UP TO ME SO MUCH...?
...
THANKS...
FOR TAKING CARE OF ME YES-TERDAY.
...!
TH...

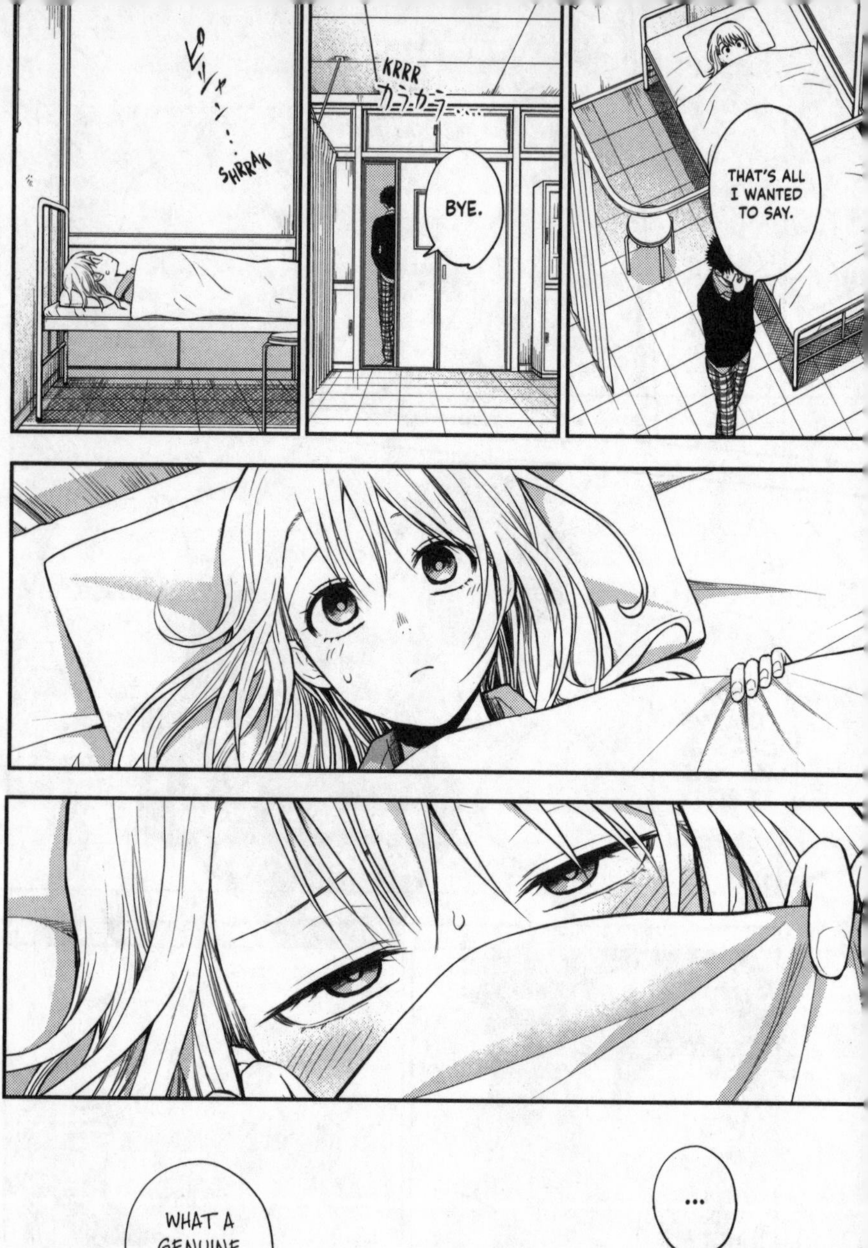
THAT'S ALL I WANTED TO SAY.
KRRR
カラカラ
BYE.
ピシャン・・
SHRRAK
...
WHAT A GENUINE JERK...

Chapter 23 ★ That Jerk and His Wallpaper

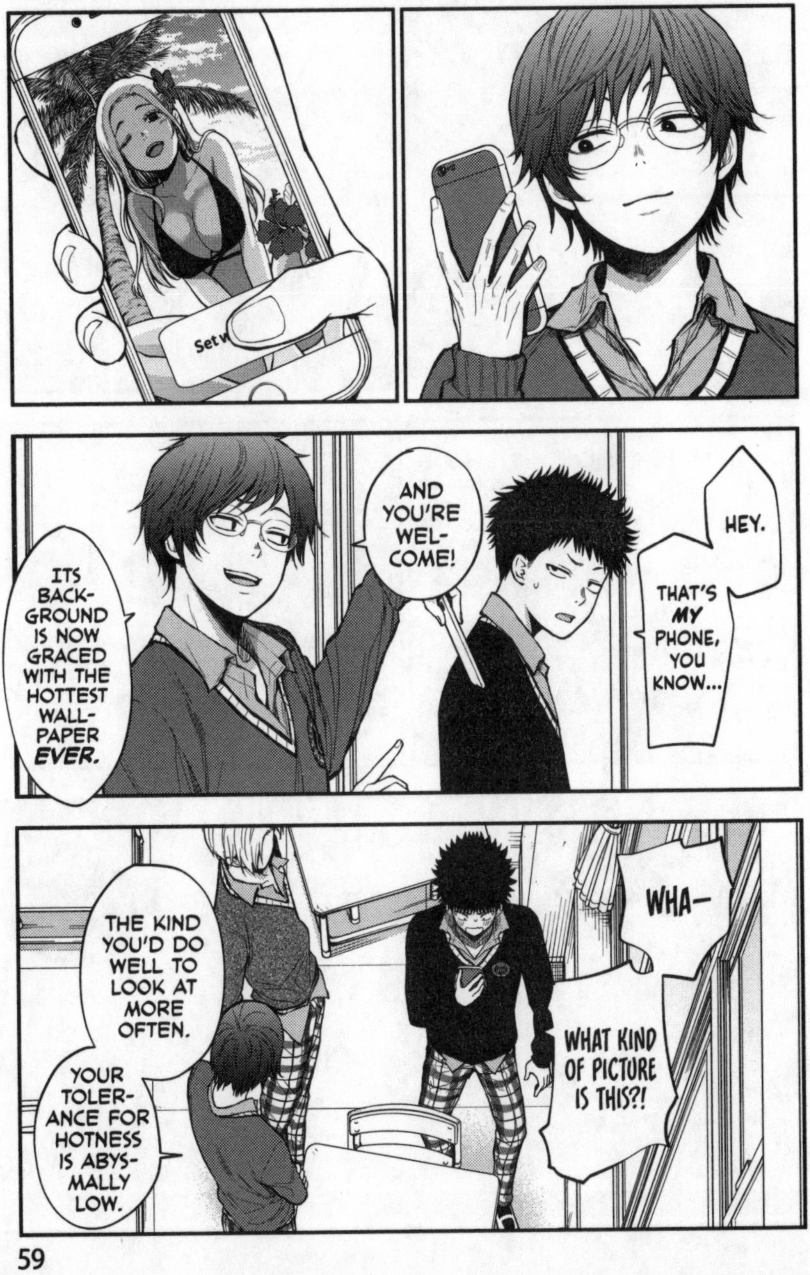
HEY.
THAT'S *MY* PHONE, YOU KNOW...
AND YOU'RE WEL-COME!
ITS BACK-GROUND IS NOW GRACED WITH THE HOTTEST WALL-PAPER ***EVER.***
WHA-
WHAT KIND OF PICTURE IS THIS?!
THE KIND YOU'D DO WELL TO LOOK AT MORE OFTEN.
YOUR TOLER-ANCE FOR HOTNESS IS ABYS-MALLY LOW.

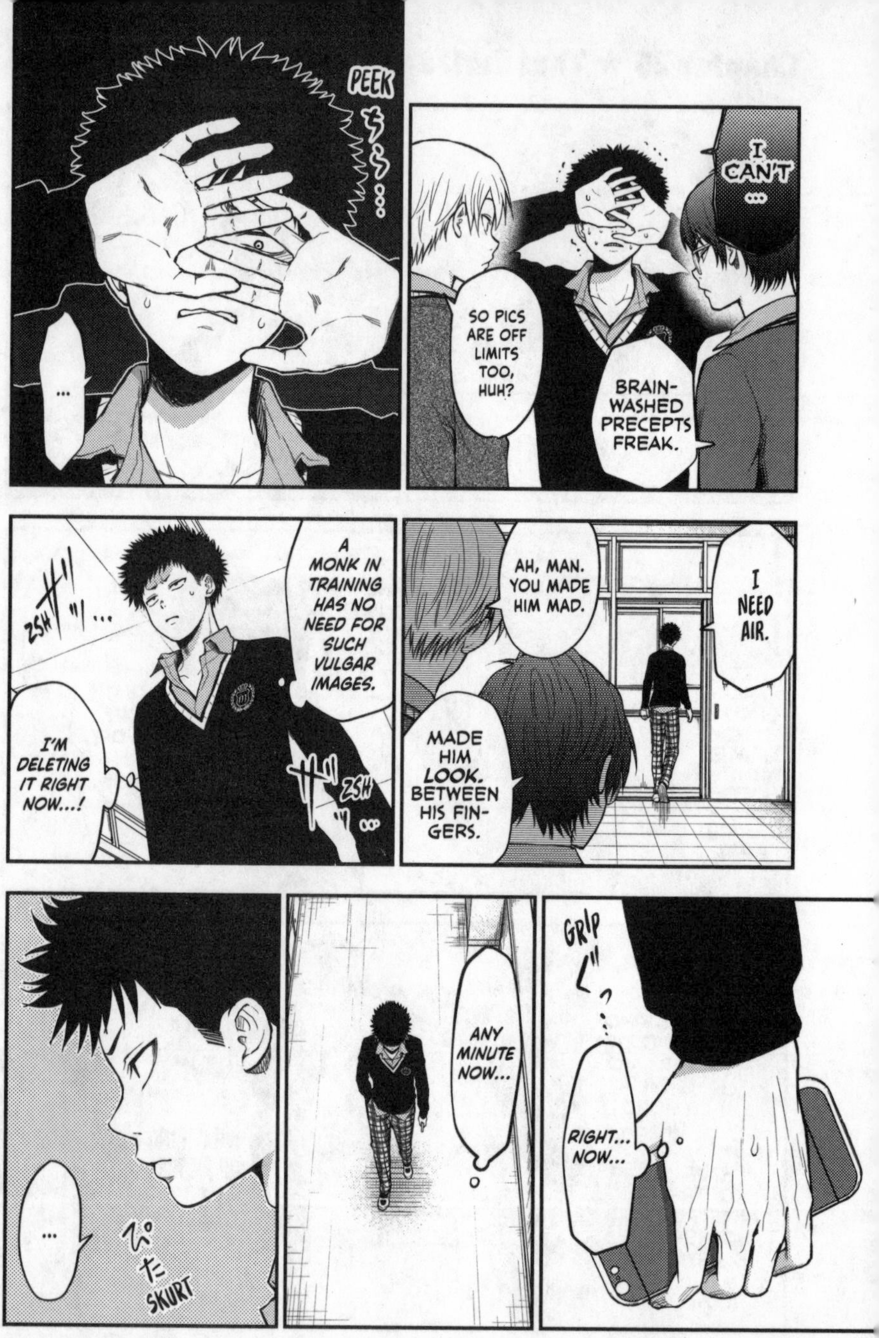
I CAN'T ...
SO PICS ARE OFF LIMITS TOO, HUH?
BRAIN-WASHED PRECEPTS FREAK.
PEEK
ちら...
...
I NEED AIR.
AH, MAN. YOU MADE HIM MAD.
MADE HIM LOOK. BETWEEN HIS FINGERS.
A MONK IN TRAINING HAS NO NEED FOR SUCH VULGAR IMAGES.
ZSH
I'M DELETING IT RIGHT NOW...!
ZSH
GRIP
...?
RIGHT... NOW...
ANY MINUTE NOW...
...
ぴた
SKURT

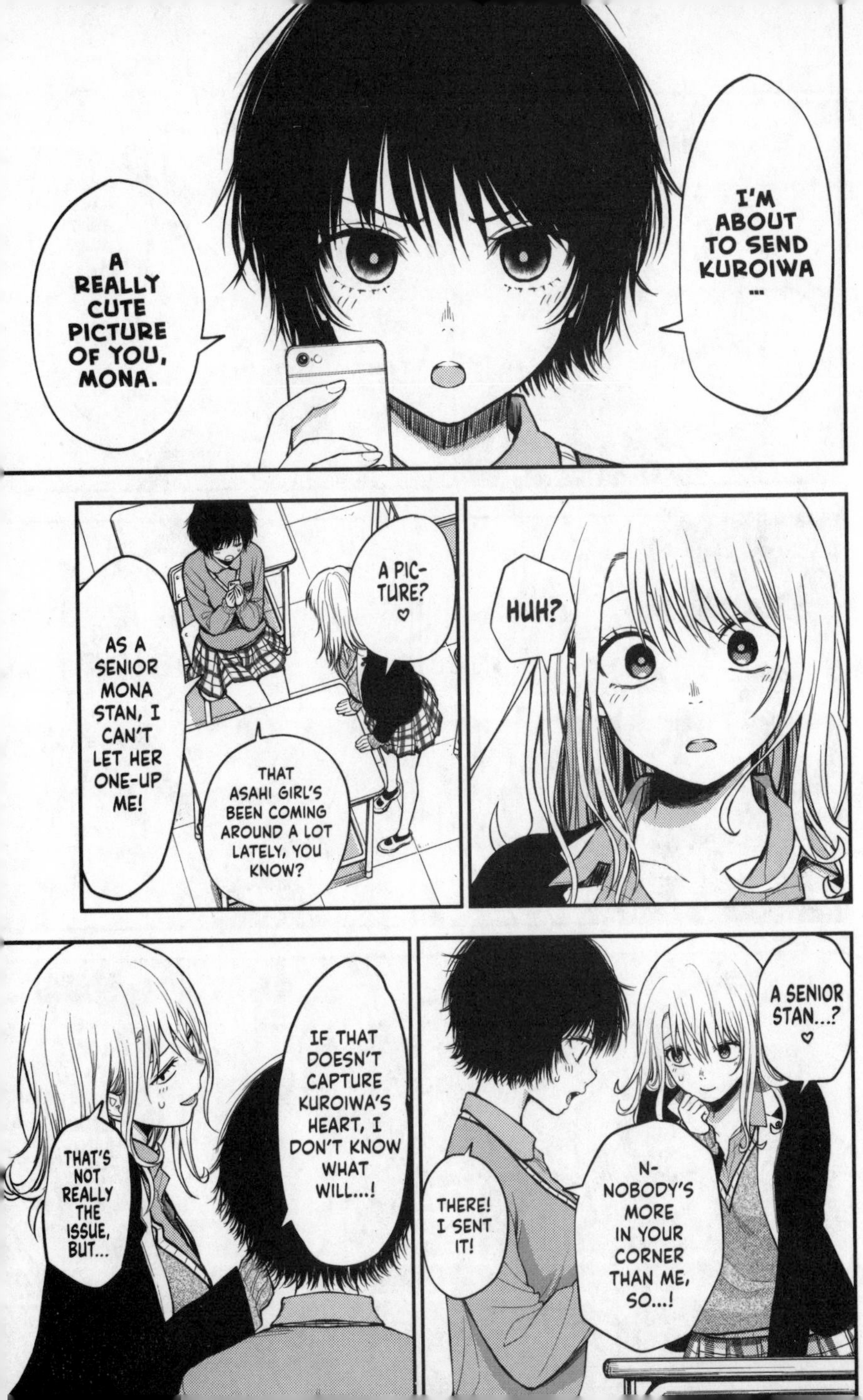
I'M ABOUT TO SEND KUROIWA...
A REALLY CUTE PICTURE OF YOU, MONA.
HUH?
A PICTURE? ♡
THAT ASAHI GIRL'S BEEN COMING AROUND A LOT LATELY, YOU KNOW?
AS A SENIOR MONA STAN, I CAN'T LET HER ONE-UP ME!
A SENIOR STAN...? ♡
N-NOBODY'S MORE IN YOUR CORNER THAN ME, SO...!
THERE! I SENT IT!
IF THAT DOESN'T CAPTURE KUROIWA'S HEART, I DON'T KNOW WHAT WILL...!
THAT'S NOT REALLY THE ISSUE, BUT...

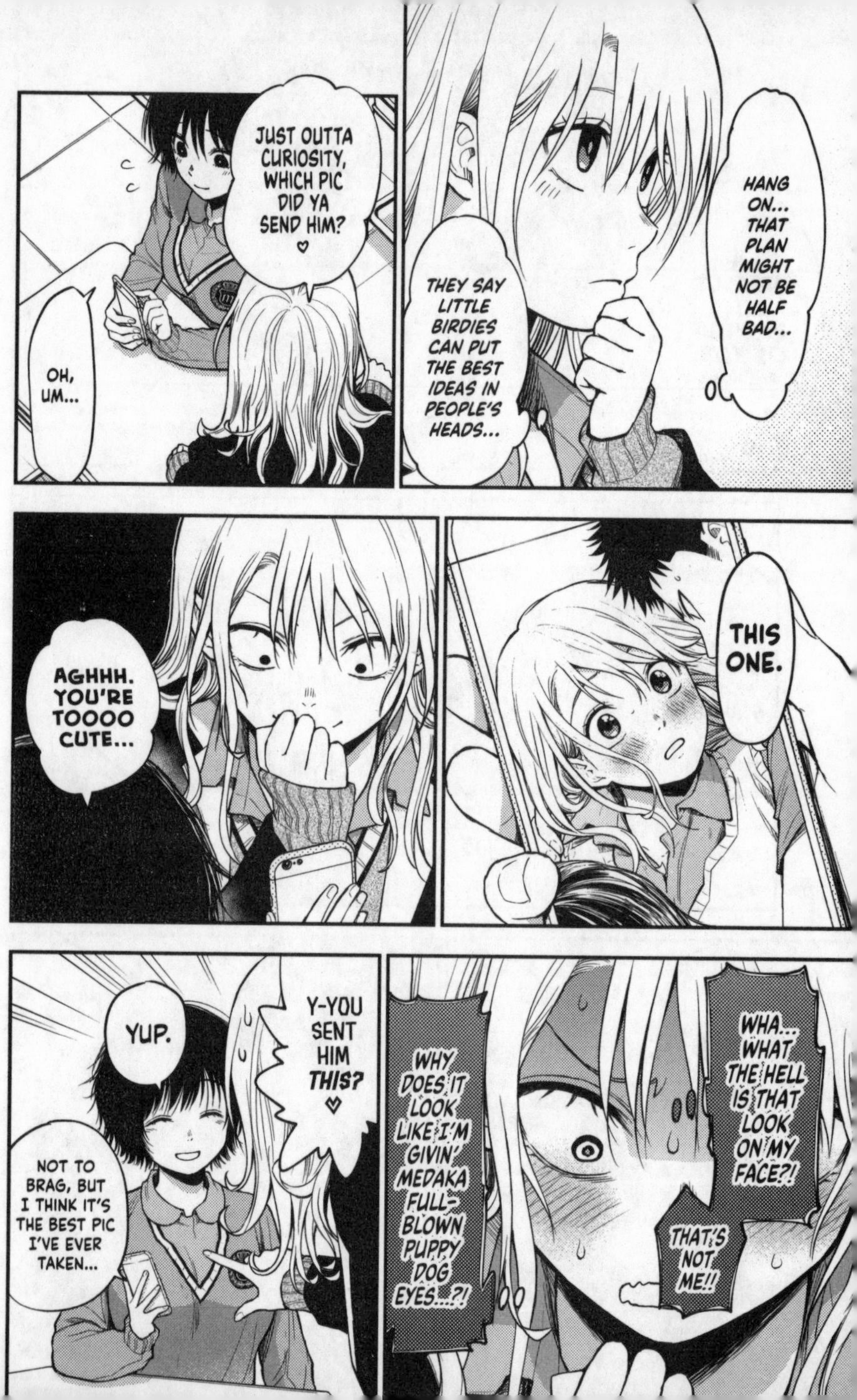
HANG ON... THAT PLAN MIGHT NOT BE HALF BAD...
THEY SAY LITTLE BIRDIES CAN PUT THE BEST IDEAS IN PEOPLE'S HEADS...
JUST OUTTA CURIOSITY, WHICH PIC DID YA SEND HIM? ♡
OH, UM...
THIS ONE.
AGHHH. YOU'RE TOOOO CUTE...
WHA... WHAT THE HELL IS THAT LOOK ON MY FACE?!
WHY DOES IT LOOK LIKE I'M GIVIN' MEDAKA FULL-BLOWN PUPPY DOG EYES...?!
THAT'S NOT ME!!
Y-YOU SENT HIM THIS? ♡
YUP.
NOT TO BRAG, BUT I THINK IT'S THE BEST PIC I'VE EVER TAKEN...

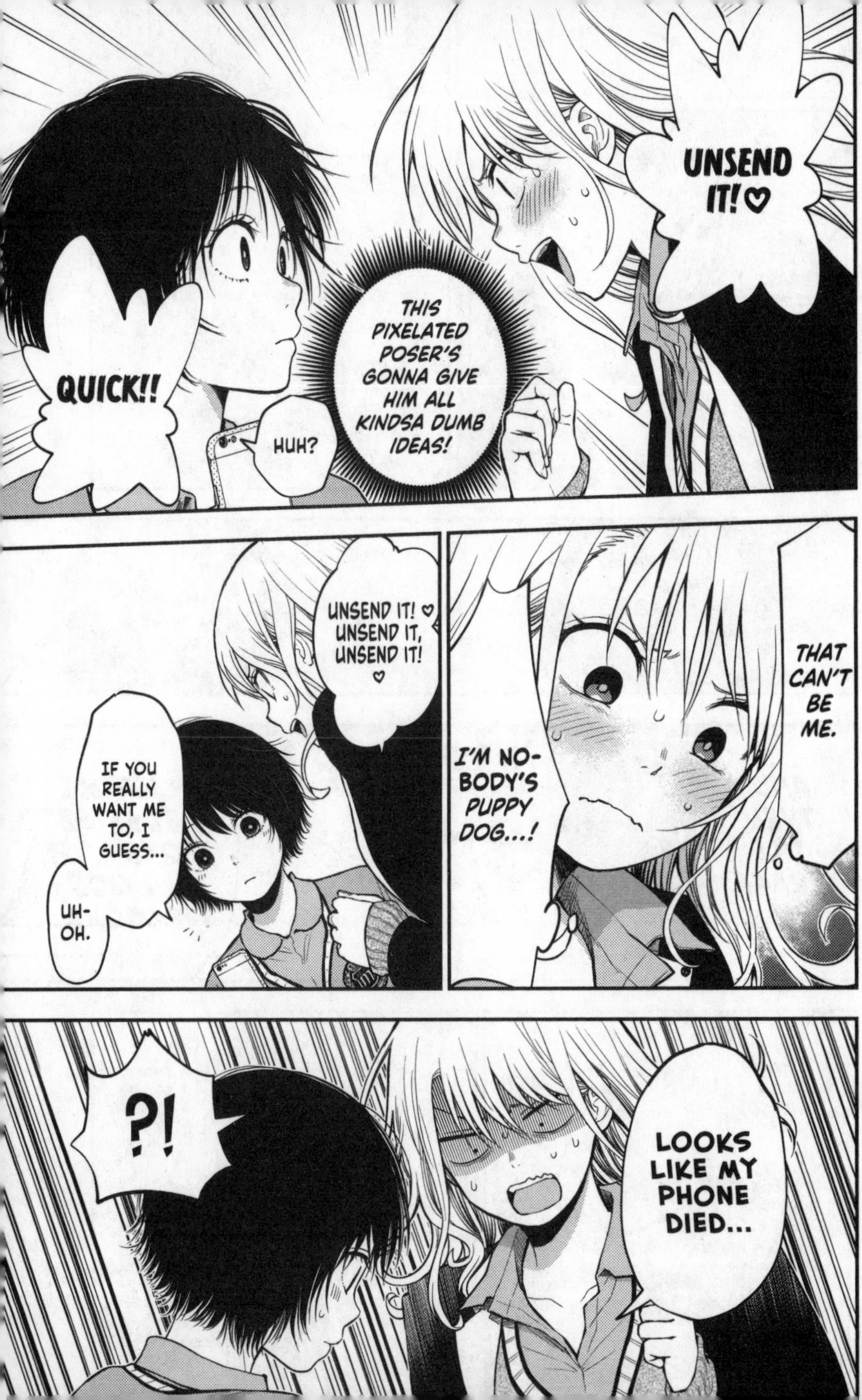
UNSEND IT!♡
THIS PIXELATED POSER'S GONNA GIVE HIM ALL KINDSA DUMB IDEAS!
HUH?
QUICK!!
THAT CAN'T BE ME.
I'M NOBODY'S PUPPY DOG...!
UNSEND IT! ♡ UNSEND IT, UNSEND IT! ♡
IF YOU REALLY WANT ME TO, I GUESS...
UH-OH.
LOOKS LIKE MY PHONE DIED...
?!

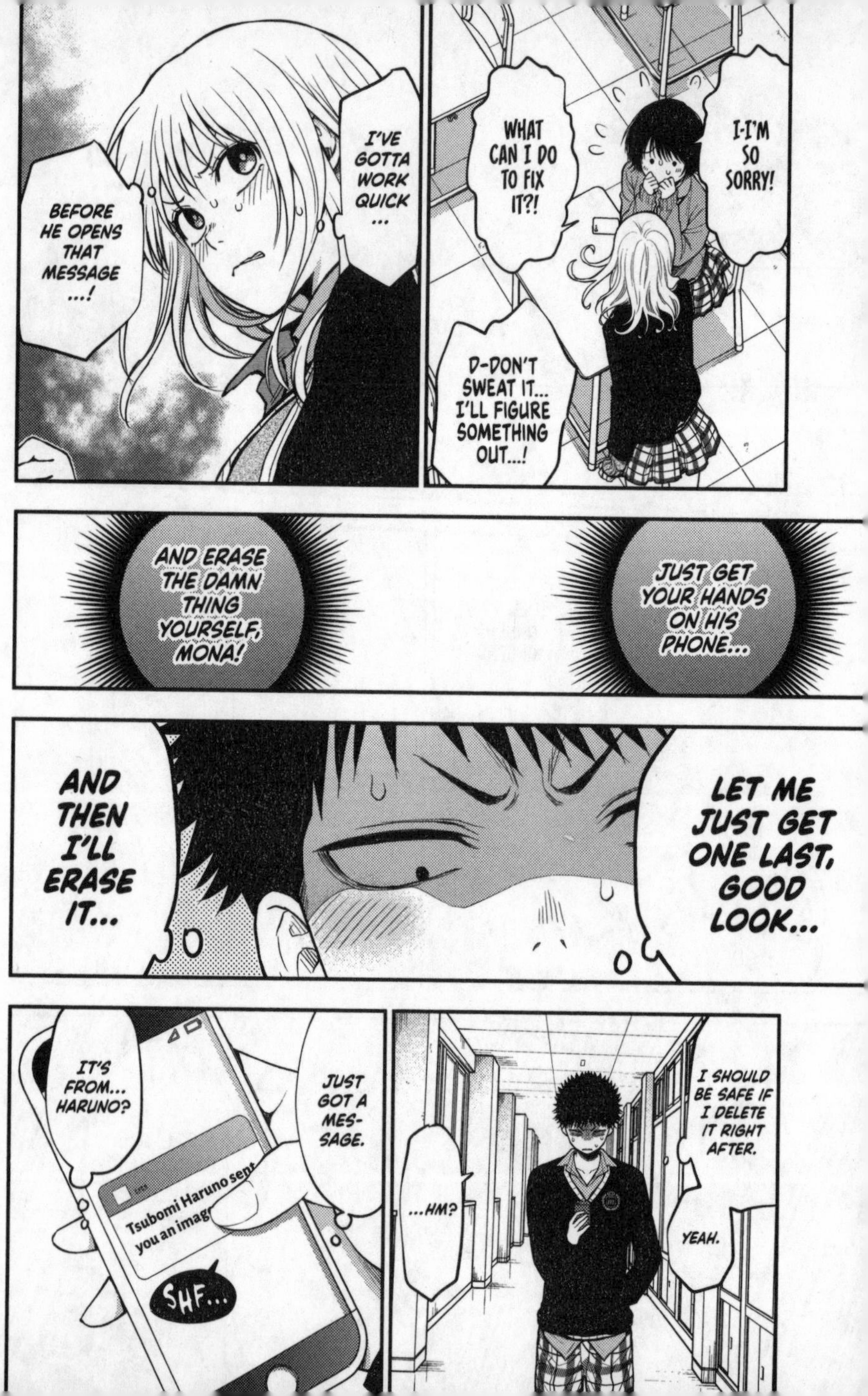
I-I'M SO SORRY!
WHAT CAN I DO TO FIX IT?!
D-DON'T SWEAT IT... I'LL FIGURE SOMETHING OUT...!
I'VE GOTTA WORK QUICK...
BEFORE HE OPENS THAT MESSAGE...!
JUST GET YOUR HANDS ON HIS PHONE...
AND ERASE THE DAMN THING YOURSELF, MONA!
LET ME JUST GET ONE LAST, GOOD LOOK...
AND THEN I'LL ERASE IT...
I SHOULD BE SAFE IF I DELETE IT RIGHT AFTER.
YEAH.
...HM?
JUST GOT A MES-SAGE.
IT'S FROM... HARUNO?
Tsubomi Haruno sent you an image
SHF...

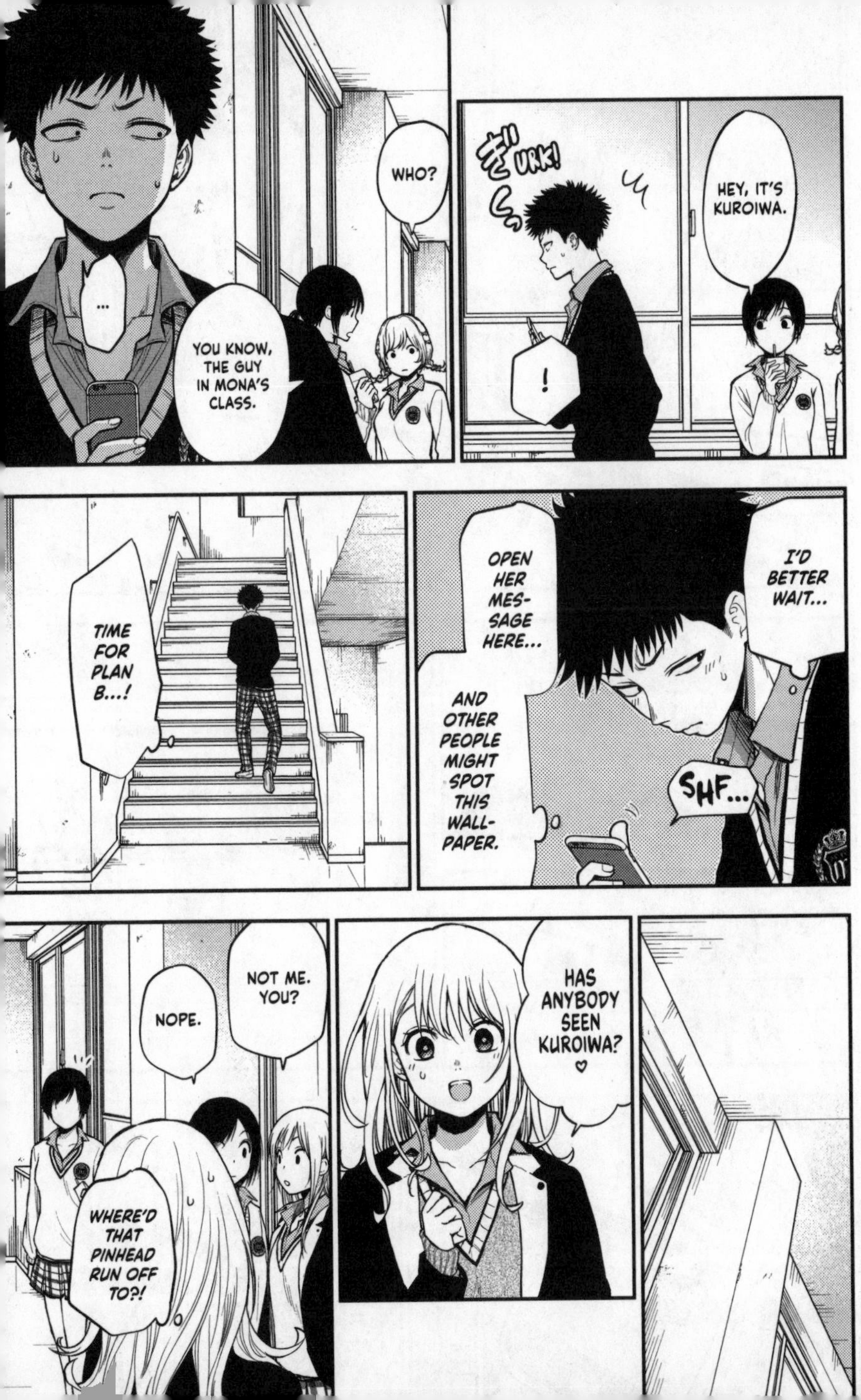
HEY, IT'S KUROIWA.
URK!
!
WHO?
YOU KNOW, THE GUY IN MONA'S CLASS.
...
I'D BETTER WAIT...
OPEN HER MES-SAGE HERE...
AND OTHER PEOPLE MIGHT SPOT THIS WALL-PAPER.
SHF...
TIME FOR PLAN B...!
HAS ANYBODY SEEN KUROIWA? ♡
NOT ME. YOU?
NOPE.
WHERE'D THAT PINHEAD RUN OFF TO?!

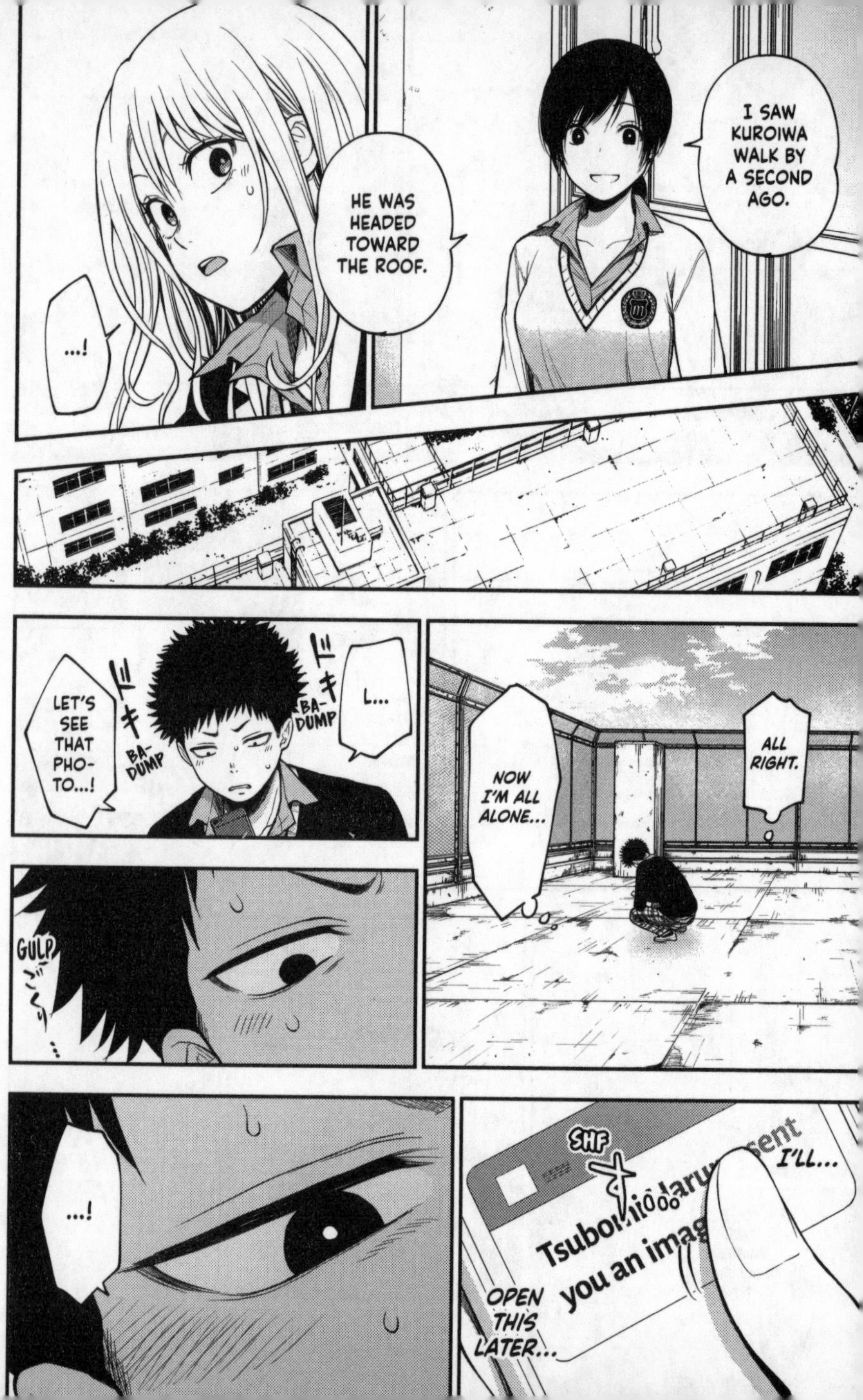
I SAW KUROIWA WALK BY A SECOND AGO.
HE WAS HEADED TOWARD THE ROOF.
...!
ALL RIGHT.
NOW I'M ALL ALONE...
L...
ドキ
BA-DUMP
LET'S SEE THAT PHO-TO...!
ドキ
BA-DUMP
GULP
ごくり...
SHF
I'LL...
Tsubo
sent
you an imag
OPEN THIS LATER...
...!

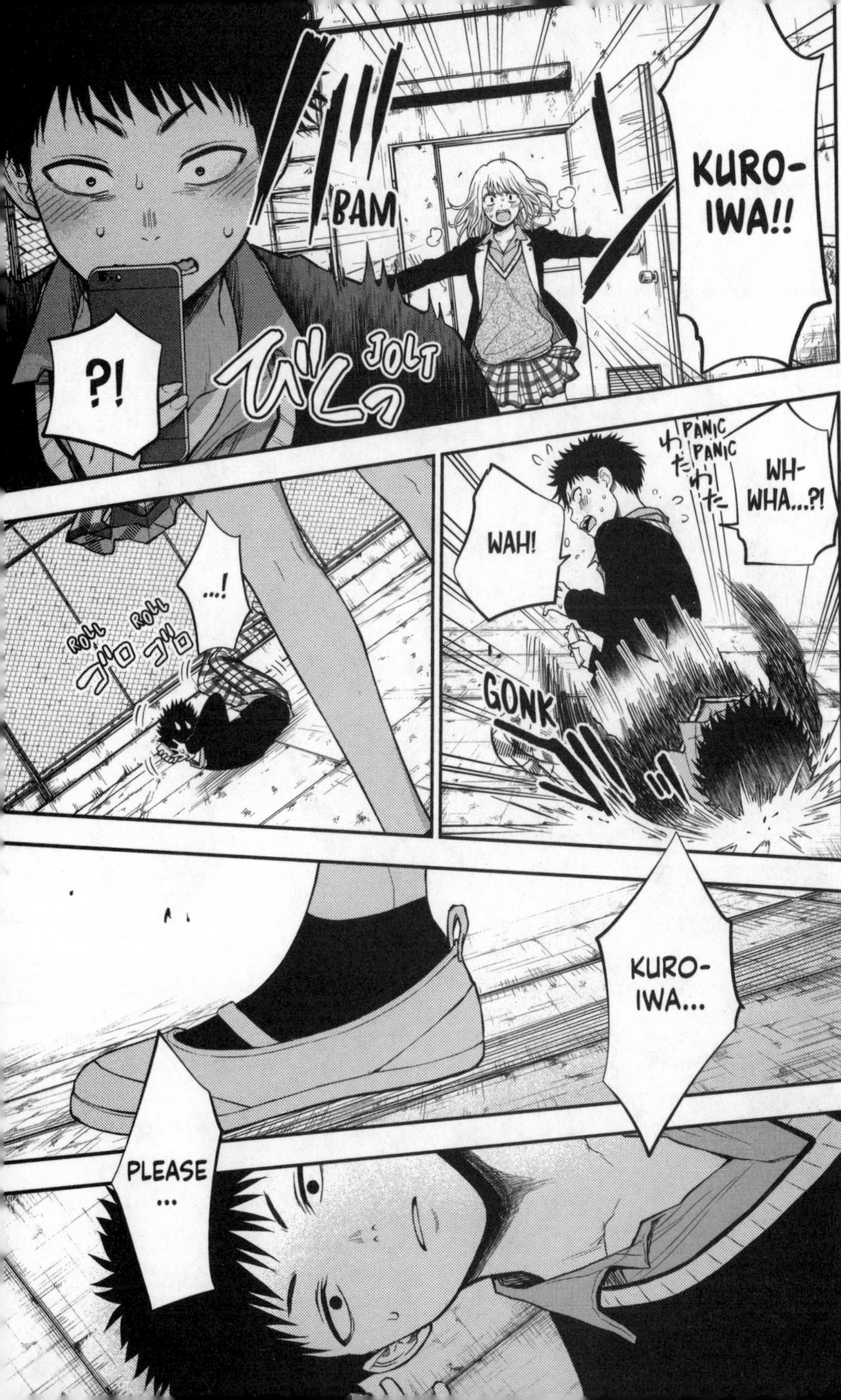
KURO-IWA!!
BAM
?!
JOLT
びくっ
WH-WHA...?!
PANIC PANIC
わたわた
WAH!
GONK
...!
ROLL ROLL
ゴロゴロ
KURO-IWA...
PLEASE ...

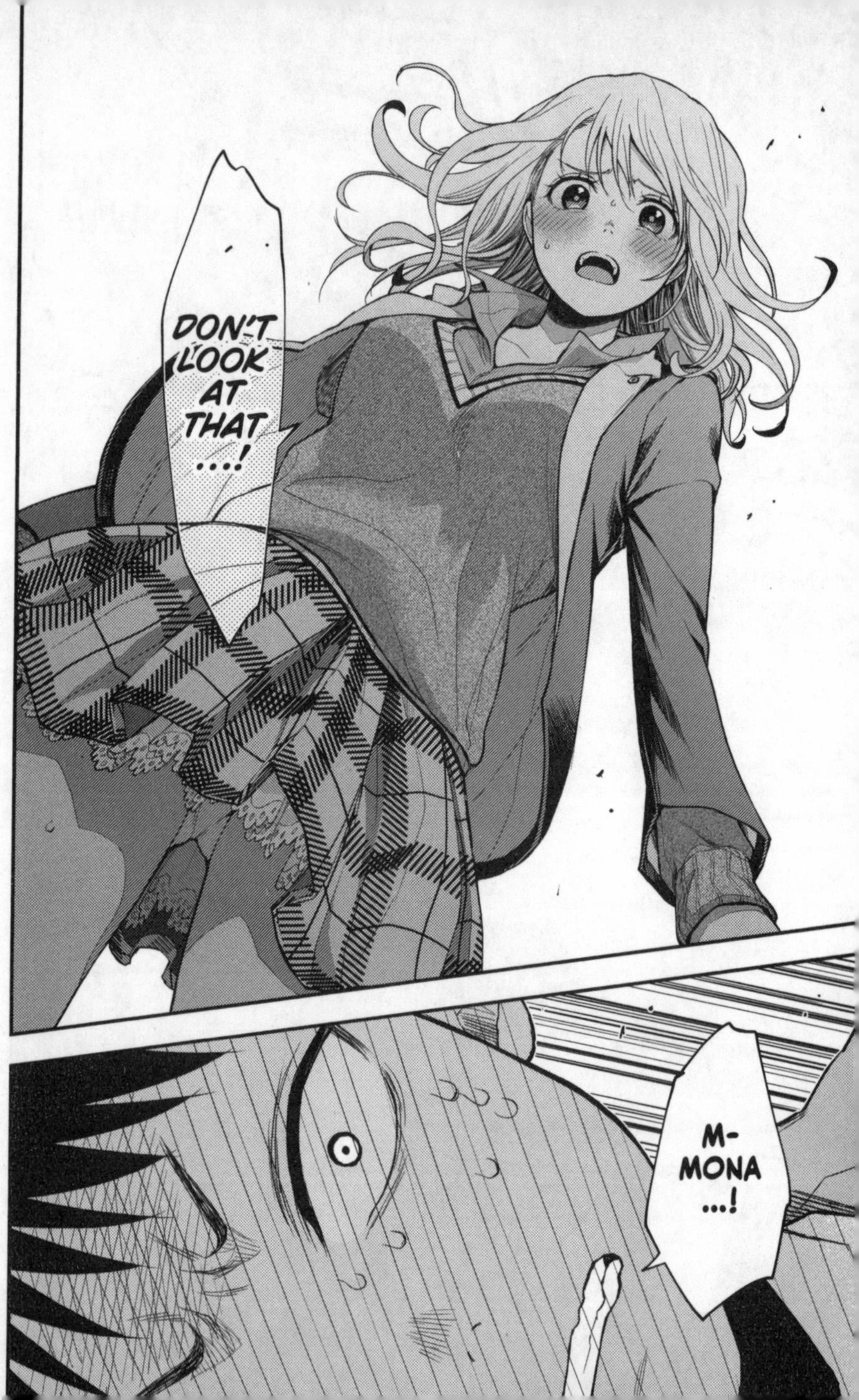
DON'T LOOK AT THAT ...!
M-MONA ...!

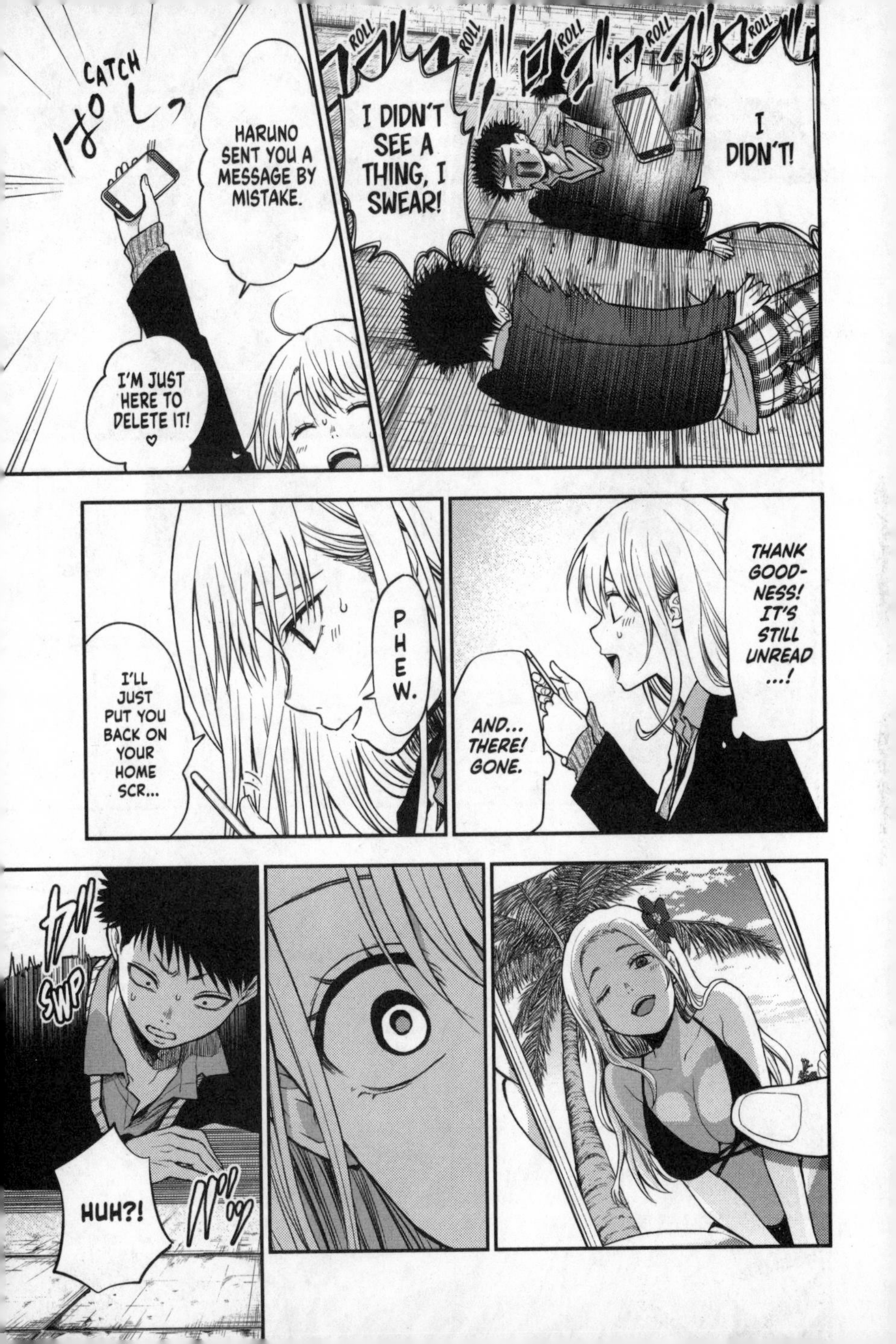
ROLL ROLL ROLL ROLL ROLL
I DIDN'T!
I DIDN'T SEE A THING, I SWEAR!
CATCH
はしっ
HARUNO SENT YOU A MESSAGE BY MISTAKE.
I'M JUST HERE TO DELETE IT! ♡
THANK GOODNESS! IT'S STILL UNREAD ...!
AND... THERE! GONE.
PHEW.
I'LL JUST PUT YOU BACK ON YOUR HOME SCR...
SWP
HUH?!

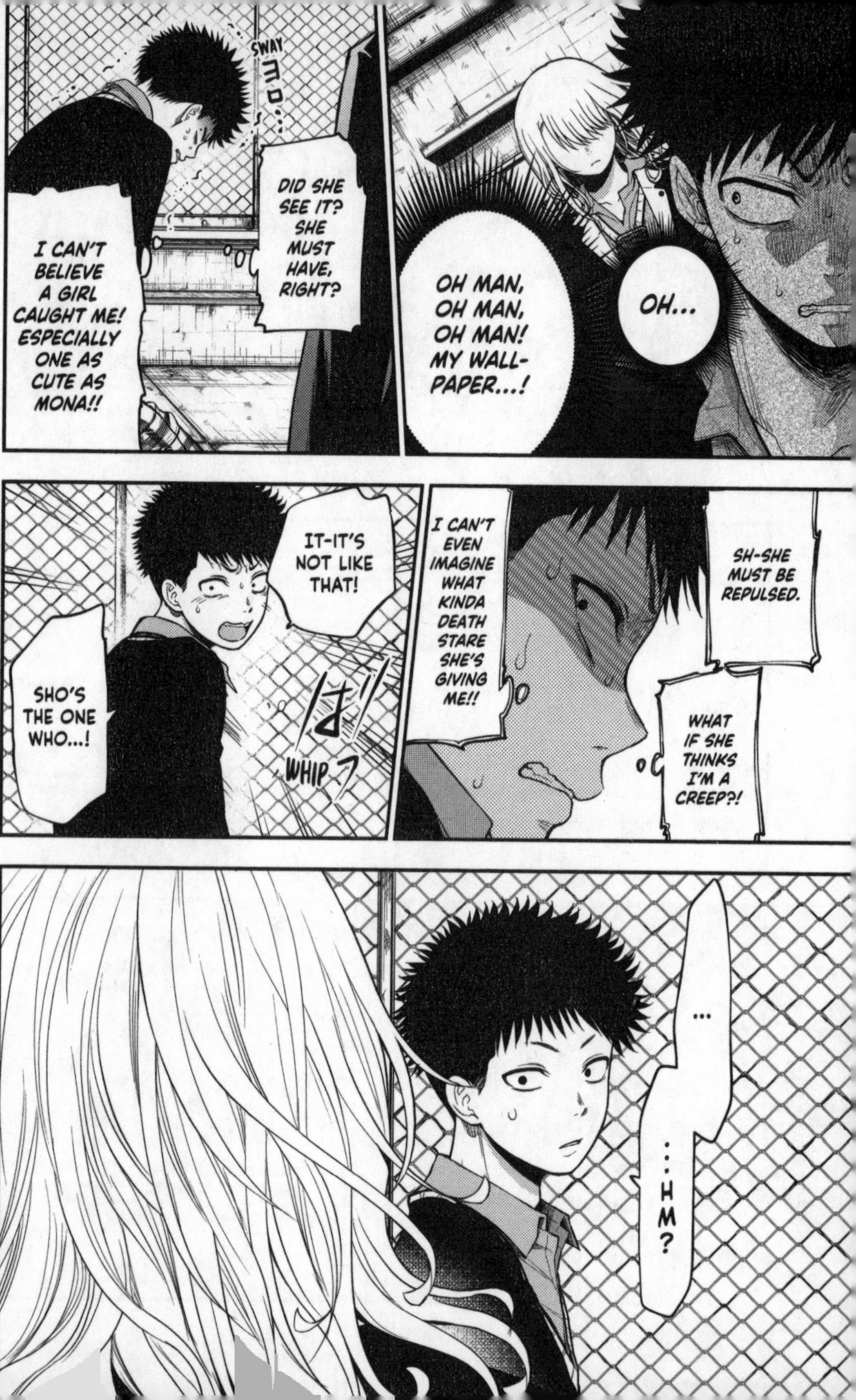
OH...
OH MAN, OH MAN, OH MAN! MY WALL-PAPER...!
SWAY
ヨロ...
DID SHE SEE IT? SHE MUST HAVE, RIGHT?
I CAN'T BELIEVE A GIRL CAUGHT ME! ESPECIALLY ONE AS CUTE AS MONA!!
SH-SHE MUST BE REPULSED.
I CAN'T EVEN IMAGINE WHAT KINDA DEATH STARE SHE'S GIVING ME!!
WHAT IF SHE THINKS I'M A CREEP?!
IT-IT'S NOT LIKE THAT!
はっ!!
WHIP
SHO'S THE ONE WHO...!
...
...HM?

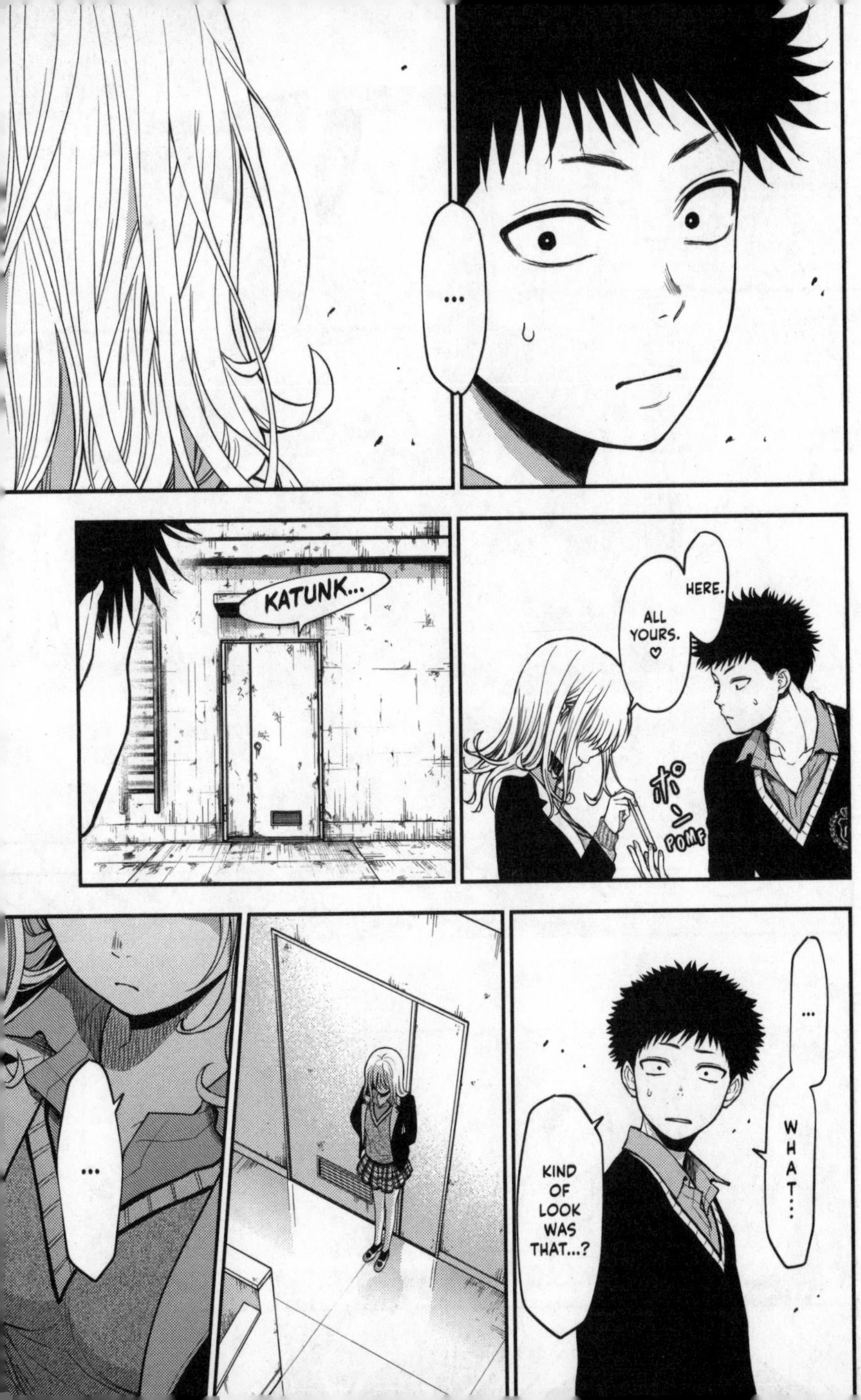
...
HERE.
ALL YOURS. ♡
ポン
POMF
KATUNK...
... WHAT...
KIND OF LOOK WAS THAT...?
...

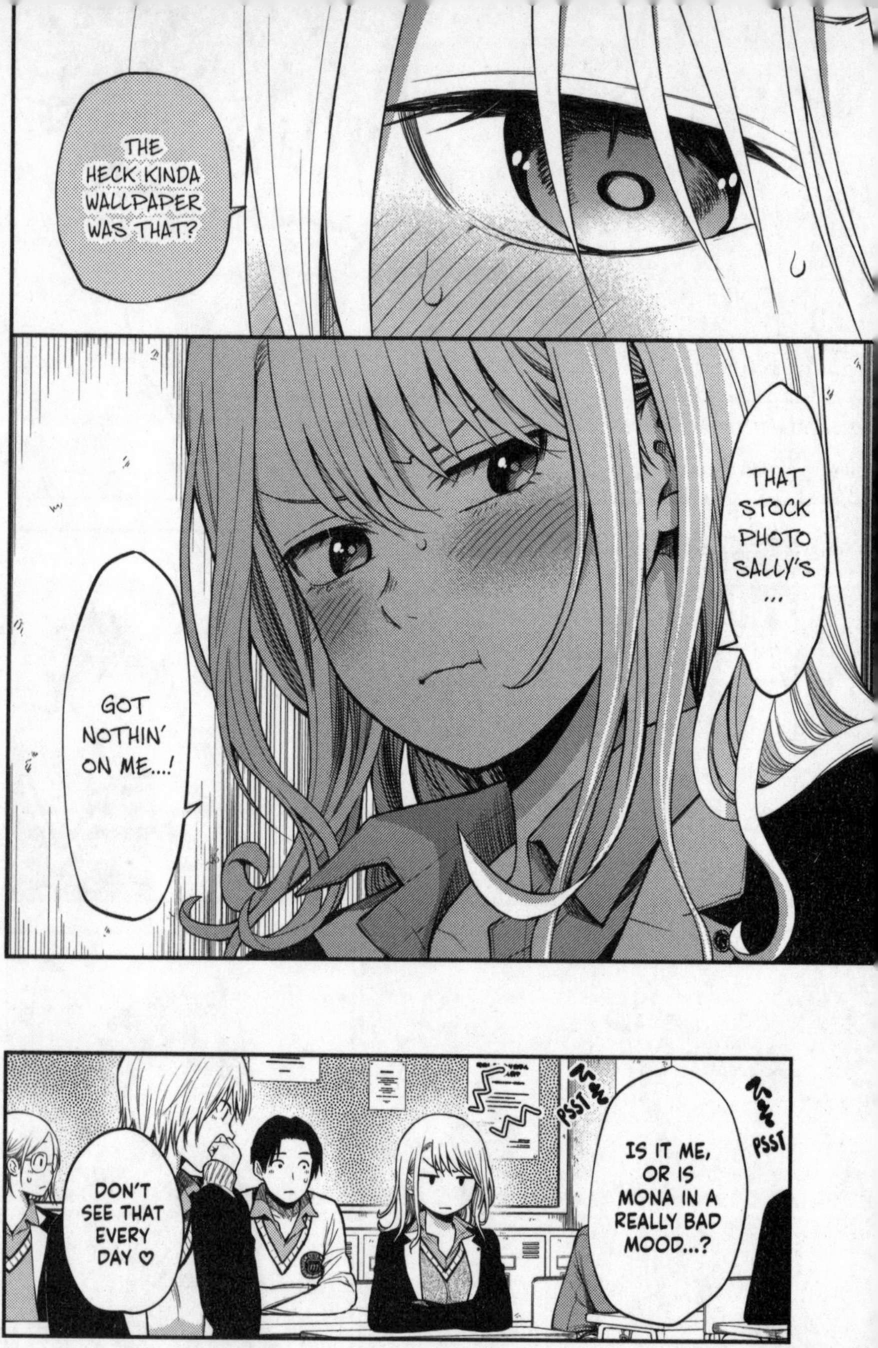
THE HECK KINDA WALLPAPER WAS THAT?
THAT STOCK PHOTO SALLY'S ...
GOT NOTHIN' ON ME...!
PSST
PSST
IS IT ME, OR IS MONA IN A REALLY BAD MOOD...?
DON'T SEE THAT EVERY DAY ♡

THE WALL-PAPER ON MEDAKA'S PHONE...
WAS OF SOME BABE IN A BIKINI.
じ STAARE
IF LOOKS...
COULD KILL...

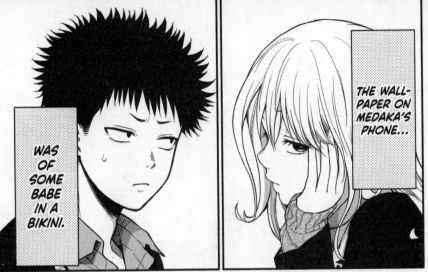

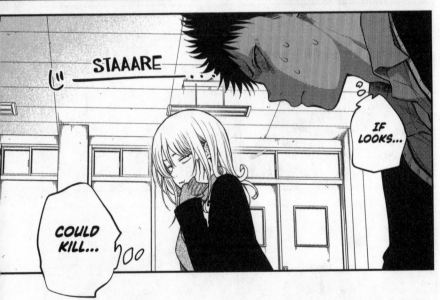

Chapter 24 ★ A Picture for That Jerk

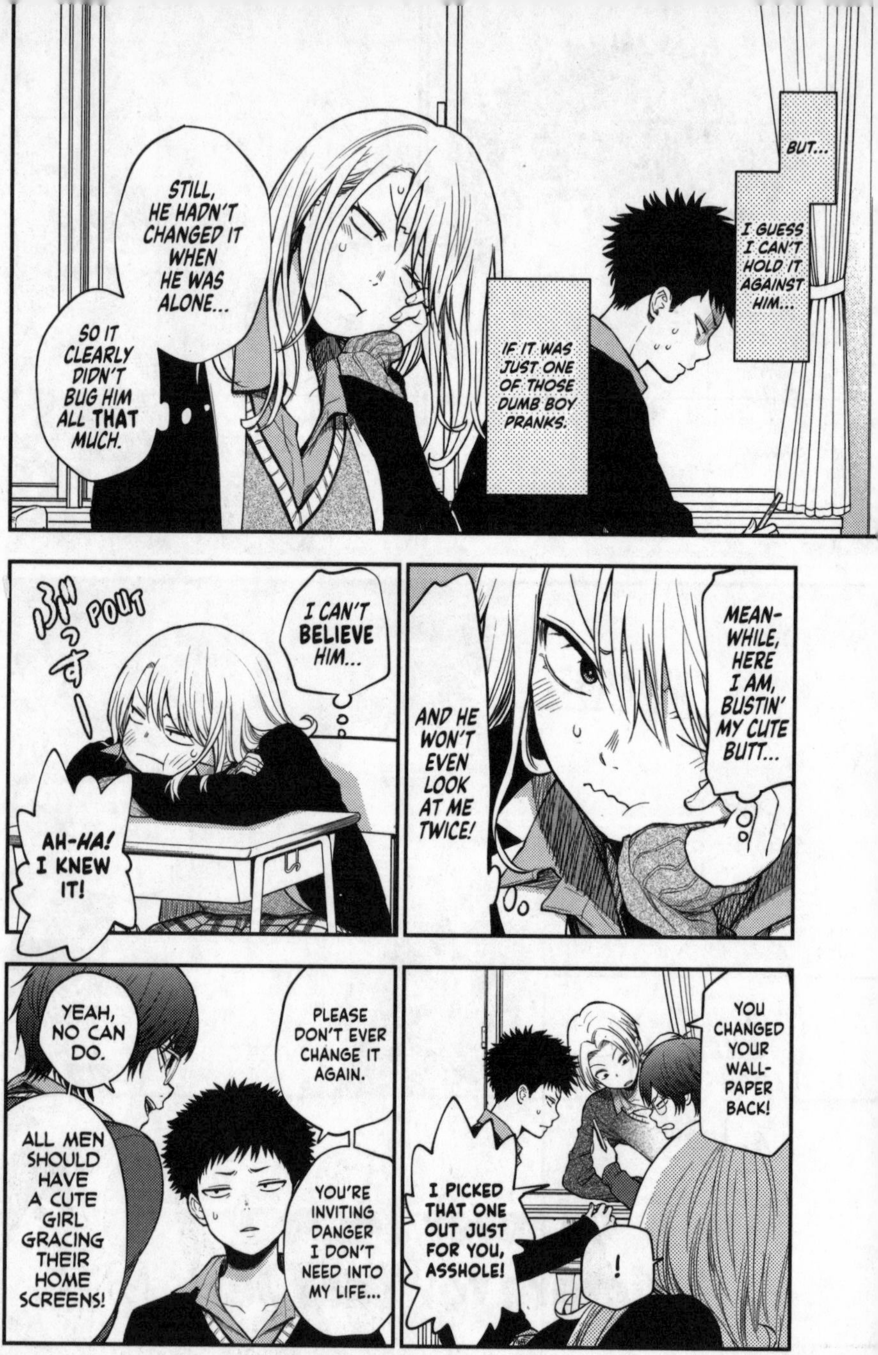

BUT...
I GUESS I CAN'T HOLD IT AGAINST HIM...
IF IT WAS JUST ONE OF THOSE DUMB BOY PRANKS.
STILL, HE HADN'T CHANGED IT WHEN HE WAS ALONE...
SO IT CLEARLY DIDN'T BUG HIM ALL THAT MUCH.
MEAN-WHILE, HERE I AM, BUSTIN' MY CUTE BUTT...
AND HE WON'T EVEN LOOK AT ME TWICE!
I CAN'T BELIEVE HIM...
ぶっすー
POUT
AH-HA! I KNEW IT!
YOU CHANGED YOUR WALL-PAPER BACK!
I PICKED THAT ONE OUT JUST FOR YOU, ASSHOLE!
!
PLEASE DON'T EVER CHANGE IT AGAIN.
YEAH, NO CAN DO.
YOU'RE INVITING DANGER I DON'T NEED INTO MY LIFE...
ALL MEN SHOULD HAVE A CUTE GIRL GRACING THEIR HOME SCREENS!

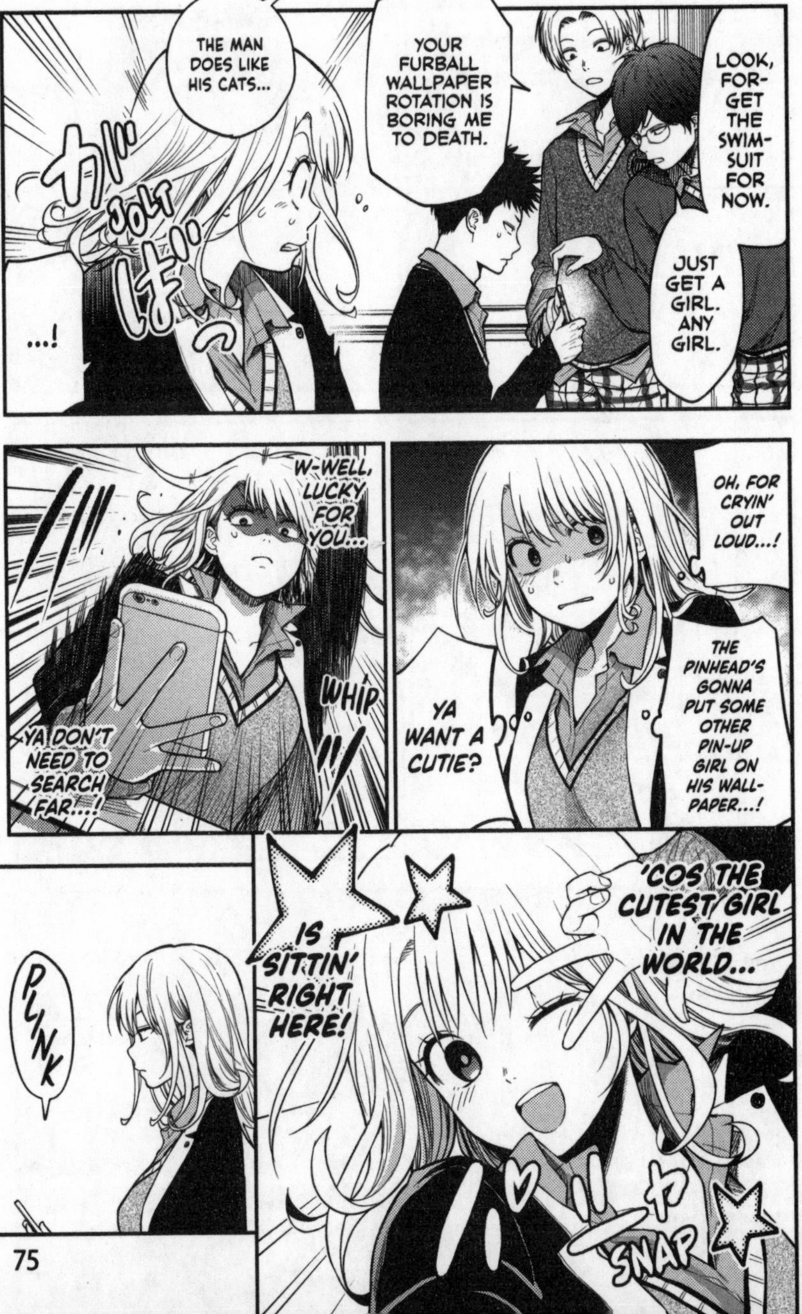

LOOK, FOR-GET THE SWIM-SUIT FOR NOW.
JUST GET A GIRL. ANY GIRL.
YOUR FURBALL WALLPAPER ROTATION IS BORING ME TO DEATH.
THE MAN DOES LIKE HIS CATS...
JOLT
...!
OH, FOR CRYIN' OUT LOUD...!
THE PINHEAD'S GONNA PUT SOME OTHER PIN-UP GIRL ON HIS WALL-PAPER...!
YA WANT A CUTIE?
W-WELL, LUCKY FOR YOU...
WHIP
YA DON'T NEED TO SEARCH FAR...!
'COS THE CUTEST GIRL IN THE WORLD...
IS SITTIN' RIGHT HERE!
SNAP
PLINK

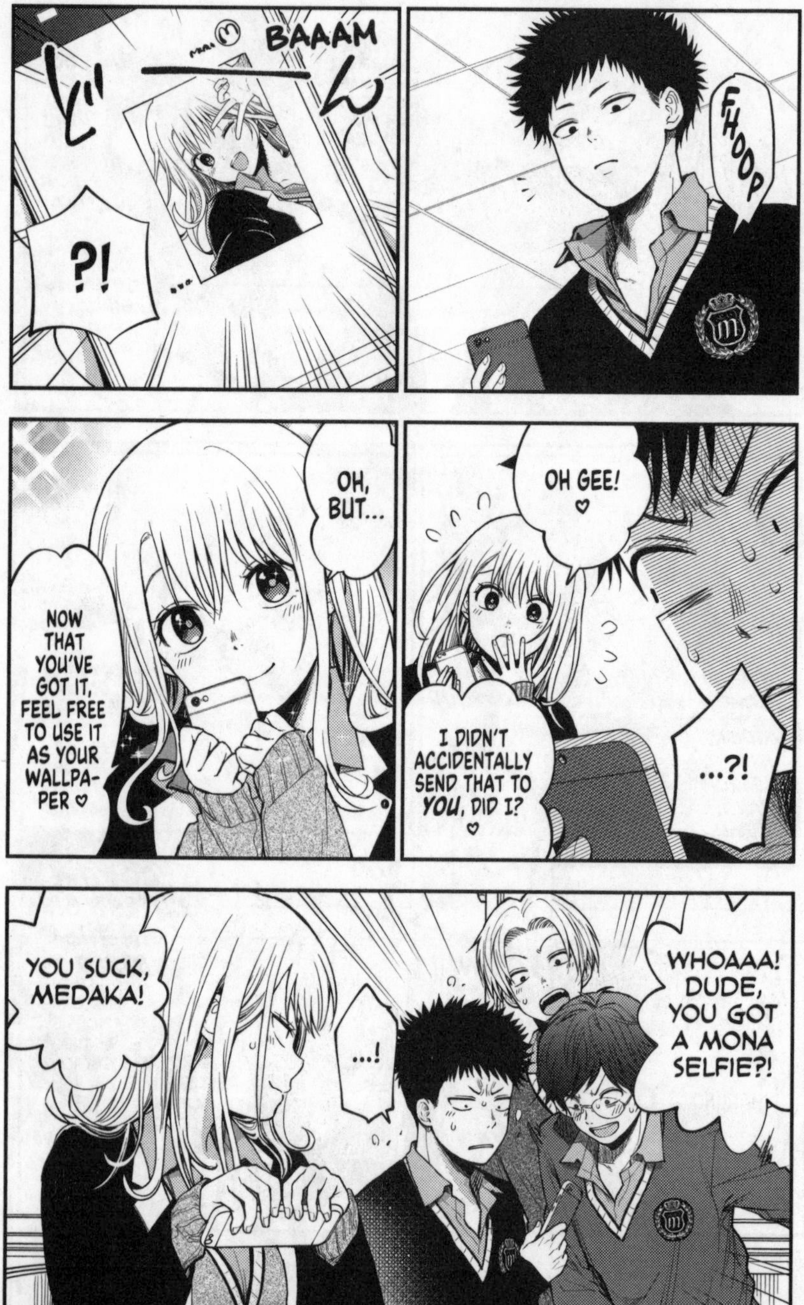
FHOOP
BAAAM
?!
OH GEE! ♡
...?!
I DIDN'T ACCIDENTALLY SEND THAT TO *YOU*, DID I? ♡
OH, BUT...
NOW THAT YOU'VE GOT IT, FEEL FREE TO USE IT AS YOUR WALLPA-PER ♡
WHOAAA! DUDE, YOU GOT A MONA SELFIE?!
...!
YOU SUCK, MEDAKA!

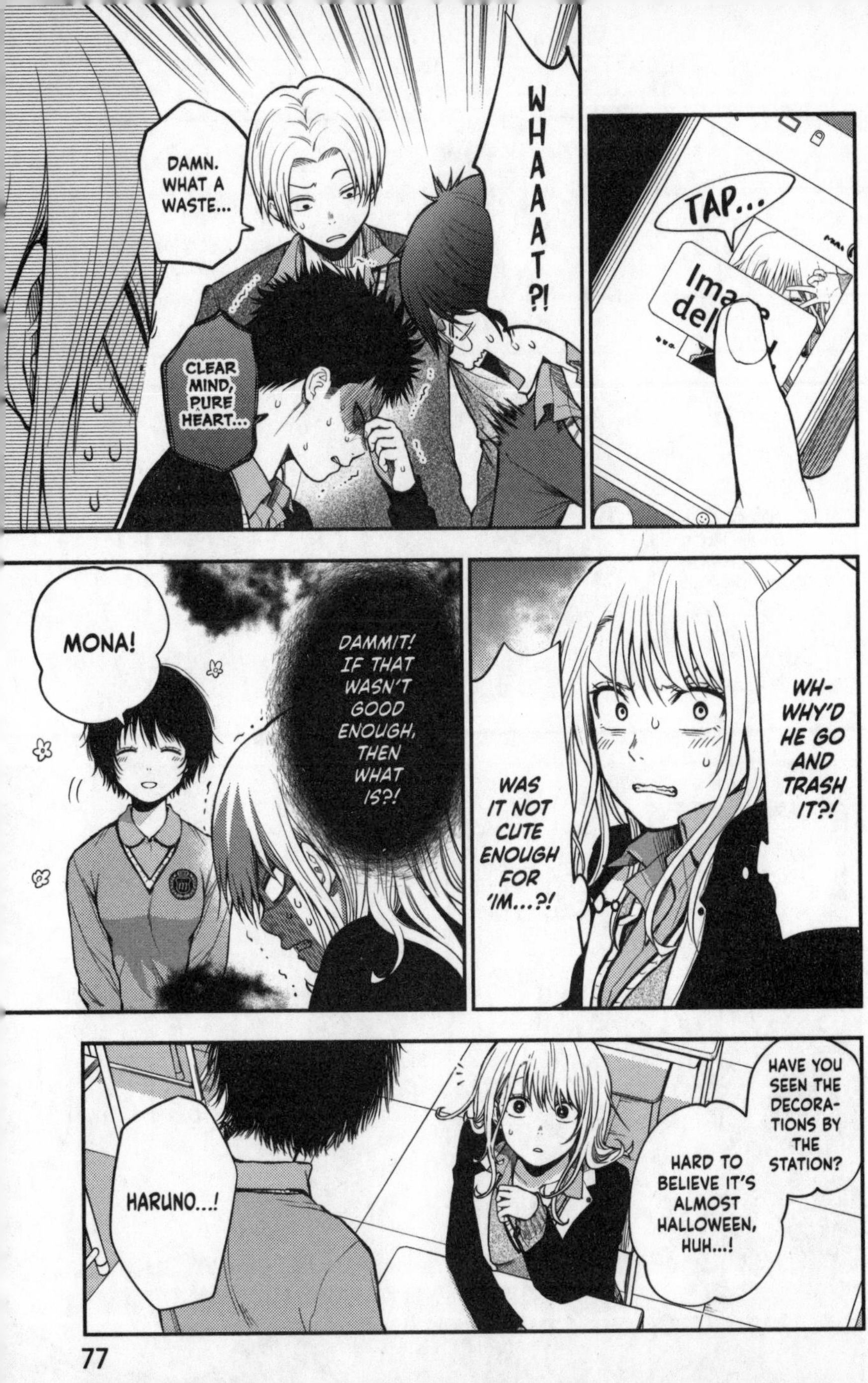
TAP...
WHAAAAT?!
DAMN. WHAT A WASTE...
CLEAR MIND, PURE HEART...
WH-WHY'D HE GO AND TRASH IT?!
WAS IT NOT CUTE ENOUGH FOR 'IM...?!
DAMMIT! IF THAT WASN'T GOOD ENOUGH, THEN WHAT IS?!
MONA!
HAVE YOU SEEN THE DECORATIONS BY THE STATION?
HARD TO BELIEVE IT'S ALMOST HALLOWEEN, HUH...!
HARUNO...!

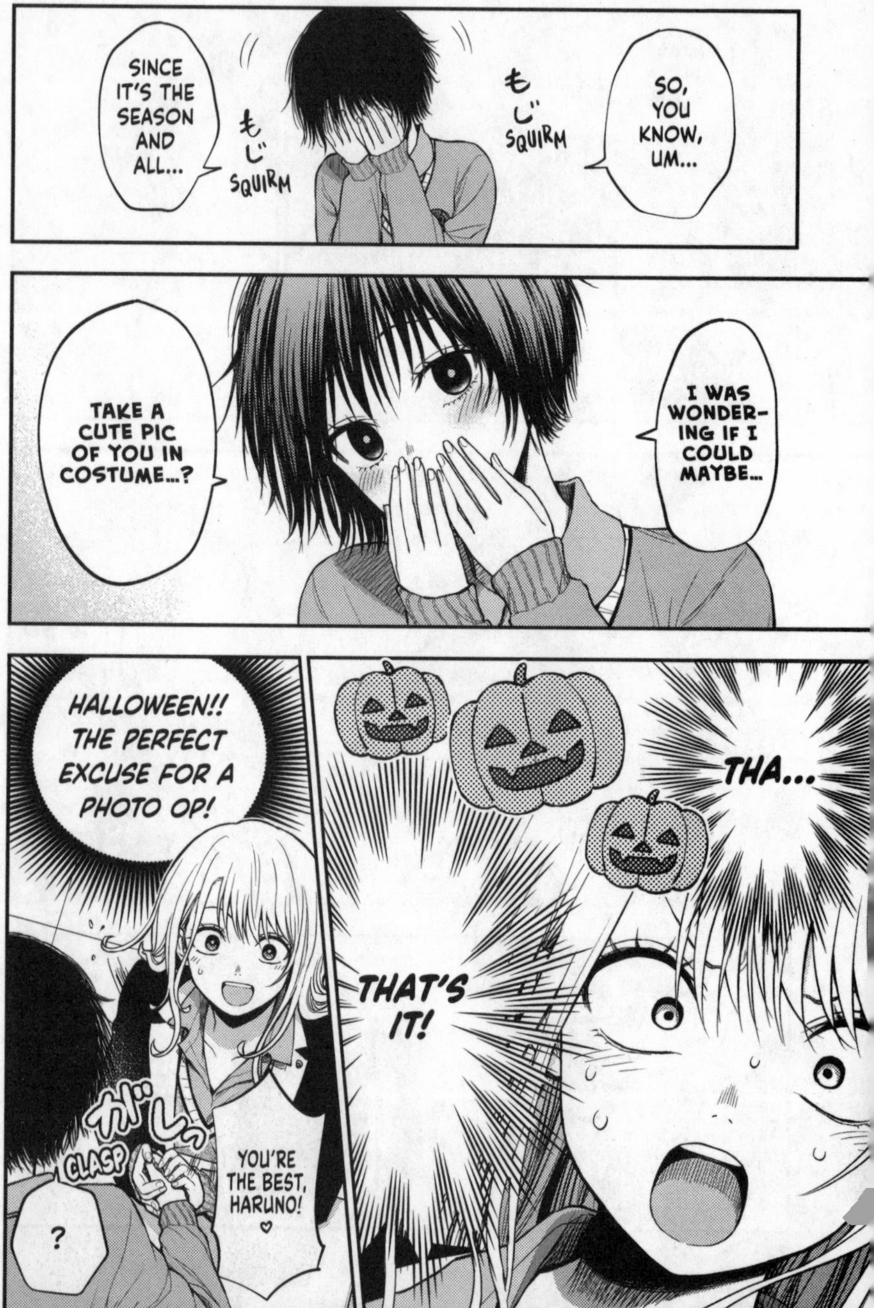
SO, YOU KNOW, UM...
もじ SQUIRM
もじ SQUIRM
SINCE IT'S THE SEASON AND ALL...
I WAS WONDERING IF I COULD MAYBE...
TAKE A CUTE PIC OF YOU IN COSTUME...?
THA...
THAT'S IT!
HALLOWEEN!! THE PERFECT EXCUSE FOR A PHOTO OP!
YOU'RE THE BEST, HARUNO! ♡
がしっ CLASP
?

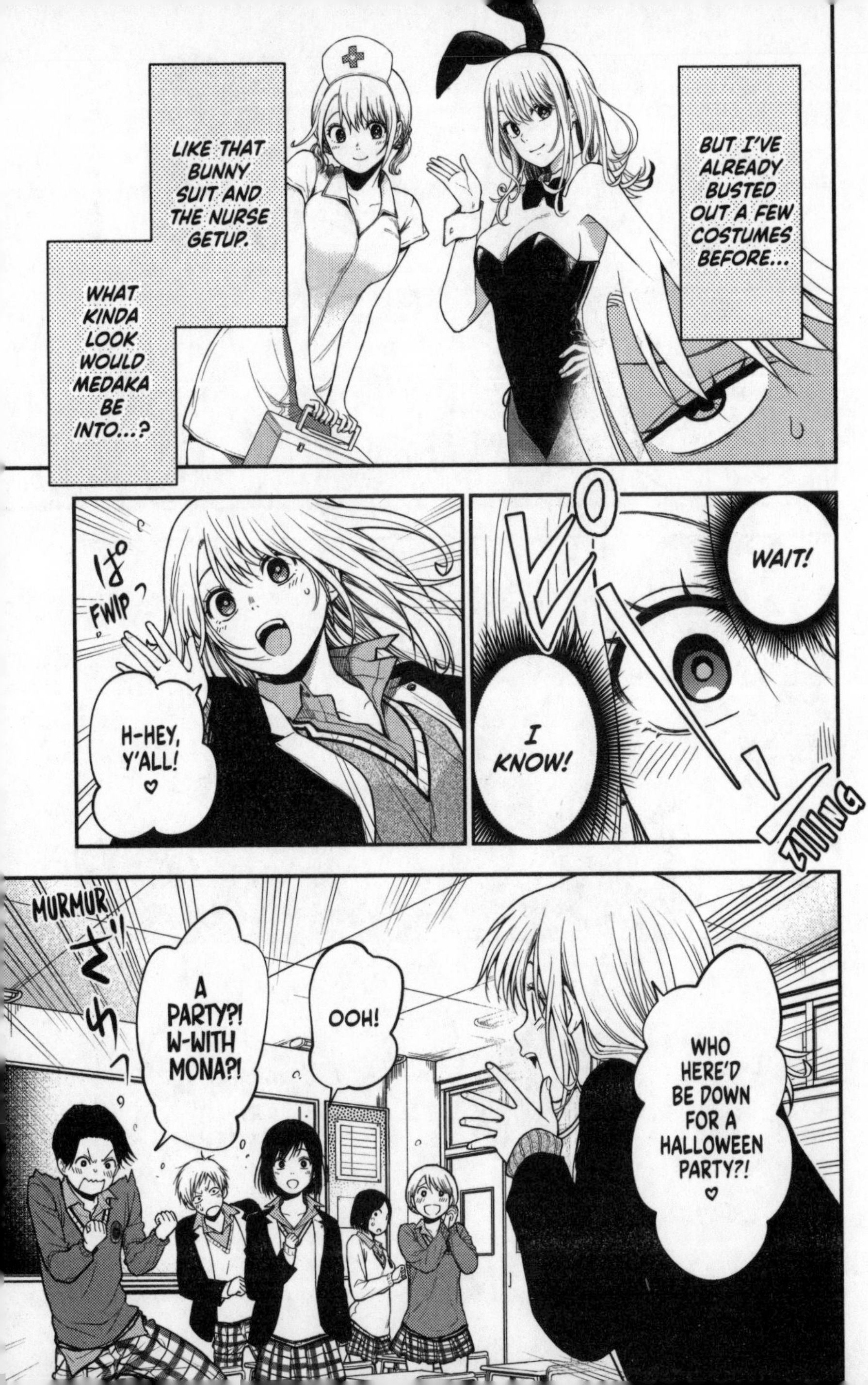
BUT I'VE ALREADY BUSTED OUT A FEW COSTUMES BEFORE...
LIKE THAT BUNNY SUIT AND THE NURSE GETUP.
WHAT KINDA LOOK WOULD MEDAKA BE INTO...?
WAIT!
I KNOW!
ZIIING
ぱ
FWIP
H-HEY, Y'ALL! ♡
WHO HERE'D BE DOWN FOR A HALLOWEEN PARTY?! ♡
OOH!
A PARTY?! W-WITH MONA?!
ざわ
MURMUR

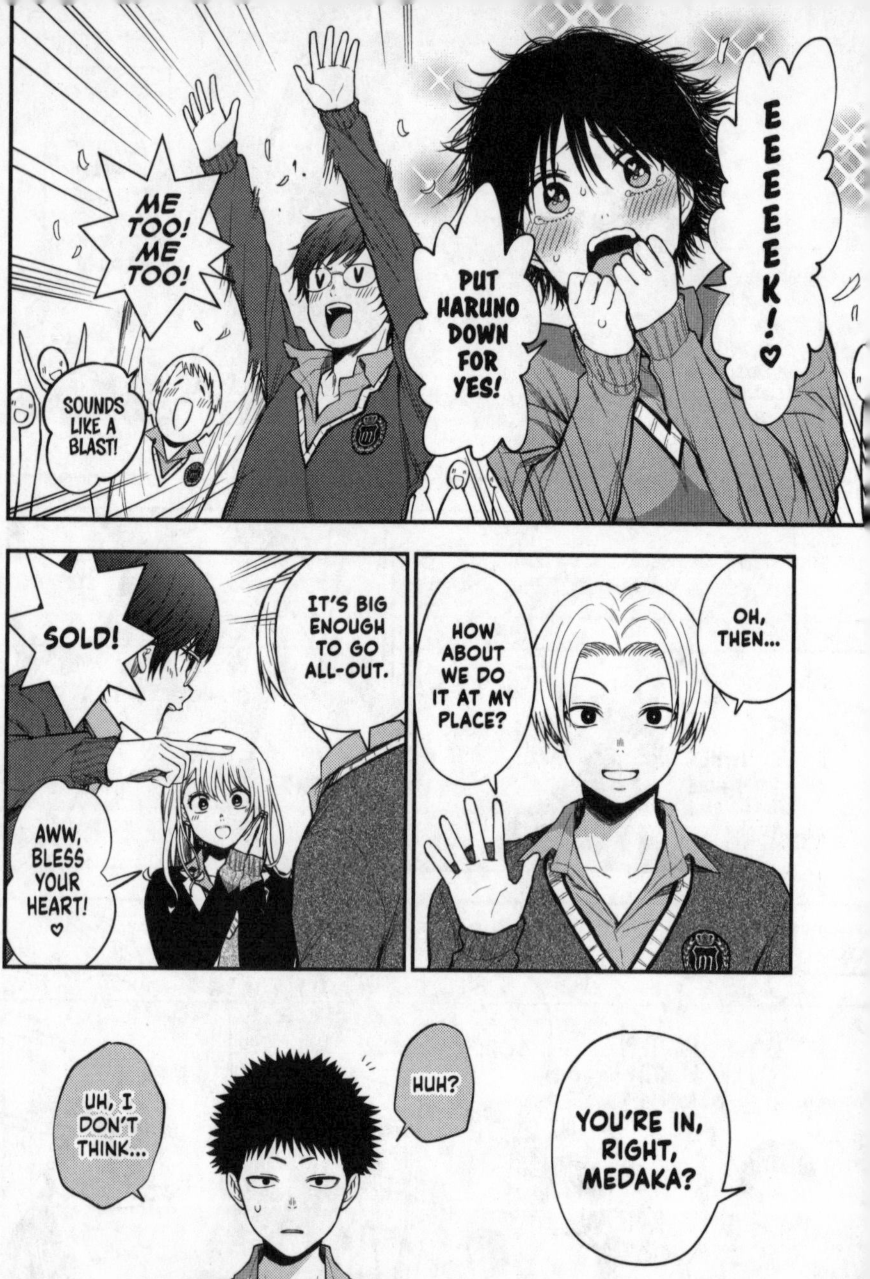
EEEEEK!♥
PUT HARUNO DOWN FOR YES!
ME TOO! ME TOO!
SOUNDS LIKE A BLAST!
OH, THEN...
HOW ABOUT WE DO IT AT MY PLACE?
IT'S BIG ENOUGH TO GO ALL-OUT.
SOLD!
AWW, BLESS YOUR HEART! ♥
YOU'RE IN, RIGHT, MEDAKA?
HUH?
UH, I DON'T THINK...

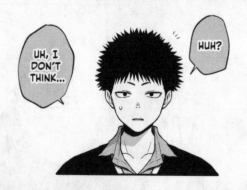

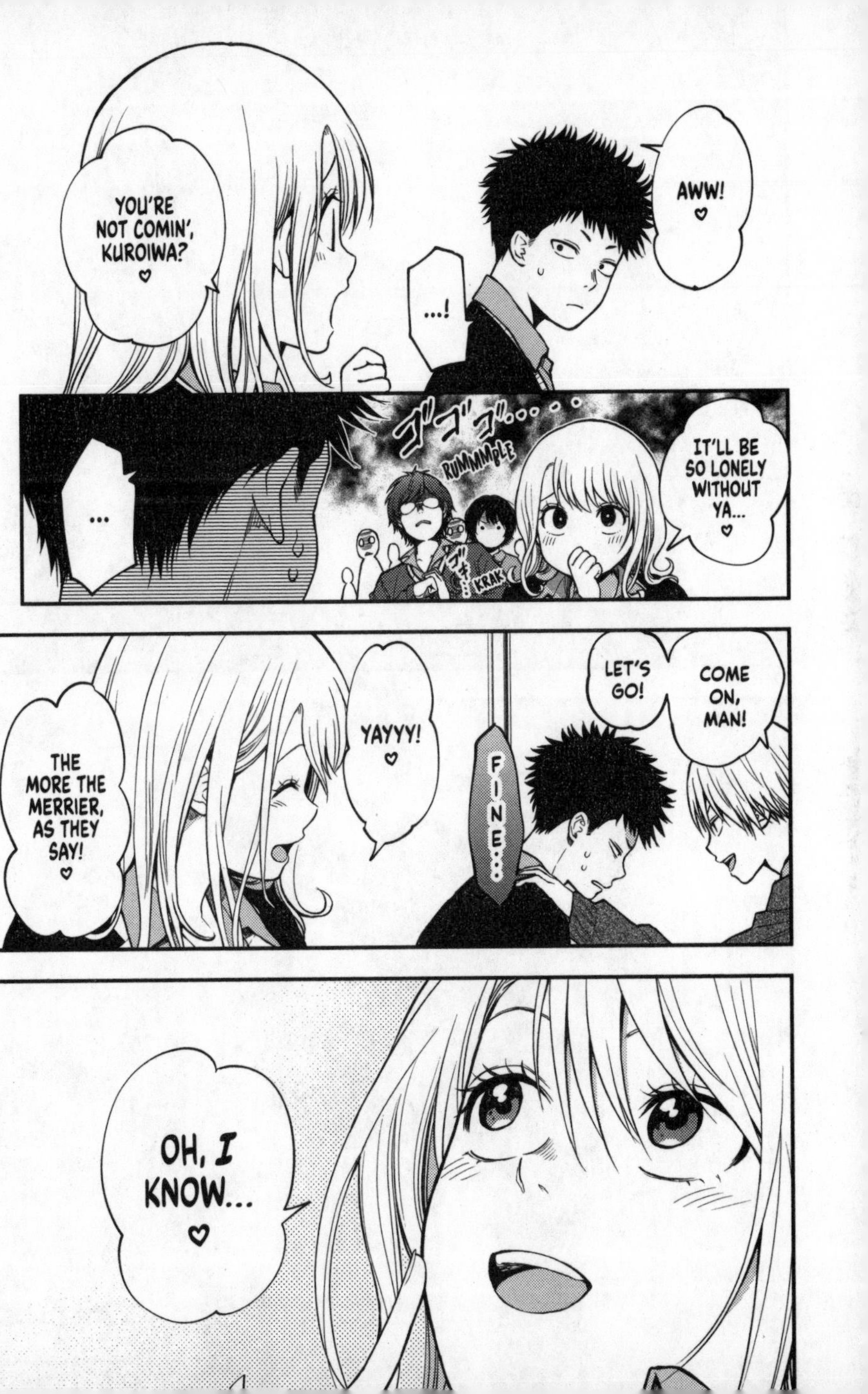

AWW! ♡
...!
YOU'RE NOT COMIN', KUROIWA? ♡
IT'LL BE SO LONELY WITHOUT YA... ♡
ゴゴゴ...
RUMMMBLE
KRAK
...
COME ON, MAN!
LET'S GO!
FINE...
YAYYY! ♡
THE MORE THE MERRIER, AS THEY SAY! ♡
OH, I KNOW... ♡

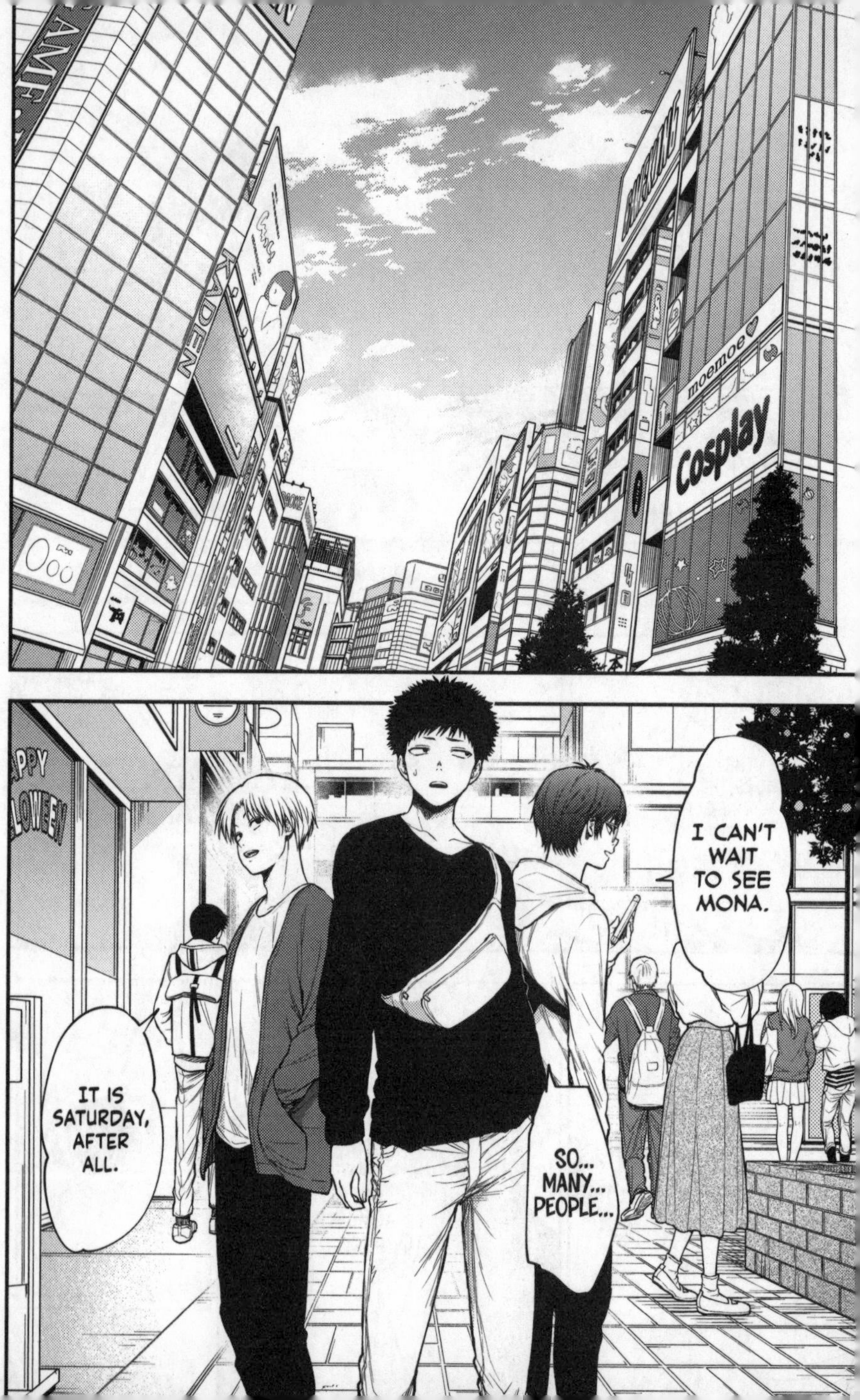
KADEN
moemoe
Cosplay
I CAN'T WAIT TO SEE MONA.
SO... MANY... PEOPLE...
IT IS SATURDAY, AFTER ALL.

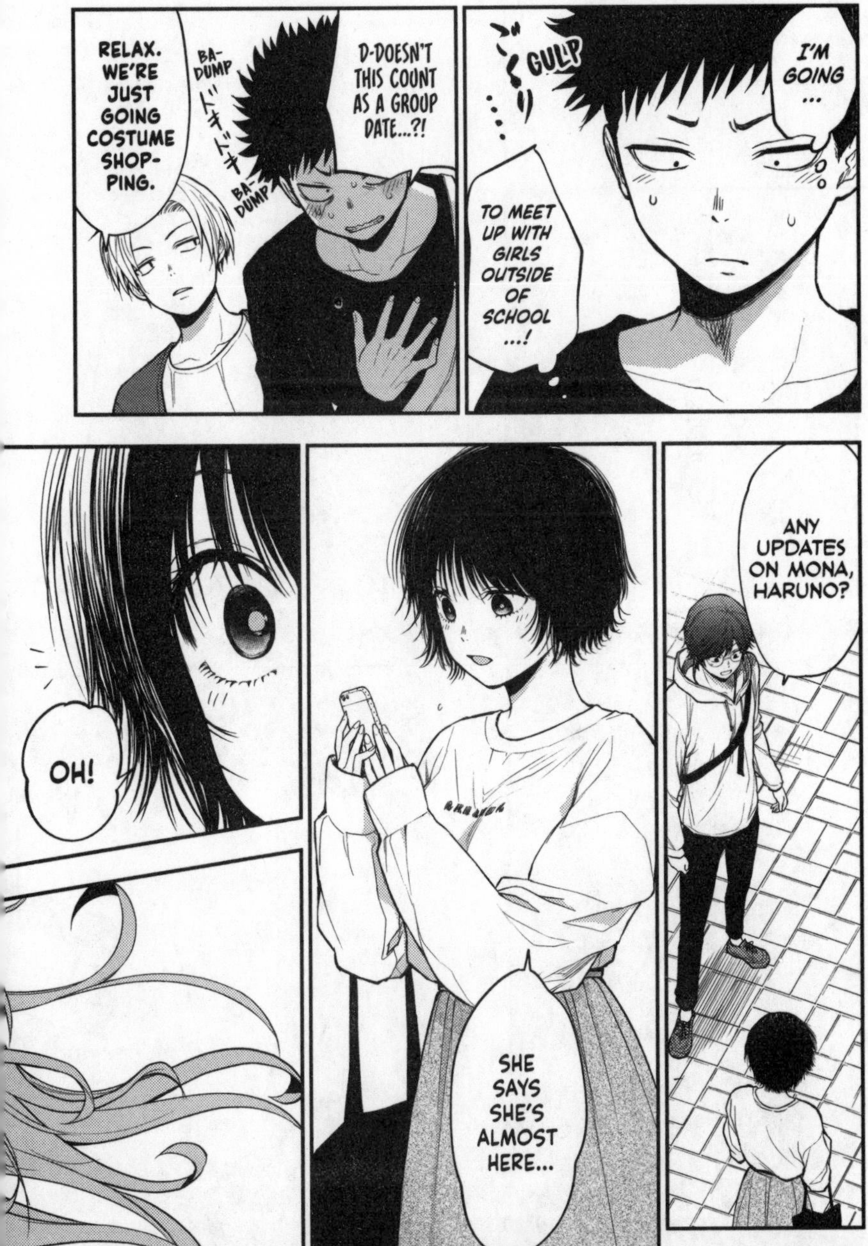
I'M GOING...
GULP
TO MEET UP WITH GIRLS OUTSIDE OF SCHOOL...!
D-DOESN'T THIS COUNT AS A GROUP DATE...?!
BA-DUMP
ドキドキ
BA-DUMP
RELAX. WE'RE JUST GOING COSTUME SHOP-PING.
ANY UPDATES ON MONA, HARUNO?
SHE SAYS SHE'S ALMOST HERE...
OH!

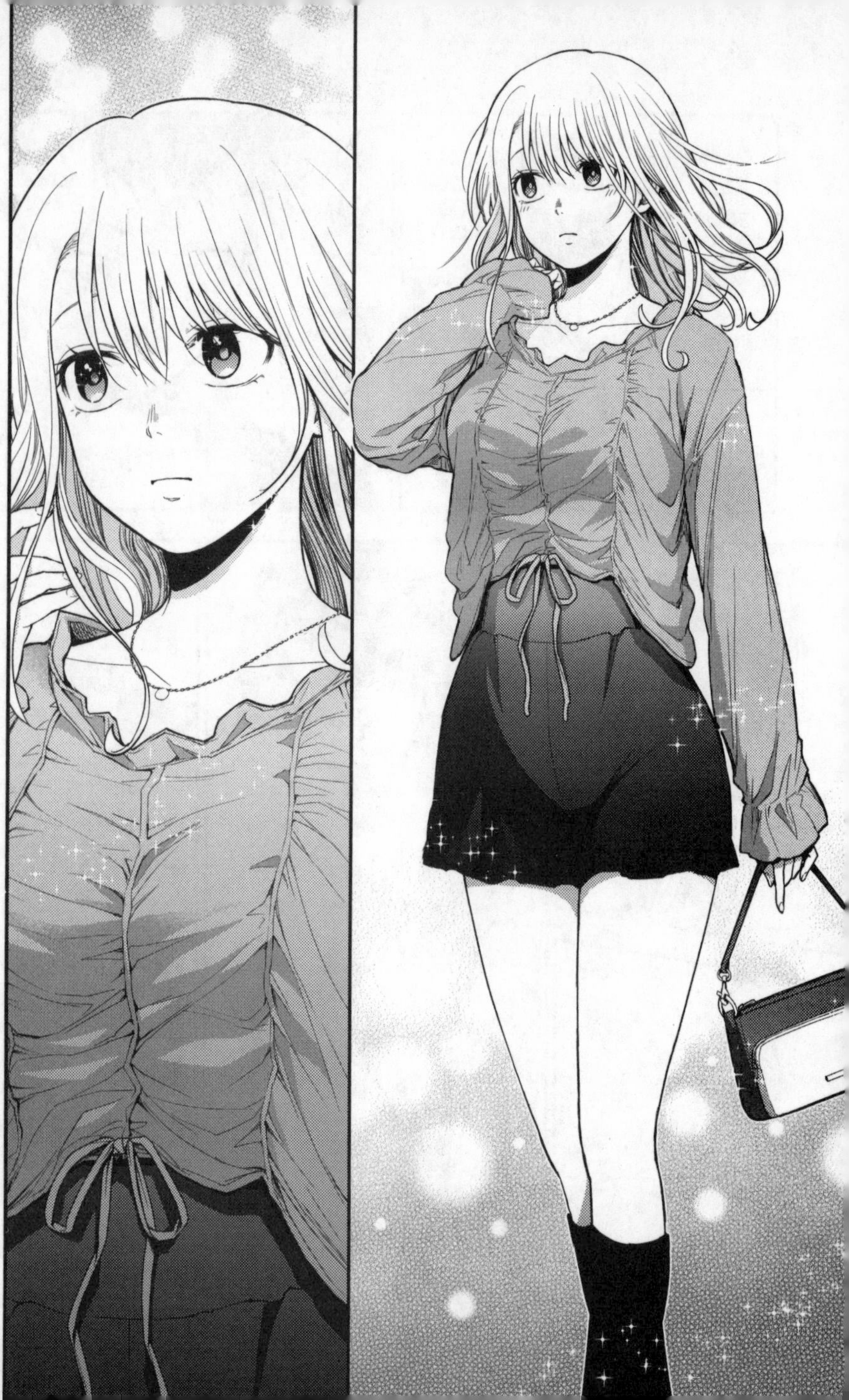

......!

MONA!

OVER HERE!

MY QUEE- EEN!

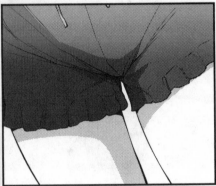

Y'ALL ARE HERE SO EARLY! ♥

YOUR OUTFIT IS SO-O-O CUTE...!

BEAM

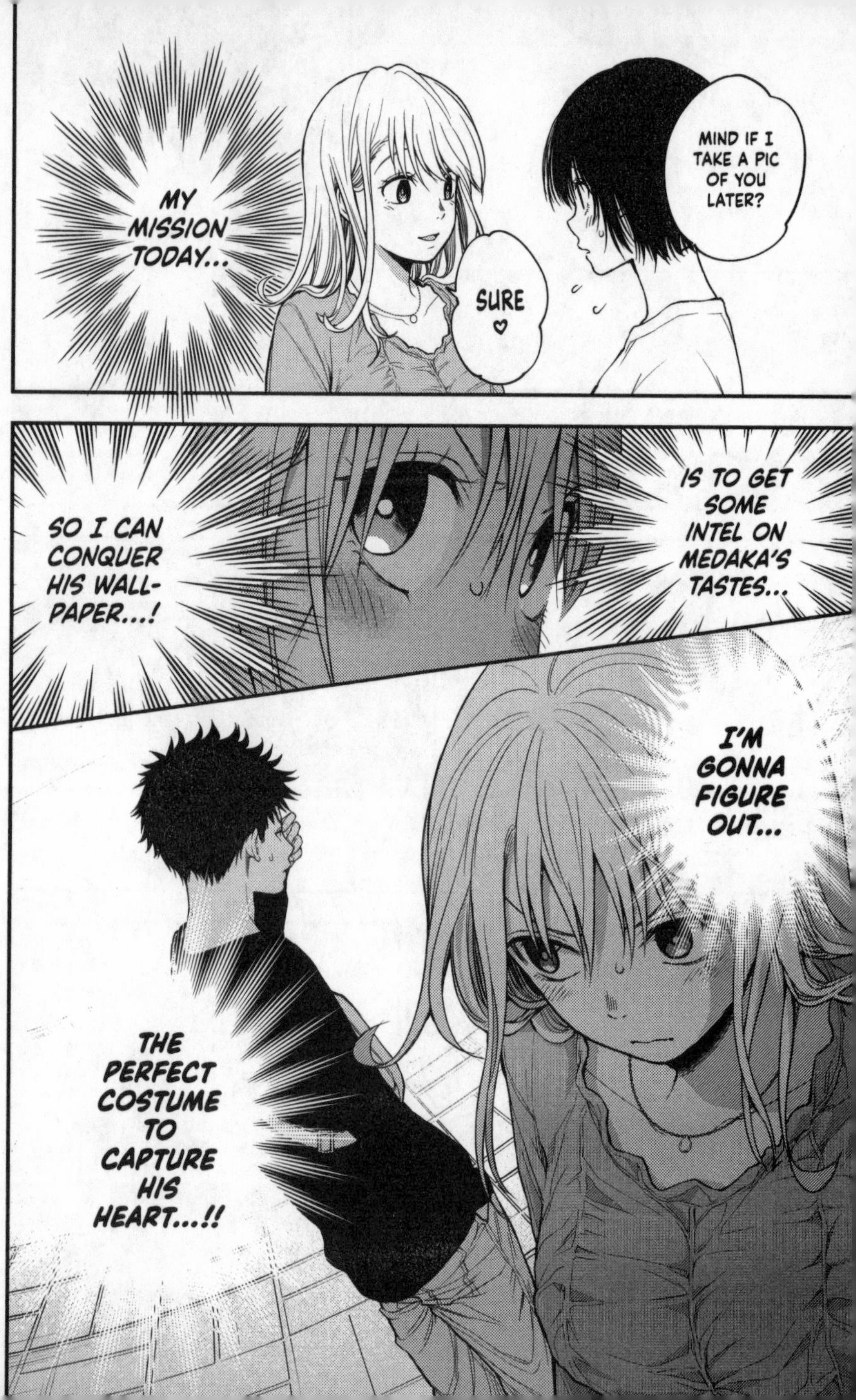
MIND IF I TAKE A PIC OF YOU LATER?
SURE ♡
MY MISSION TODAY...
IS TO GET SOME INTEL ON MEDAKA'S TASTES...
SO I CAN CONQUER HIS WALL-PAPER...!
I'M GONNA FIGURE OUT...
THE PERFECT COSTUME TO CAPTURE HIS HEART...!!

Chapter 25 ★ Shopping with That Jerk

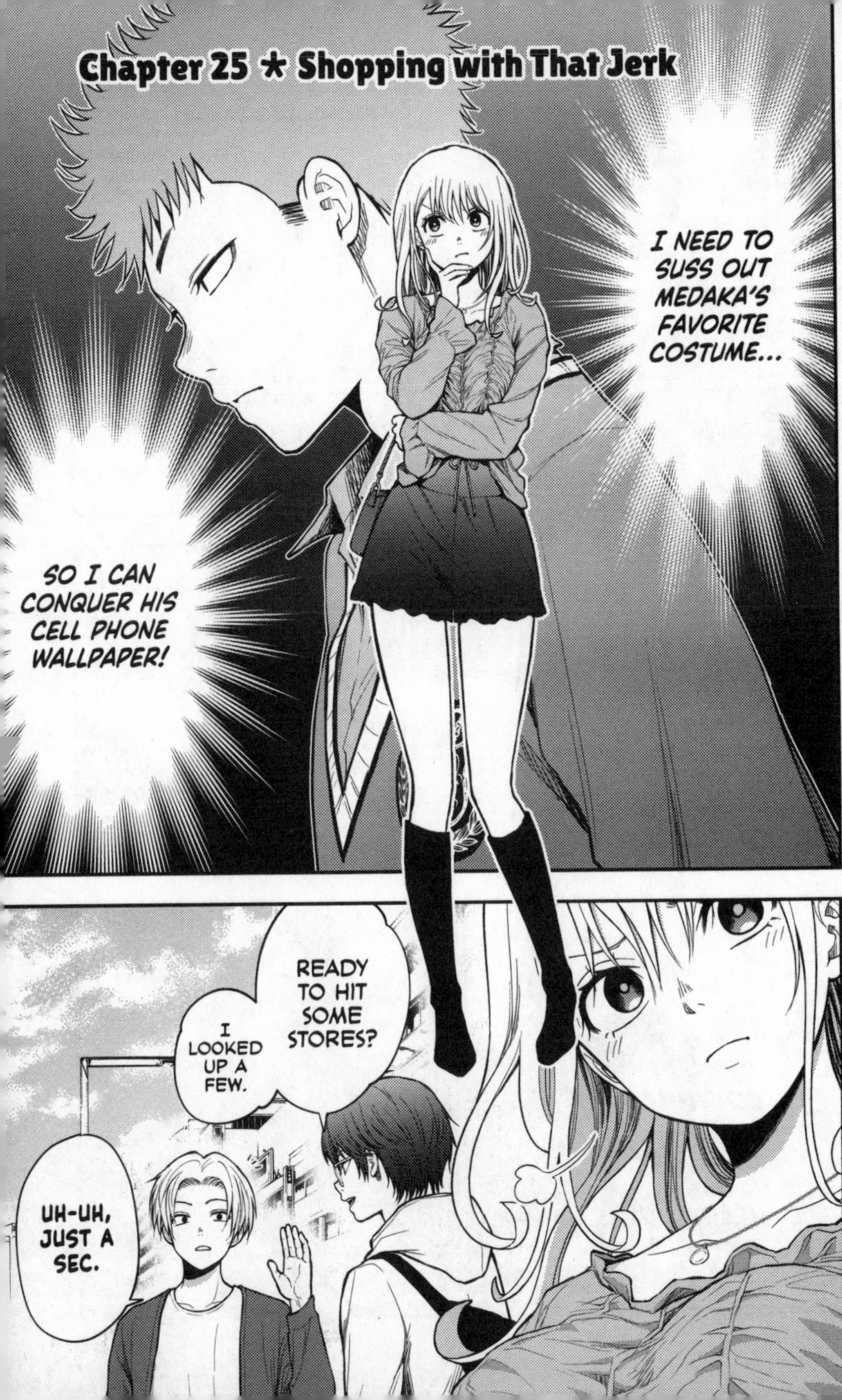
I NEED TO SUSS OUT MEDAKA'S FAVORITE COSTUME...
SO I CAN CONQUER HIS CELL PHONE WALLPAPER!
READY TO HIT SOME STORES?
I LOOKED UP A FEW.
UH-UH, JUST A SEC.

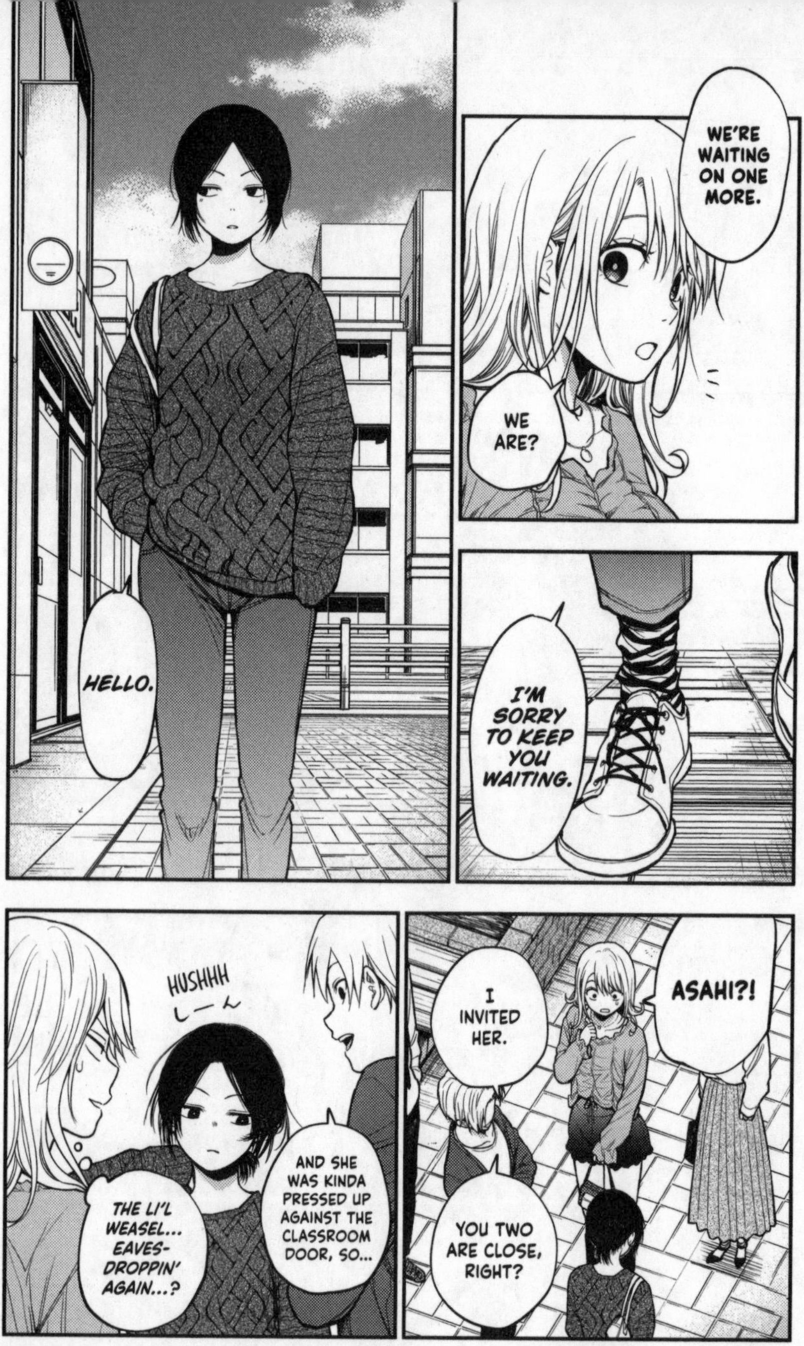
WE'RE WAITING ON ONE MORE.
WE ARE?
I'M SORRY TO KEEP YOU WAITING.
HELLO.
ASAHI?!
I INVITED HER.
YOU TWO ARE CLOSE, RIGHT?
HUSHHH
しーん
AND SHE WAS KINDA PRESSED UP AGAINST THE CLASSROOM DOOR, SO...
THE LI'L WEASEL... EAVES-DROPPIN' AGAIN...?

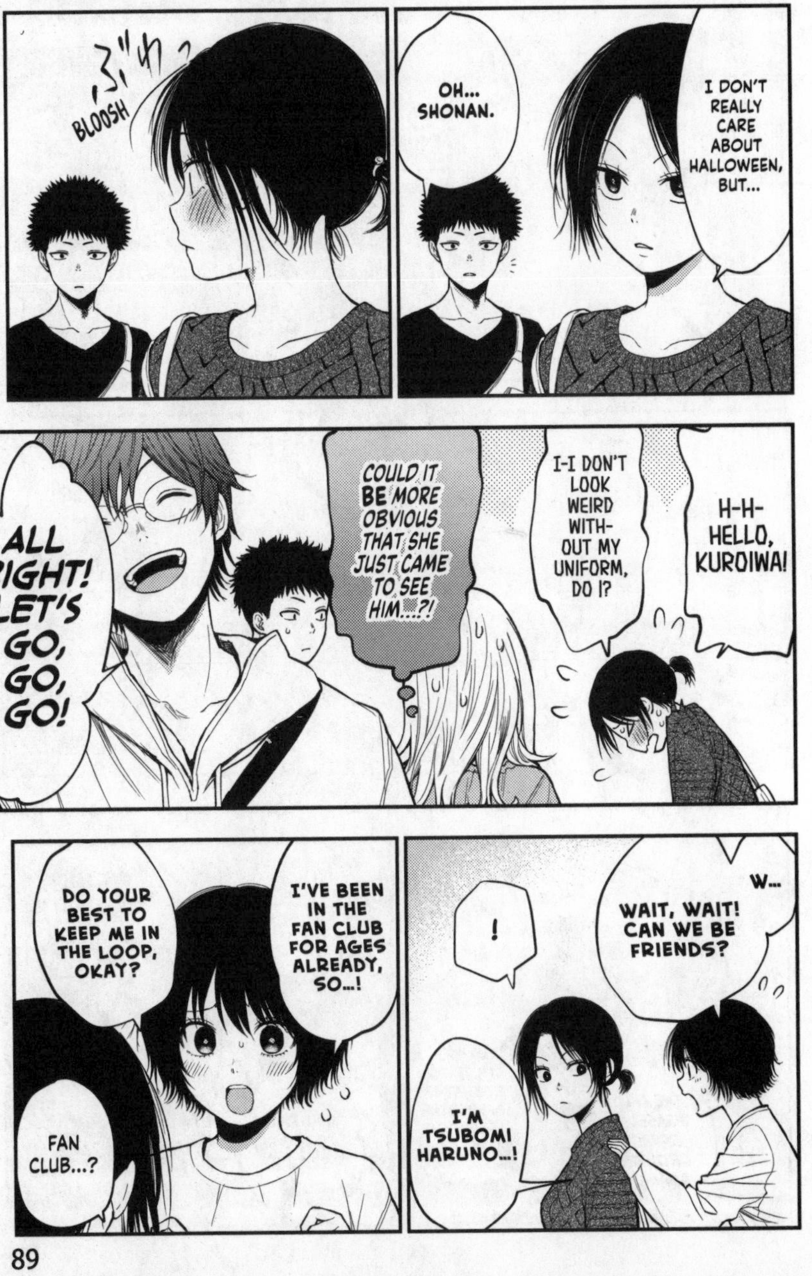
I DON'T REALLY CARE ABOUT HALLOWEEN, BUT...
OH... SHONAN.
ぶわっ
BLOOSH
H-H-HELLO, KUROIWA!
I-I DON'T LOOK WEIRD WITHOUT MY UNIFORM, DO I?
COULD IT BE MORE OBVIOUS THAT SHE JUST CAME TO SEE HIM...?!
ALL RIGHT! LET'S GO, GO, GO!
W...
WAIT, WAIT! CAN WE BE FRIENDS?
!
I'M TSUBOMI HARUNO...!
I'VE BEEN IN THE FAN CLUB FOR AGES ALREADY, SO...!
DO YOUR BEST TO KEEP ME IN THE LOOP, OKAY?
FAN CLUB...?

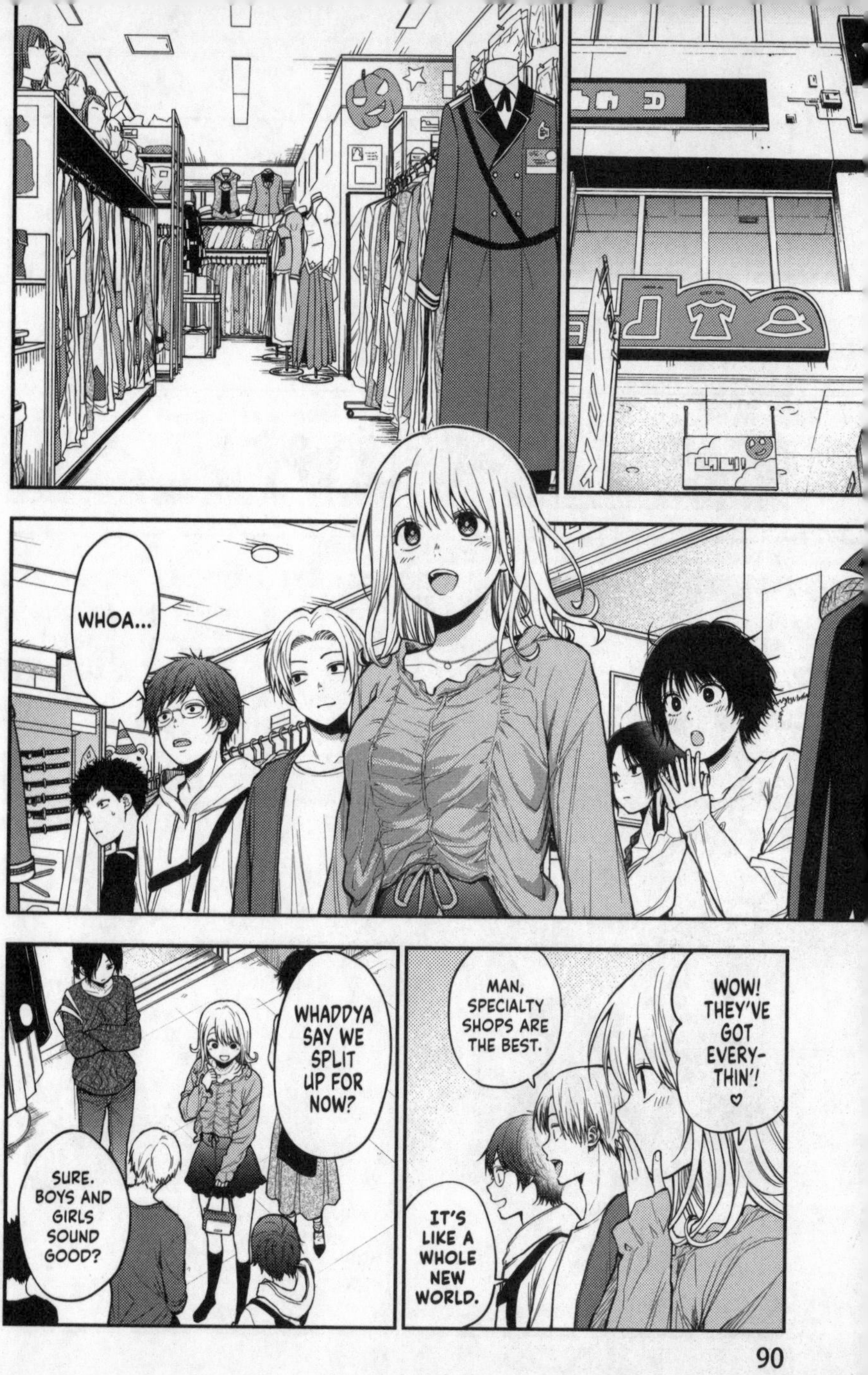
WHOA...
WOW! THEY'VE GOT EVERY-THIN'! ♥
MAN, SPECIALTY SHOPS ARE THE BEST.
IT'S LIKE A WHOLE NEW WORLD.
WHADDYA SAY WE SPLIT UP FOR NOW?
SURE. BOYS AND GIRLS SOUND GOOD?

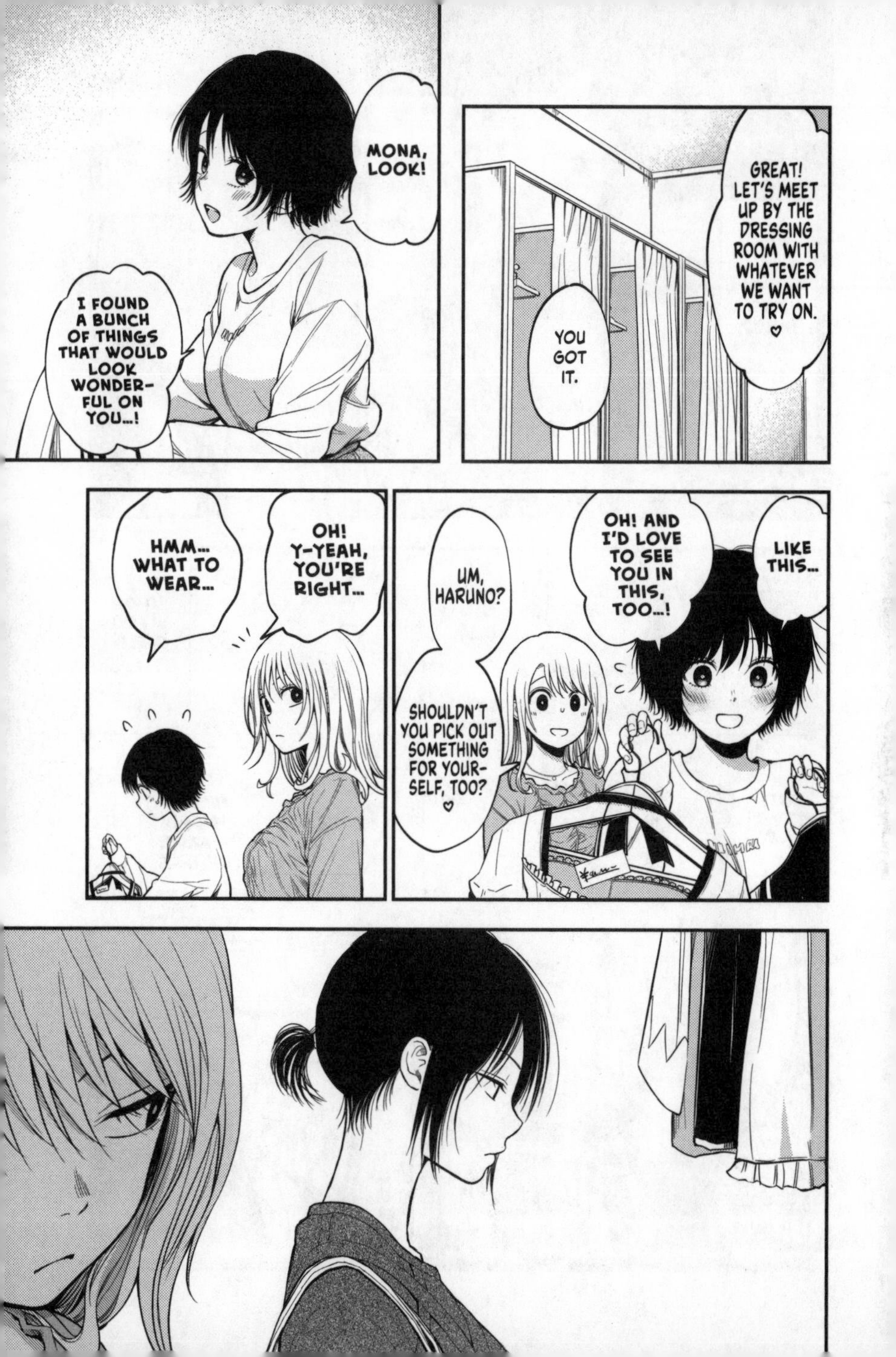
GREAT! LET'S MEET UP BY THE DRESSING ROOM WITH WHATEVER WE WANT TO TRY ON. ♡
YOU GOT IT.
MONA, LOOK!
I FOUND A BUNCH OF THINGS THAT WOULD LOOK WONDERFUL ON YOU...!
LIKE THIS...
OH! AND I'D LOVE TO SEE YOU IN THIS, TOO...!
UM, HARUNO?
SHOULDN'T YOU PICK OUT SOMETHING FOR YOURSELF, TOO? ♡
OH! Y-YEAH, YOU'RE RIGHT...
HMM... WHAT TO WEAR...

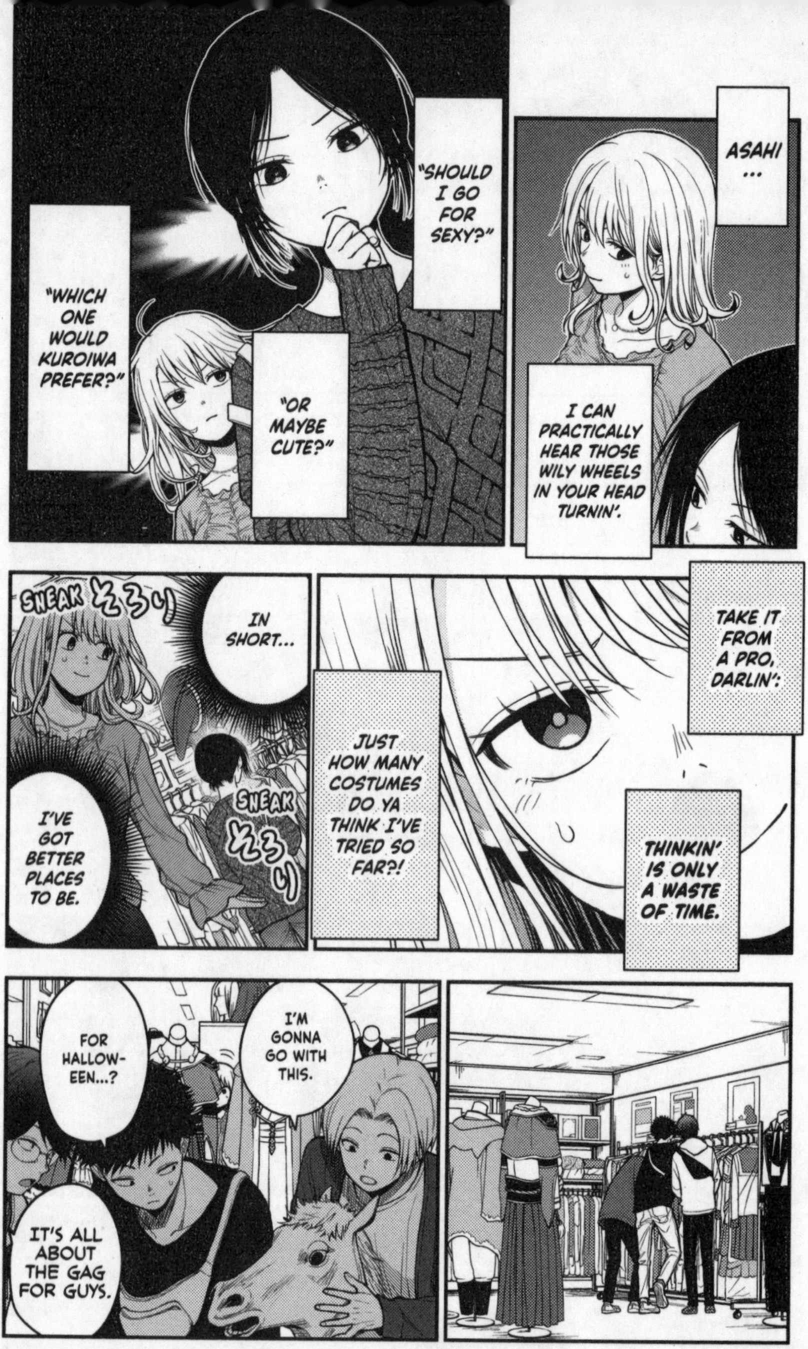
ASAHI ...
I CAN PRACTICALLY HEAR THOSE WILY WHEELS IN YOUR HEAD TURNIN'.
"SHOULD I GO FOR SEXY?"
"OR MAYBE CUTE?"
"WHICH ONE WOULD KUROIWA PREFER?"
TAKE IT FROM A PRO, DARLIN':
JUST HOW MANY COSTUMES DO YA THINK I'VE TRIED SO FAR?!
THINKIN' IS ONLY A WASTE OF TIME.
SNEAK そろり
IN SHORT...
I'VE GOT BETTER PLACES TO BE.
SNEAK そろり
I'M GONNA GO WITH THIS.
FOR HALLOW-EEN...?
IT'S ALL ABOUT THE GAG FOR GUYS.

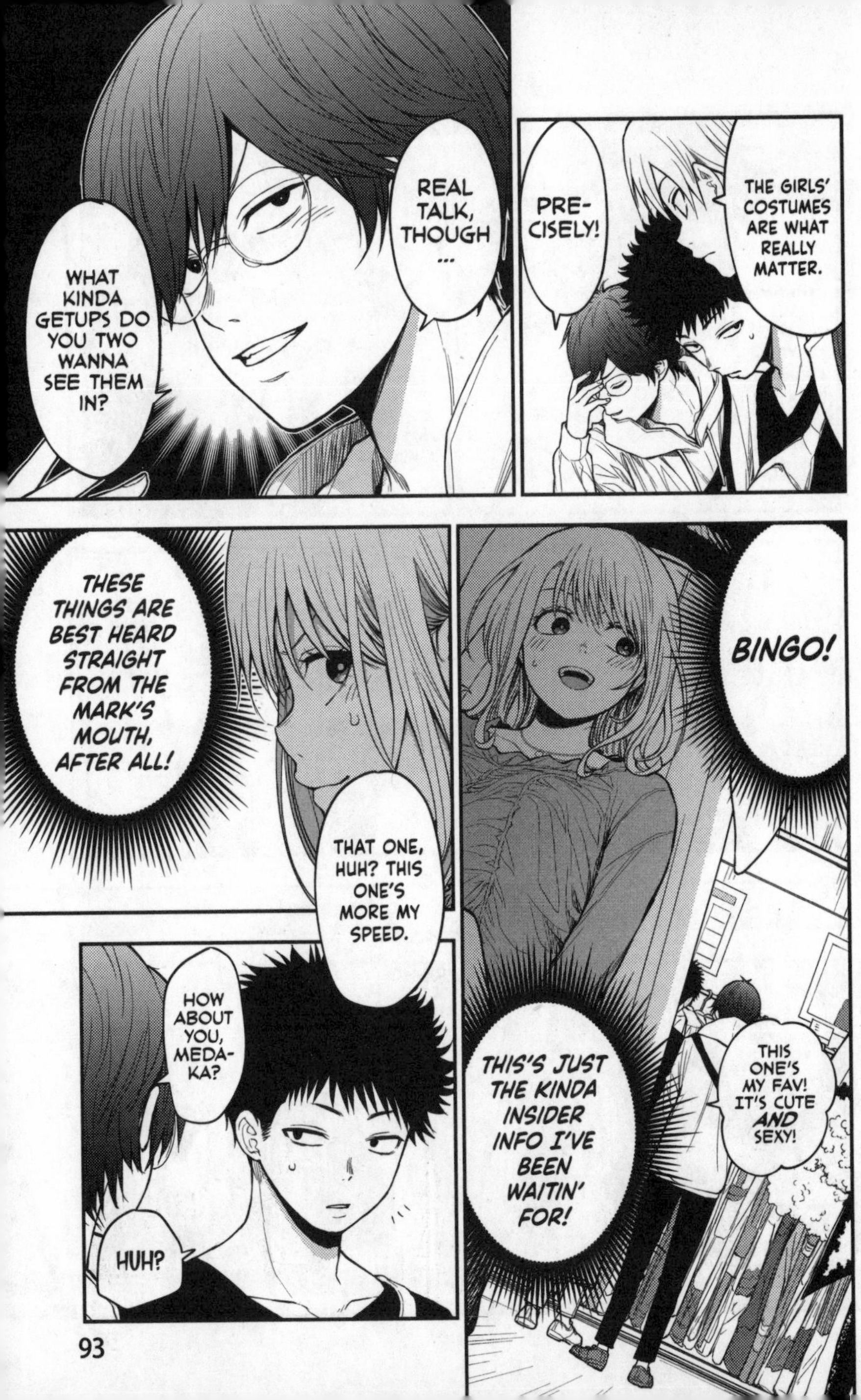
THE GIRLS' COSTUMES ARE WHAT REALLY MATTER.
PRE-CISELY!
REAL TALK, THOUGH...
WHAT KINDA GETUPS DO YOU TWO WANNA SEE THEM IN?
BINGO!
THIS ONE'S MY FAV! IT'S CUTE AND SEXY!
THIS'S JUST THE KINDA INSIDER INFO I'VE BEEN WAITIN' FOR!
THESE THINGS ARE BEST HEARD STRAIGHT FROM THE MARK'S MOUTH, AFTER ALL!
THAT ONE, HUH? THIS ONE'S MORE MY SPEED.
HOW ABOUT YOU, MEDA-KA?
HUH?

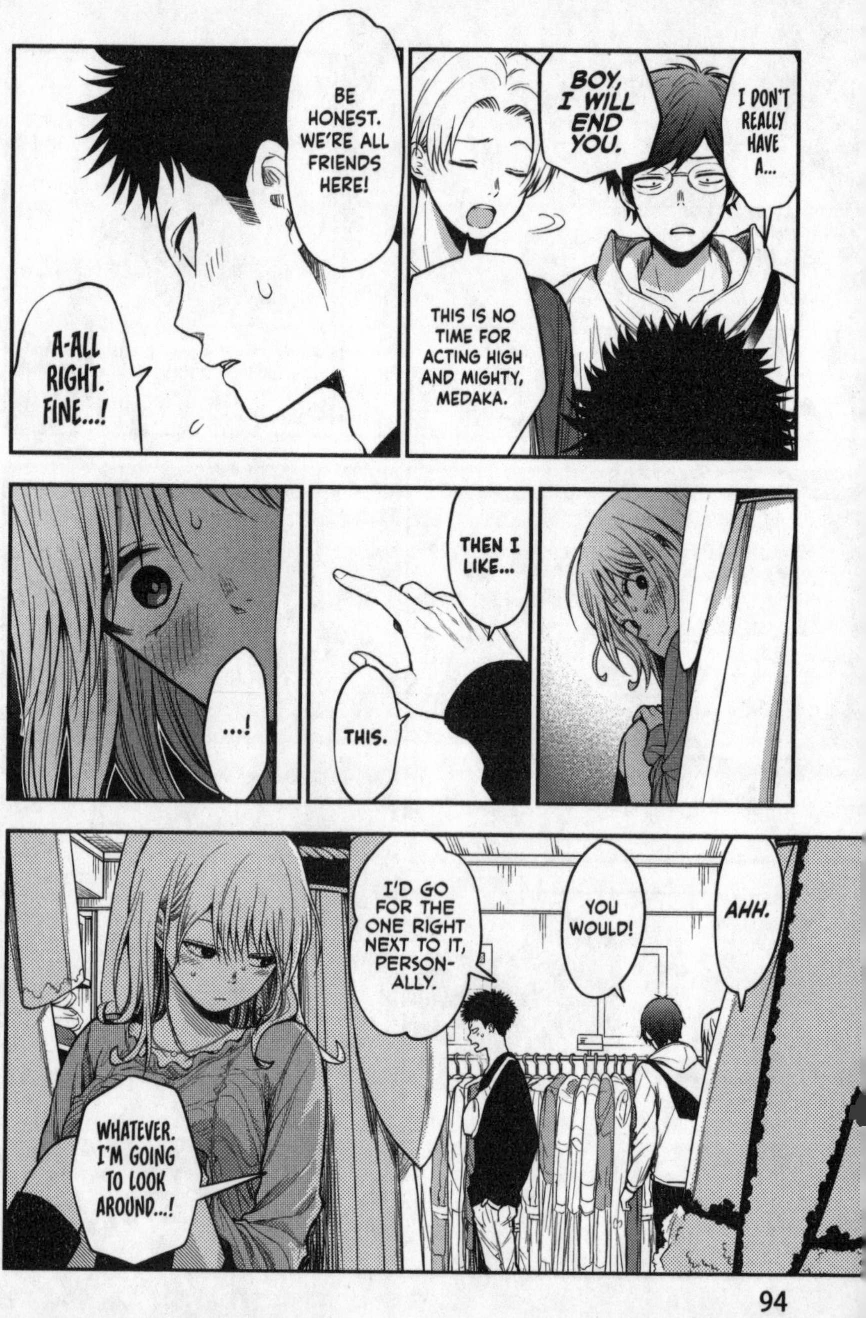
I DON'T REALLY HAVE A...
BOY, I WILL END YOU.
THIS IS NO TIME FOR ACTING HIGH AND MIGHTY, MEDAKA.
BE HONEST. WE'RE ALL FRIENDS HERE!
A-ALL RIGHT. FINE...!
THEN I LIKE...
THIS.
...!
AHH.
YOU WOULD!
I'D GO FOR THE ONE RIGHT NEXT TO IT, PERSON-ALLY.
WHATEVER. I'M GOING TO LOOK AROUND...!

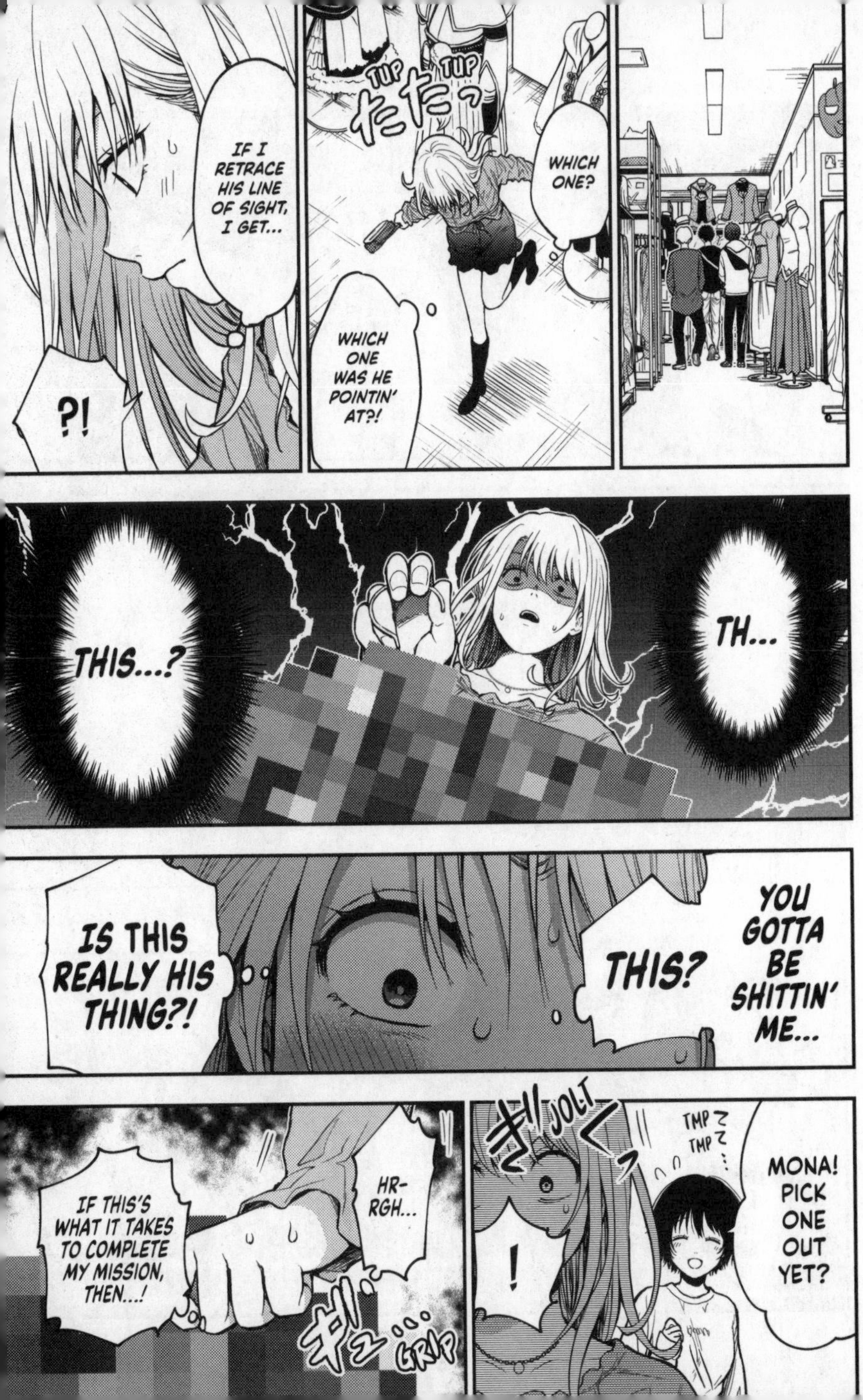
TUP TUP
たたっ
WHICH ONE?
WHICH ONE WAS HE POINTIN' AT?!
IF I RETRACE HIS LINE OF SIGHT, I GET...
?!
TH...
THIS...?
YOU GOTTA BE SHITTIN' ME...
THIS?
IS THIS REALLY HIS THING?!
MONA! PICK ONE OUT YET?
TMP TMP
JOLT
!
HR-RGH...
IF THIS'S WHAT IT TAKES TO COMPLETE MY MISSION, THEN...!
GRIP

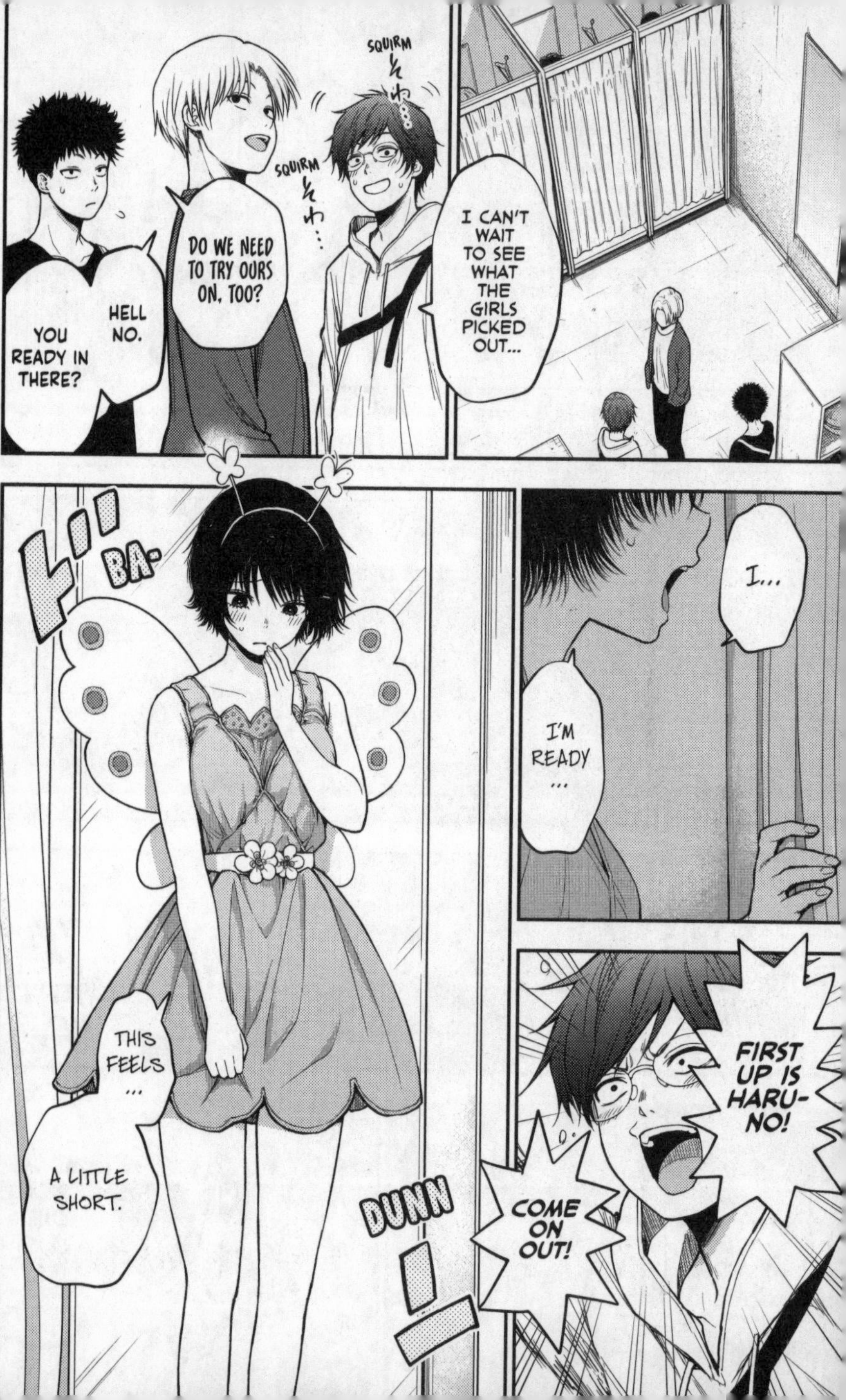

SQUIRM
そわ…
SQUIRM
そわ…
I CAN'T WAIT TO SEE WHAT THE GIRLS PICKED OUT...
DO WE NEED TO TRY OURS ON, TOO?
HELL NO.
YOU READY IN THERE?
I...
I'M READY...
FIRST UP IS HARU-NO!
COME ON OUT!
DUNN
BA-
THIS FEELS...
A LITTLE SHORT.

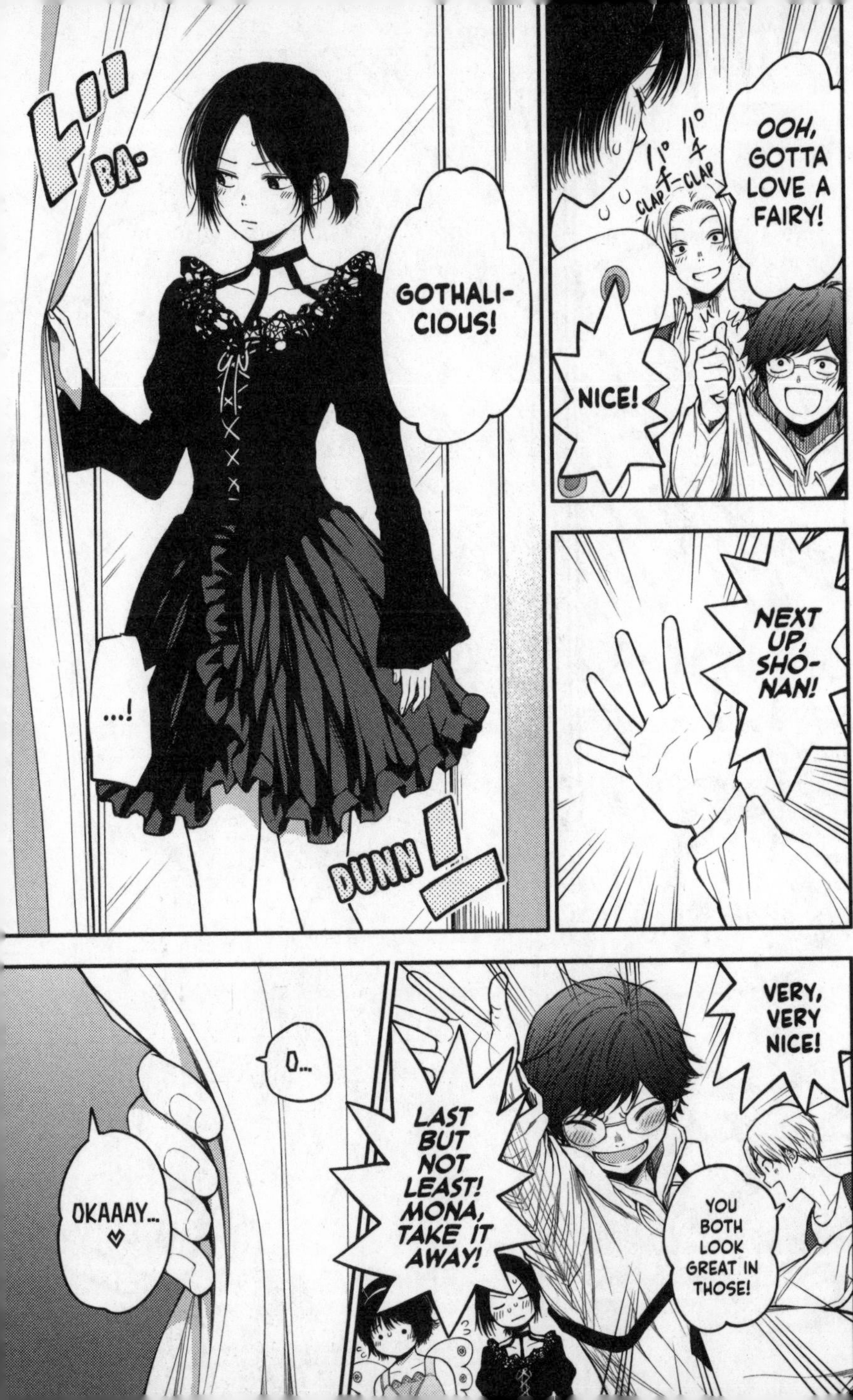

OOH, GOTTA LOVE A FAIRY!
パチパチ
CLAP CLAP
NICE!
NEXT UP, SHO-NAN!
BA-
GOTHALI-CIOUS!
...!
DUNN
VERY, VERY NICE!
LAST BUT NOT LEAST! MONA, TAKE IT AWAY!
YOU BOTH LOOK GREAT IN THOSE!
O...
OKAAAY... ♡

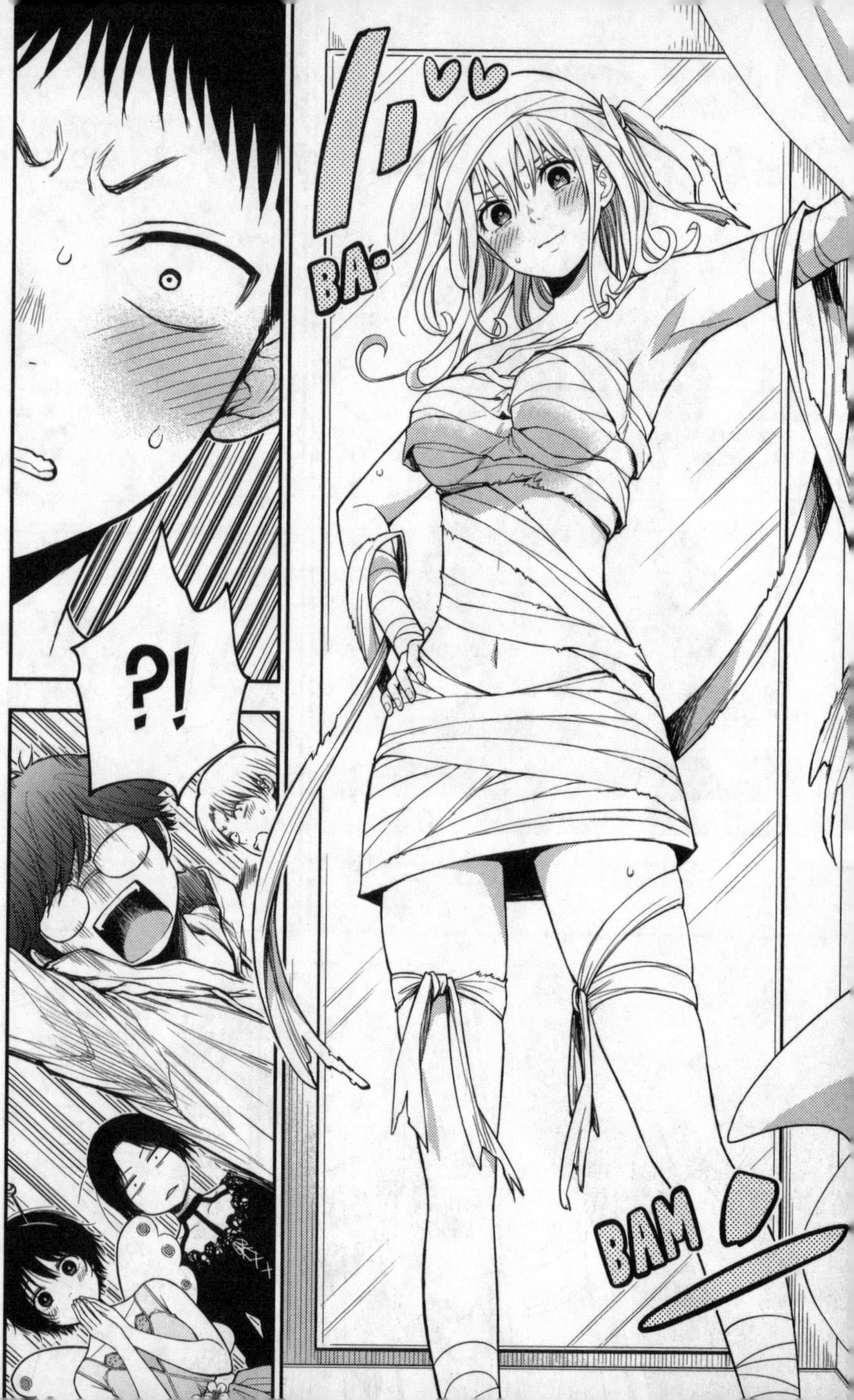
BA-
BAM
?!

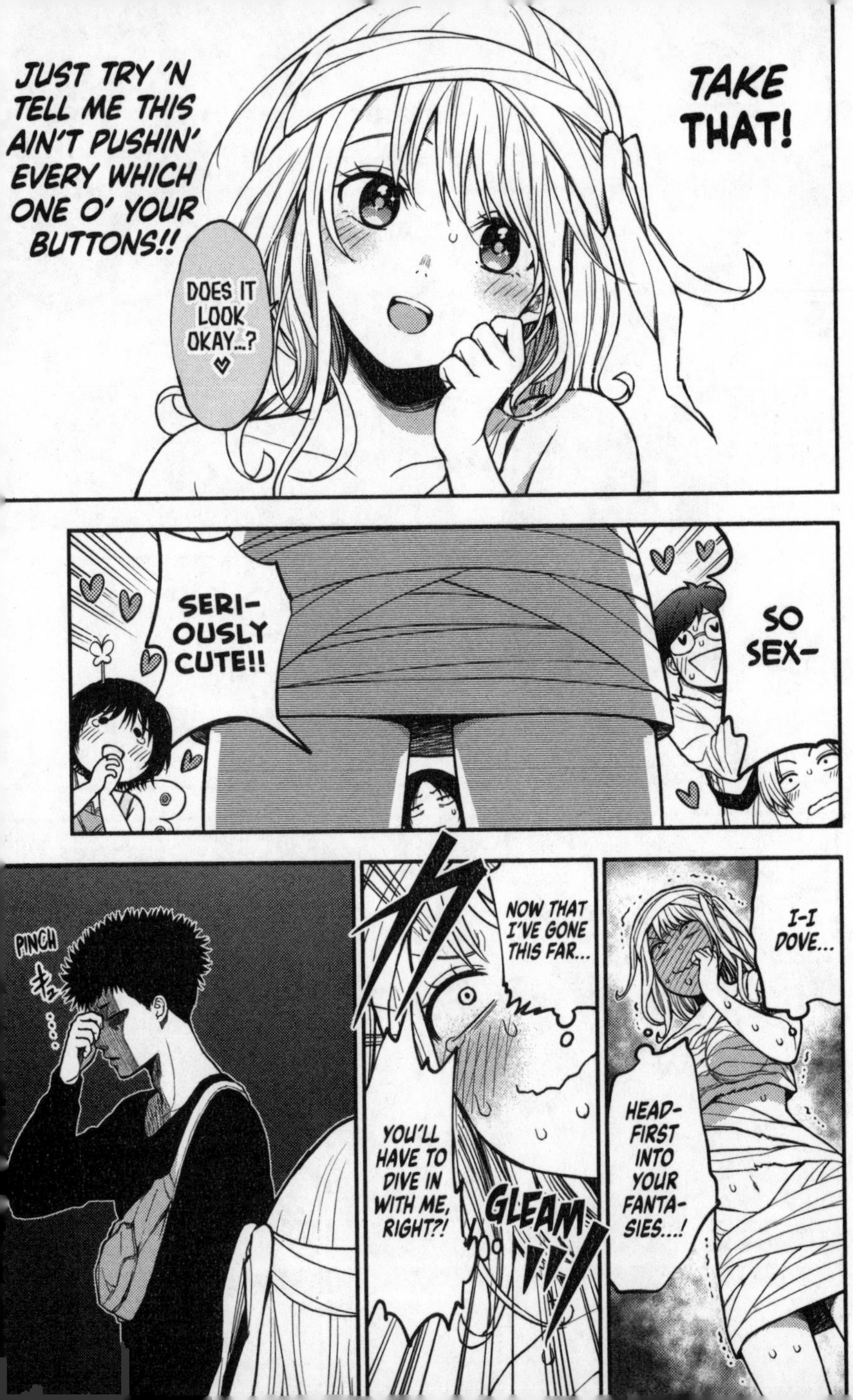
TAKE THAT!
JUST TRY 'N TELL ME THIS AIN'T PUSHIN' EVERY WHICH ONE O' YOUR BUTTONS!!
DOES IT LOOK OKAY...?
SO SEX-
SERI-OUSLY CUTE!!
I-I DOVE...
HEAD-FIRST INTO YOUR FANTA-SIES...!
NOW THAT I'VE GONE THIS FAR...
YOU'LL HAVE TO DIVE IN WITH ME, RIGHT?!
GLEAM
PINCH

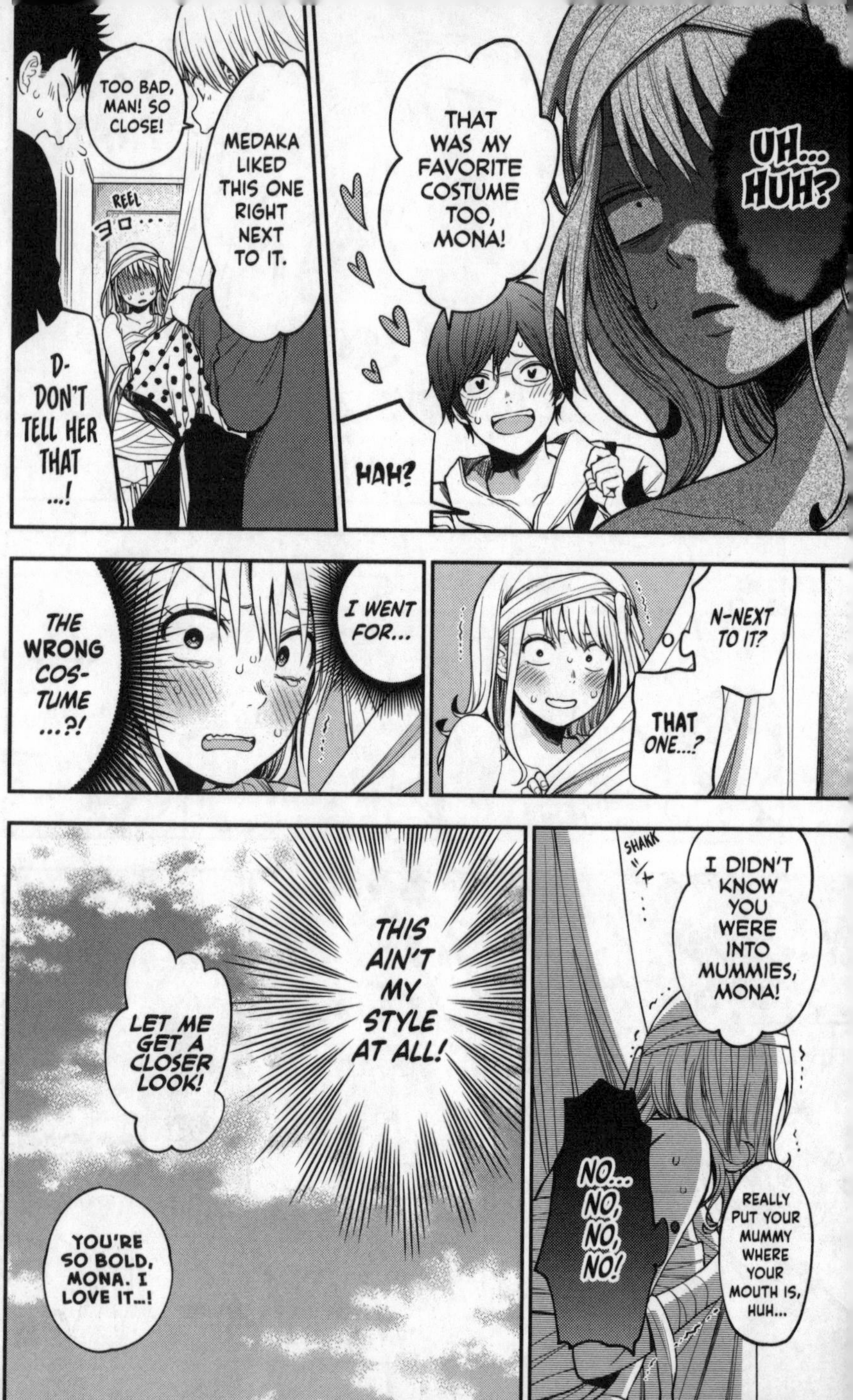
UH... HUH?
THAT WAS MY FAVORITE COSTUME TOO, MONA!
HAH?
MEDAKA LIKED THIS ONE RIGHT NEXT TO IT.
TOO BAD, MAN! SO CLOSE!
REEL
ヨロ…
D-DON'T TELL HER THAT ...!
N-NEXT TO IT?
THAT ONE...?
I WENT FOR...
THE WRONG COS-TUME ...?!
I DIDN'T KNOW YOU WERE INTO MUMMIES, MONA!
SHAKK
REALLY PUT YOUR MUMMY WHERE YOUR MOUTH IS, HUH...
NO... NO, NO, NO!
THIS AIN'T MY STYLE AT ALL!
LET ME GET A CLOSER LOOK!
YOU'RE SO BOLD, MONA. I LOVE IT...!

Chapter 26 ★ Halloween with That Jerk

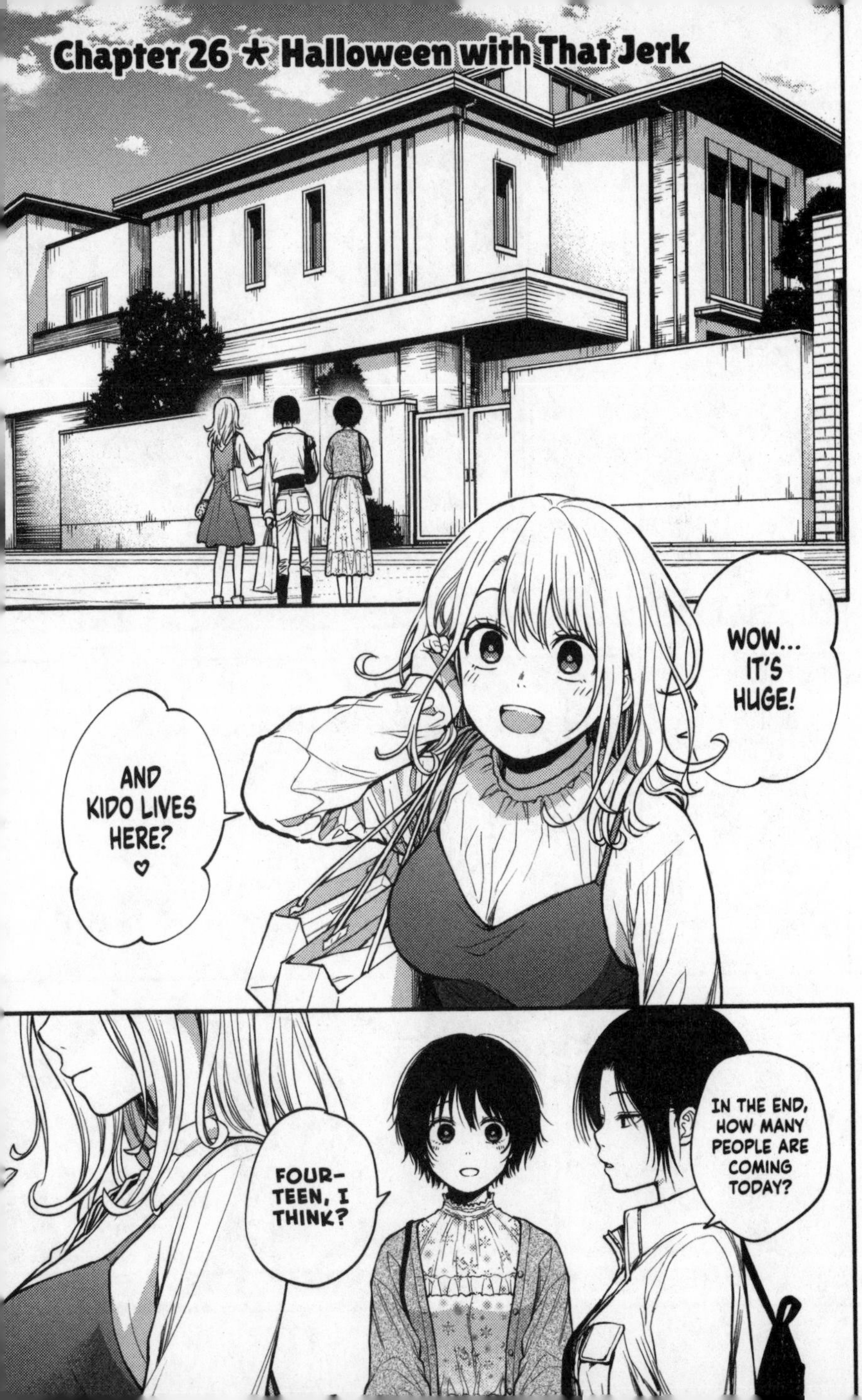
WOW... IT'S HUGE!
AND KIDO LIVES HERE? ♡
IN THE END, HOW MANY PEOPLE ARE COMING TODAY?
FOUR-TEEN, I THINK?

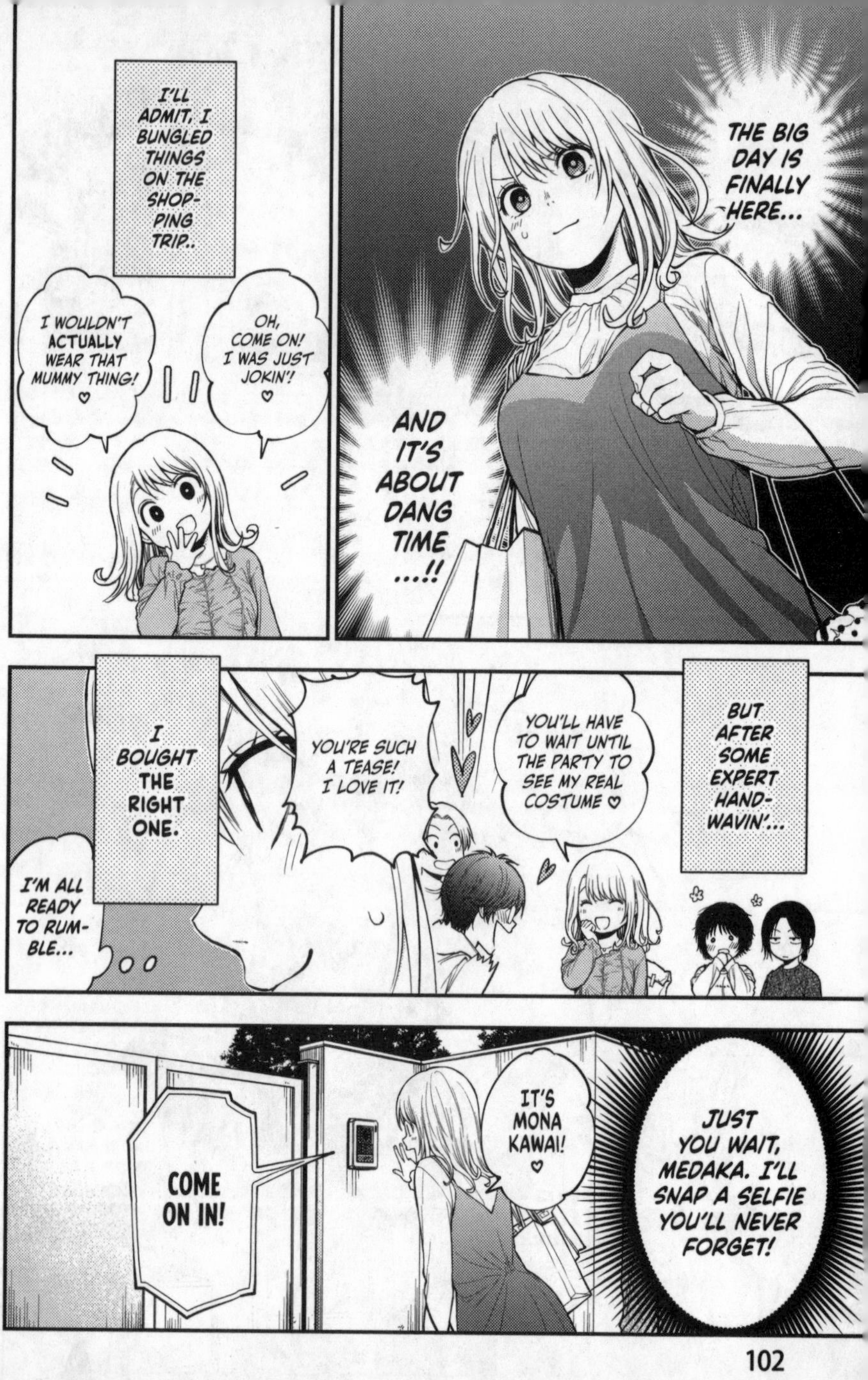
THE BIG DAY IS FINALLY HERE...
AND IT'S ABOUT DANG TIME ...!!
I'LL ADMIT, I BUNGLED THINGS ON THE SHOP-PING TRIP..
OH, COME ON! I WAS JUST JOKIN'! ♡
I WOULDN'T ACTUALLY WEAR THAT MUMMY THING! ♡
BUT AFTER SOME EXPERT HAND-WAVIN'...
YOU'LL HAVE TO WAIT UNTIL THE PARTY TO SEE MY REAL COSTUME ♡
YOU'RE SUCH A TEASE! I LOVE IT!
I BOUGHT THE RIGHT ONE.
I'M ALL READY TO RUM-BLE...
JUST YOU WAIT, MEDAKA. I'LL SNAP A SELFIE YOU'LL NEVER FORGET!
IT'S MONA KAWAI! ♡
COME ON IN!

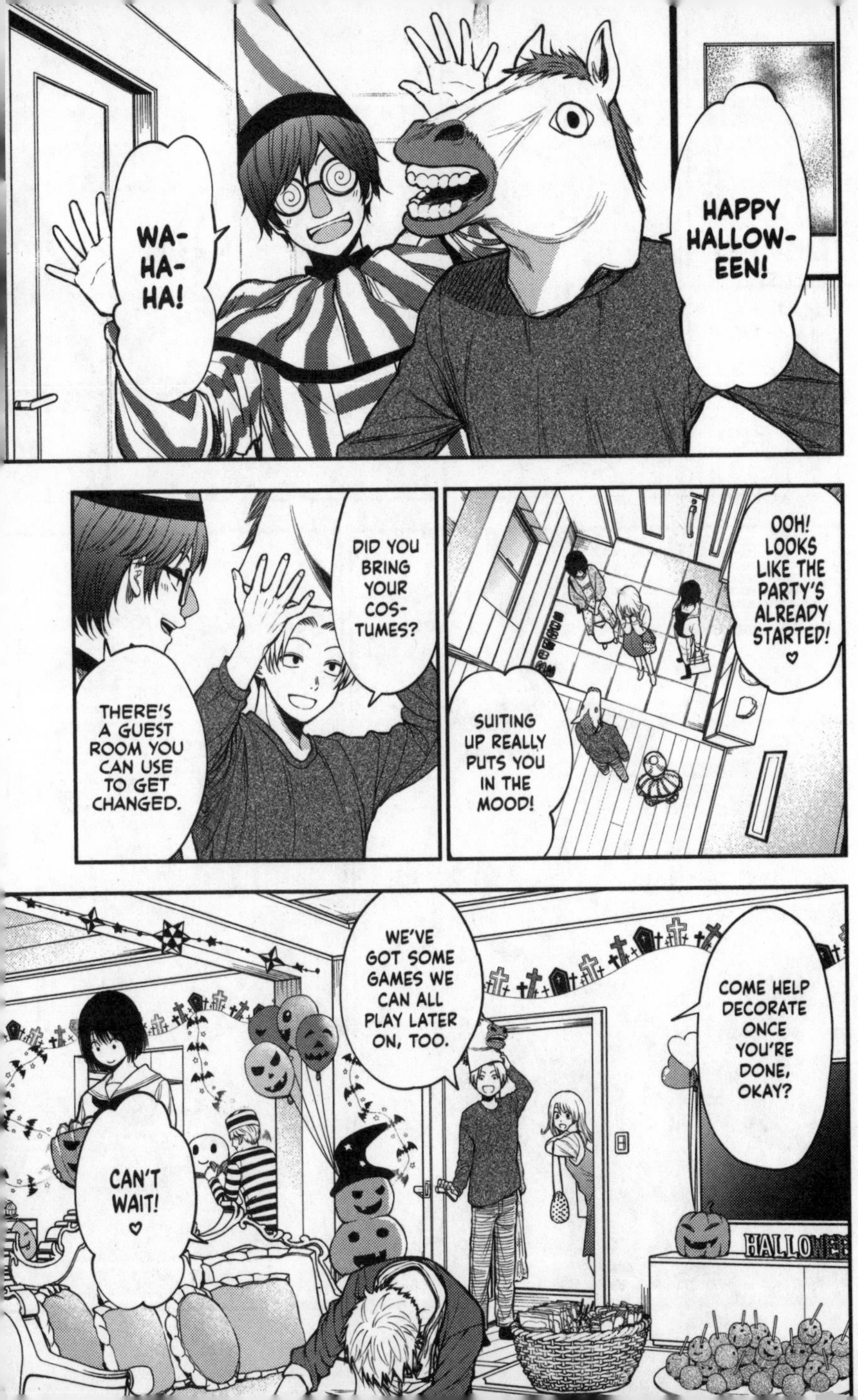
HAPPY HALLOW-EEN!
WA-HA-HA!
OOH! LOOKS LIKE THE PARTY'S ALREADY STARTED! ♡
SUITING UP REALLY PUTS YOU IN THE MOOD!
DID YOU BRING YOUR COS-TUMES?
THERE'S A GUEST ROOM YOU CAN USE TO GET CHANGED.
COME HELP DECORATE ONCE YOU'RE DONE, OKAY?
WE'VE GOT SOME GAMES WE CAN ALL PLAY LATER ON, TOO.
CAN'T WAIT! ♡

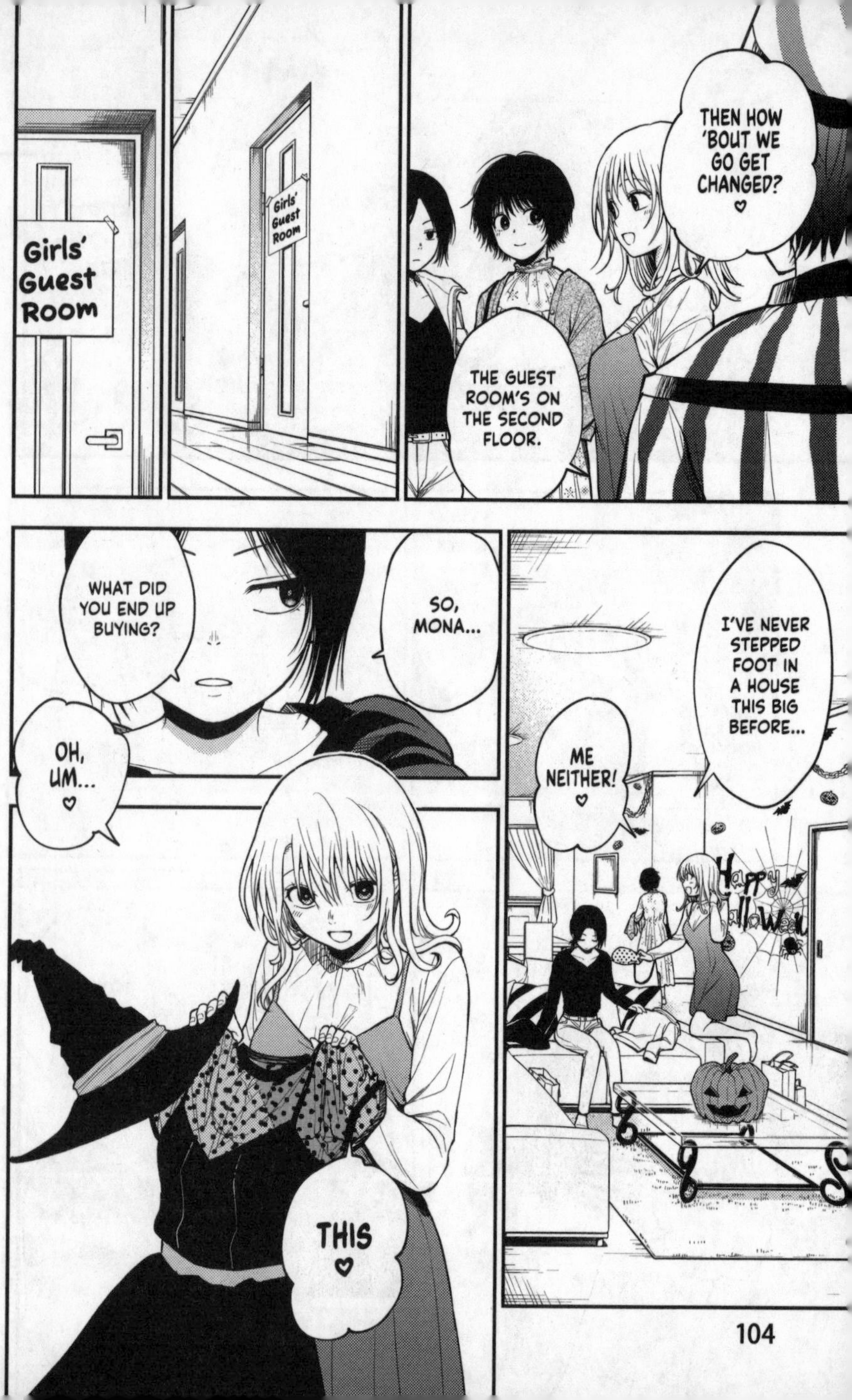
THEN HOW 'BOUT WE GO GET CHANGED? ♡
THE GUEST ROOM'S ON THE SECOND FLOOR.
Girls' Guest Room
Girls' Guest Room
I'VE NEVER STEPPED FOOT IN A HOUSE THIS BIG BEFORE...
ME NEITHER! ♡
Happy Halloween
SO, MONA...
WHAT DID YOU END UP BUYING?
OH, UM... ♡
THIS ♡

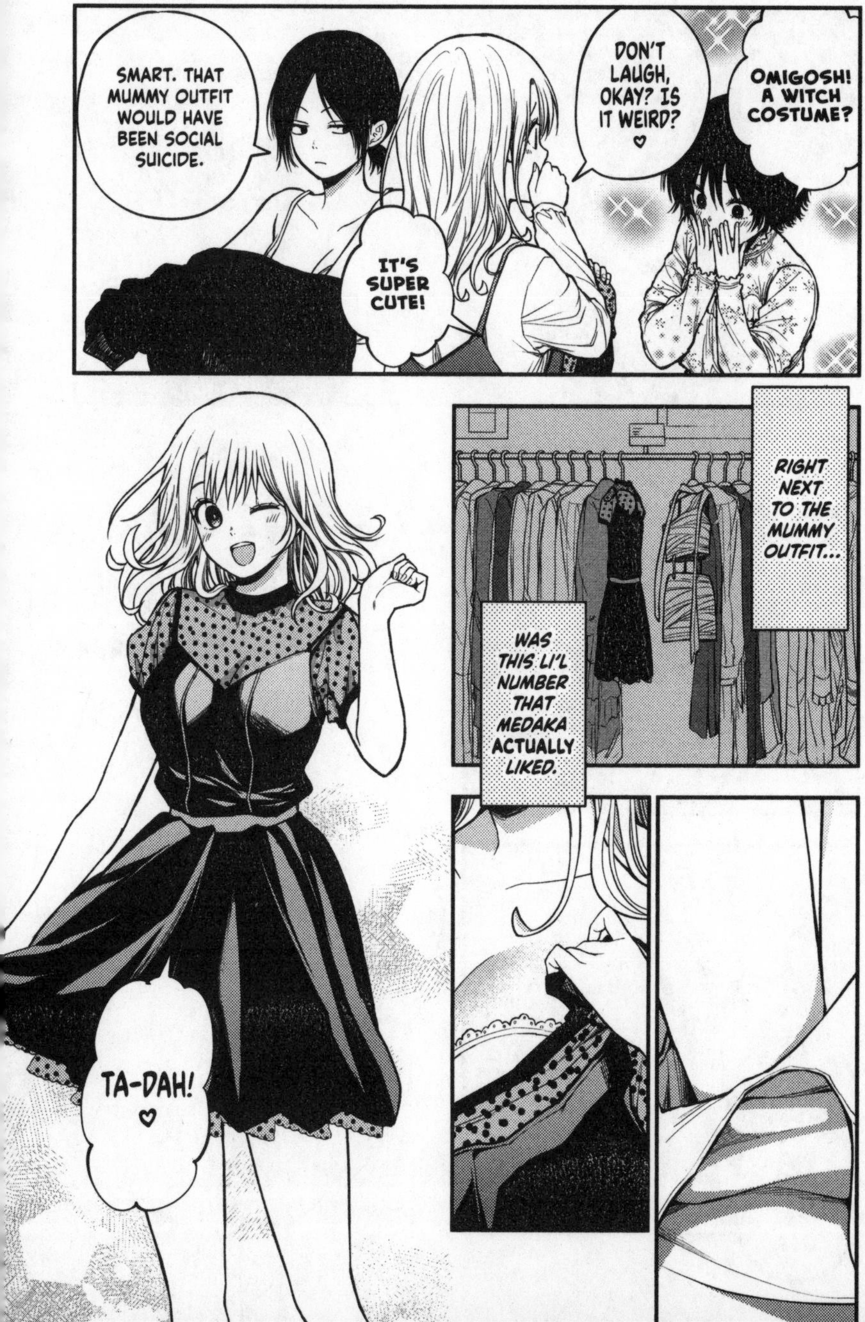
OMIGOSH! A WITCH COSTUME?
DON'T LAUGH, OKAY? IS IT WEIRD? ♡
IT'S SUPER CUTE!
SMART. THAT MUMMY OUTFIT WOULD HAVE BEEN SOCIAL SUICIDE.
RIGHT NEXT TO THE MUMMY OUTFIT...
WAS THIS LI'L NUMBER THAT MEDAKA ACTUALLY LIKED.
TA-DAH! ♡

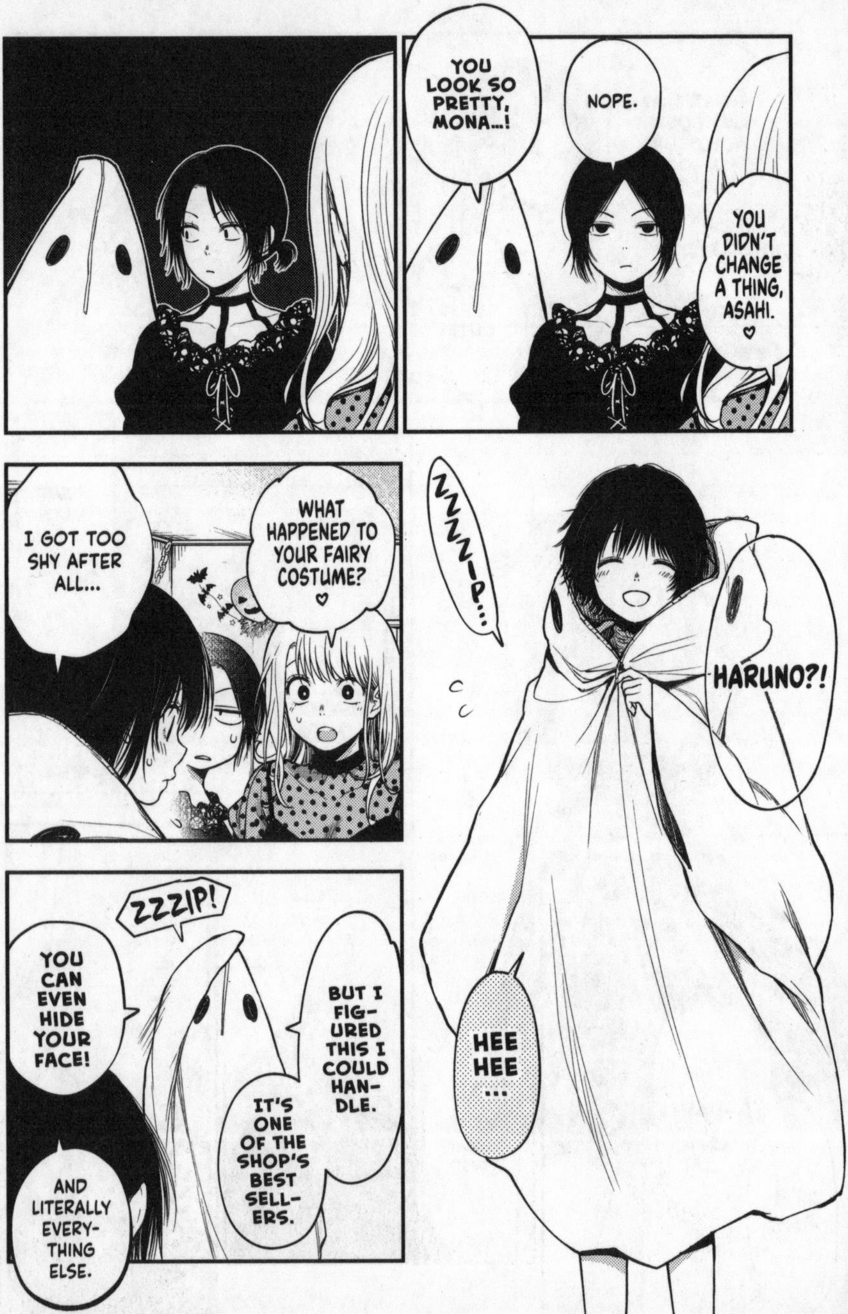
YOU LOOK SO PRETTY, MONA...!
NOPE.
YOU DIDN'T CHANGE A THING, ASAHI. ♥
ZZZIP...
HARUNO?!
HEE HEE...
WHAT HAPPENED TO YOUR FAIRY COSTUME? ♥
I GOT TOO SHY AFTER ALL...
ZZZIP!
BUT I FIGURED THIS I COULD HANDLE.
IT'S ONE OF THE SHOP'S BEST SELLERS.
YOU CAN EVEN HIDE YOUR FACE!
AND LITERALLY EVERYTHING ELSE.

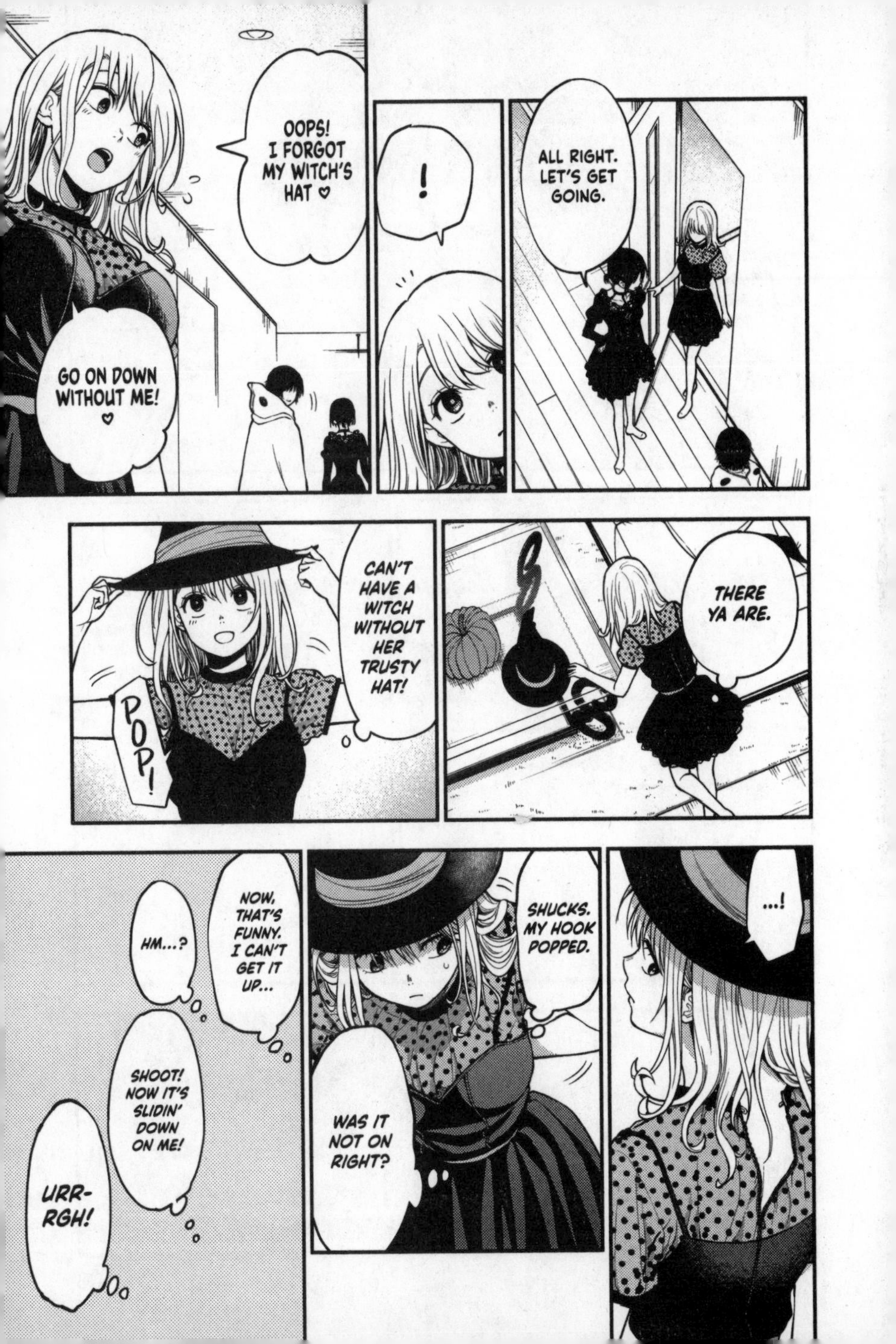
ALL RIGHT. LET'S GET GOING.
!
OOPS! I FORGOT MY WITCH'S HAT ♡
GO ON DOWN WITHOUT ME! ♡
THERE YA ARE.
CAN'T HAVE A WITCH WITHOUT HER TRUSTY HAT!
POP!
...!
SHUCKS. MY HOOK POPPED.
WAS IT NOT ON RIGHT?
NOW, THAT'S FUNNY. I CAN'T GET IT UP...
HM...?
SHOOT! NOW IT'S SLIDIN' DOWN ON ME!
URR-RGH!

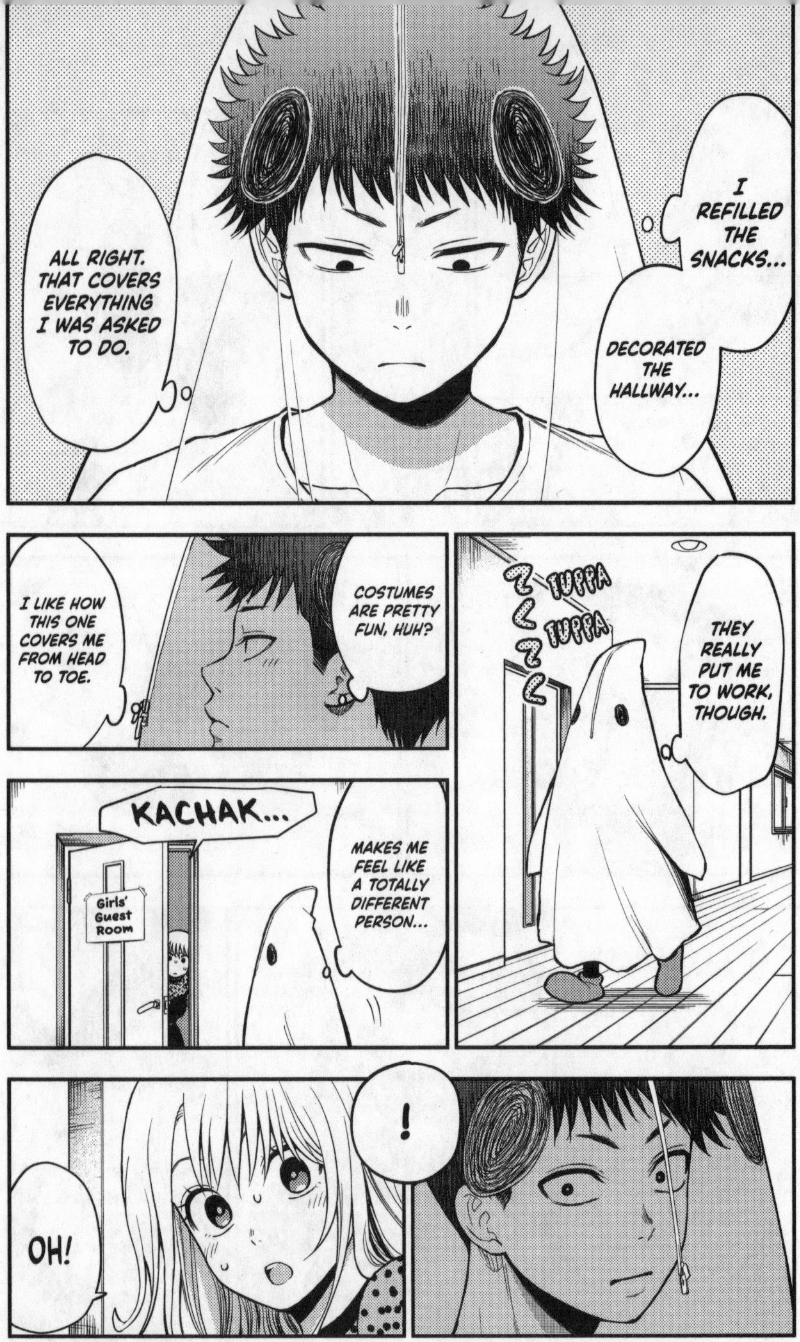
I REFILLED THE SNACKS...
DECORATED THE HALLWAY...
ALL RIGHT. THAT COVERS EVERYTHING I WAS ASKED TO DO.
TUPPA TUPPA
THEY REALLY PUT ME TO WORK, THOUGH.
COSTUMES ARE PRETTY FUN, HUH?
I LIKE HOW THIS ONE COVERS ME FROM HEAD TO TOE.
MAKES ME FEEL LIKE A TOTALLY DIFFERENT PERSON...
KACHAK...
Girls' Guest Room
!
OH!

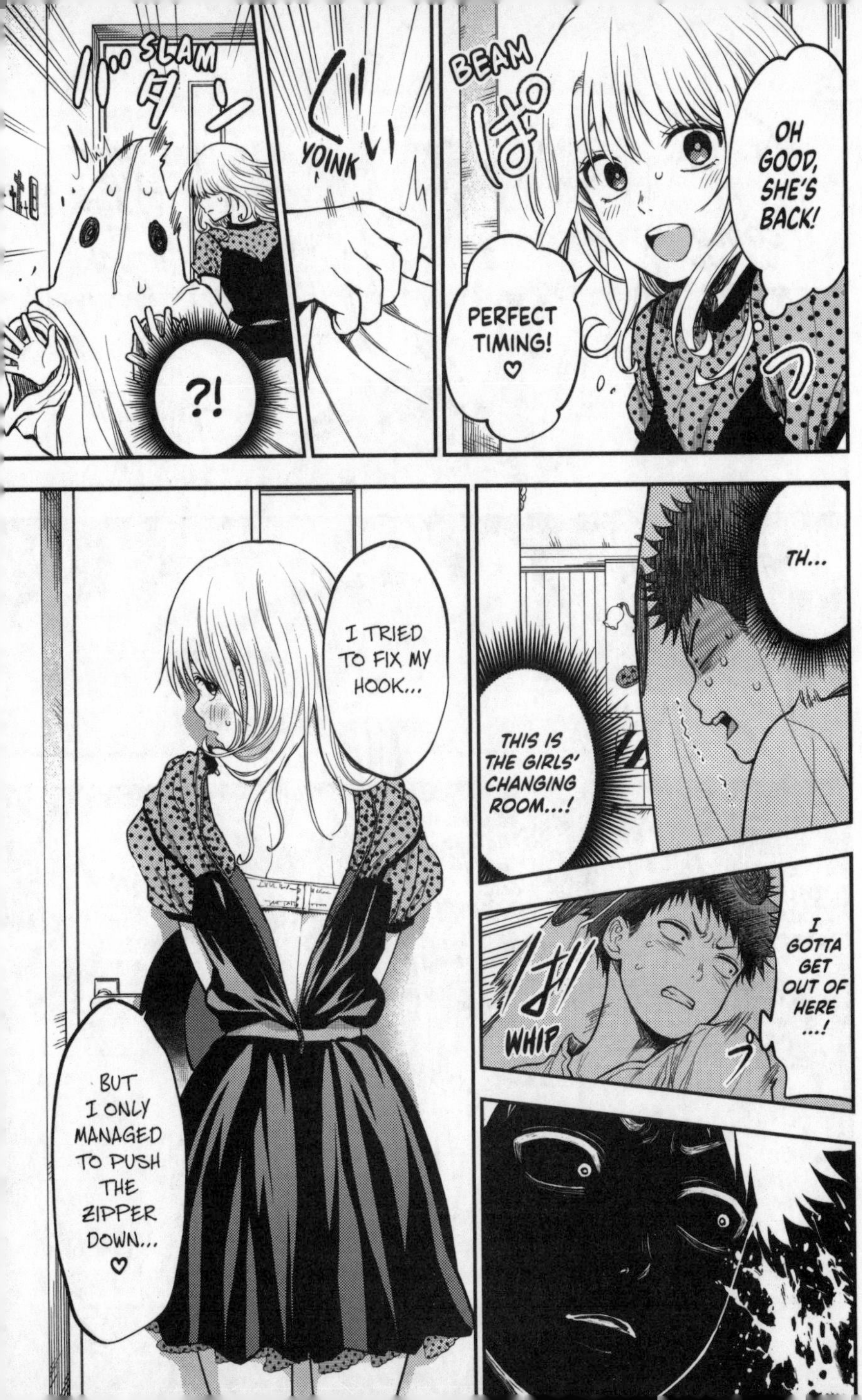
OH GOOD, SHE'S BACK!
BEAM
PERFECT TIMING! ♥
YOINK
SLAM
?!
TH...
THIS IS THE GIRLS' CHANGING ROOM...!
I GOTTA GET OUT OF HERE...!
WHIP
I TRIED TO FIX MY HOOK...
BUT I ONLY MANAGED TO PUSH THE ZIPPER DOWN... ♥

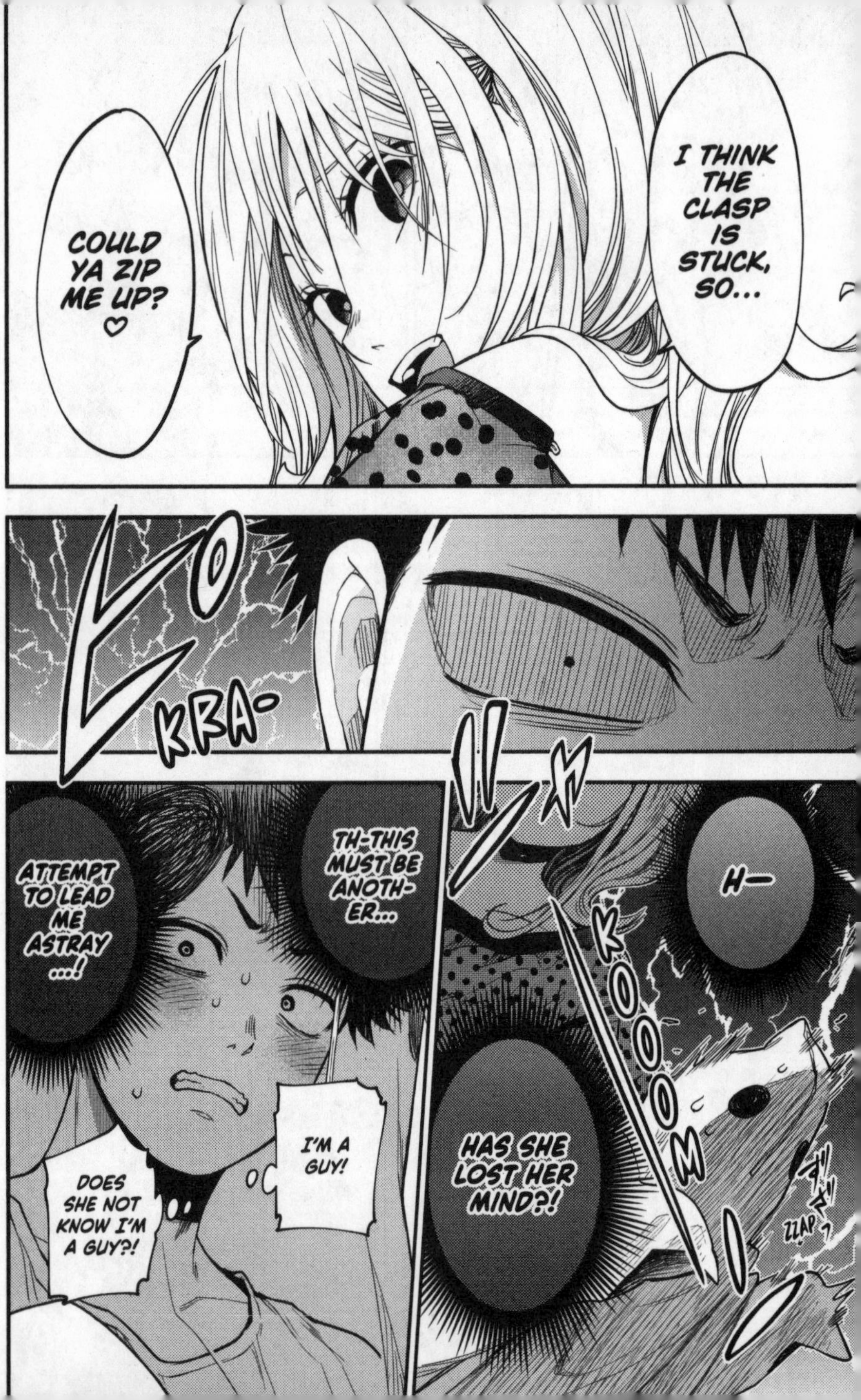
I THINK THE CLASP IS STUCK, SO...
COULD YA ZIP ME UP? ♡
KRA-
KOOOOM
H—
HAS SHE LOST HER MIND?!
ZZAP
TH-THIS MUST BE ANOTHER...
ATTEMPT TO LEAD ME ASTRAY ...!
I'M A GUY!
DOES SHE NOT KNOW I'M A GUY?!

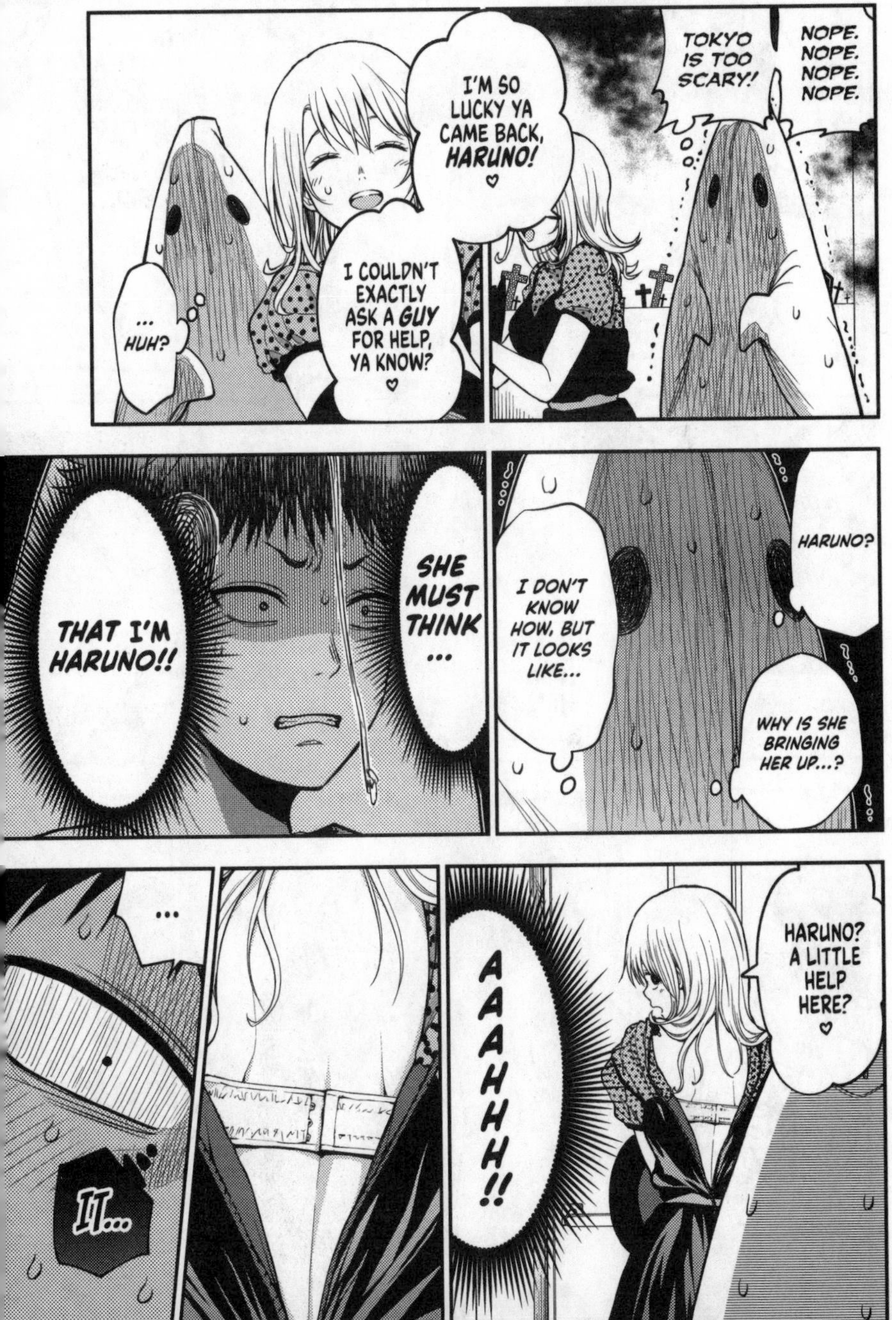
NOPE. NOPE. NOPE. NOPE.
TOKYO IS TOO SCARY!
I'M SO LUCKY YA CAME BACK, HARUNO! ♡
I COULDN'T EXACTLY ASK A GUY FOR HELP, YA KNOW? ♡
... HUH?
HARUNO?
WHY IS SHE BRINGING HER UP...?
I DON'T KNOW HOW, BUT IT LOOKS LIKE...
SHE MUST THINK ...
THAT I'M HARUNO!!
HARUNO? A LITTLE HELP HERE? ♡
AAAAHHH!!
...
IT...

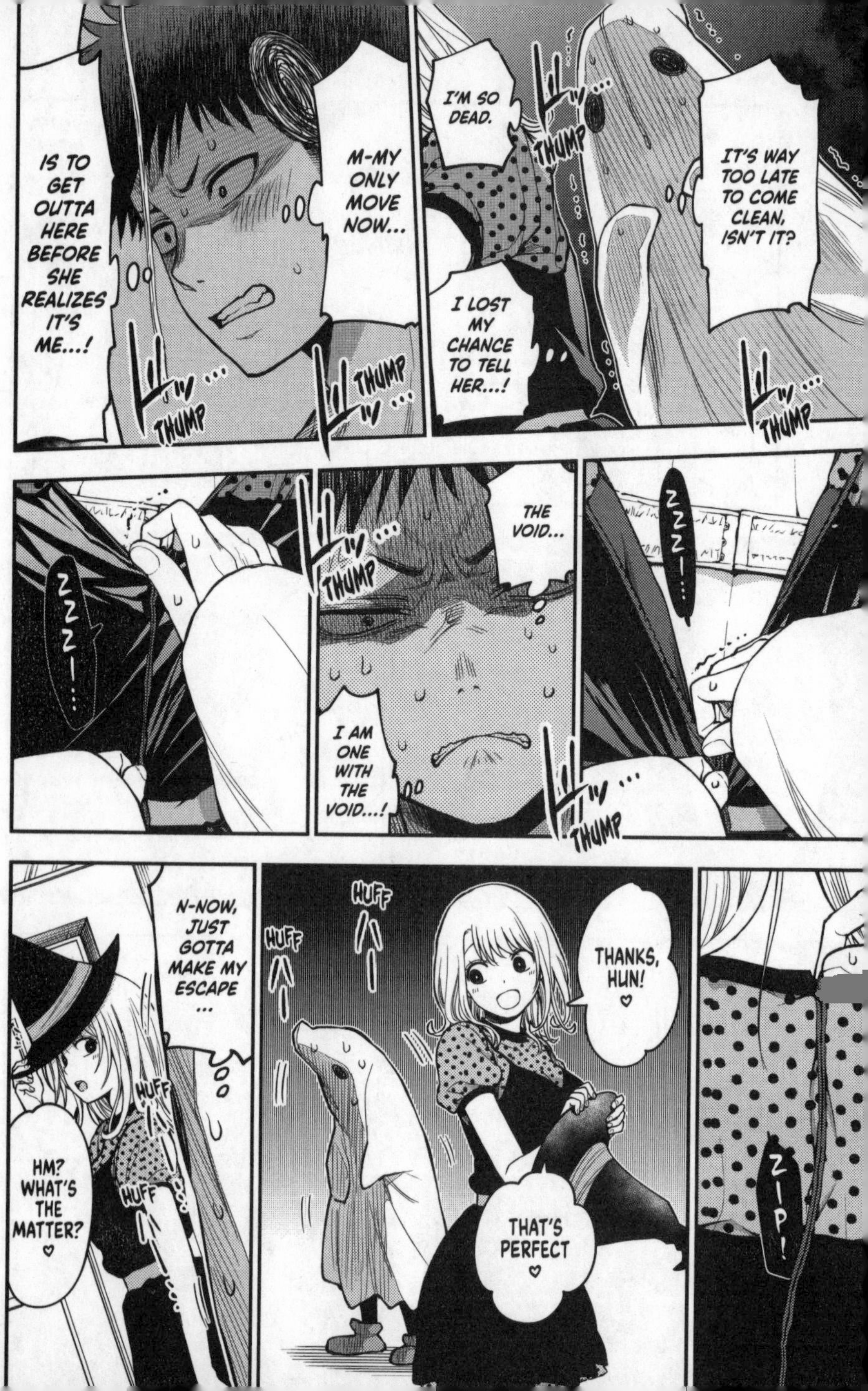

IT'S WAY TOO LATE TO COME CLEAN, ISN'T IT?
THUMP
I'M SO DEAD.
THUMP
I LOST MY CHANCE TO TELL HER...!
THUMP
M-MY ONLY MOVE NOW...
IS TO GET OUTTA HERE BEFORE SHE REALIZES IT'S ME...!
THUMP
ZZZ!...
THUMP
THUMP
THE VOID...
I AM ONE WITH THE VOID...!
ZZZ!...
ZIP!
THANKS, HUN! ♡
HUFF
HUFF
THAT'S PERFECT ♡
N-NOW, JUST GOTTA MAKE MY ESCAPE ...
HUFF
HUFF
HM? WHAT'S THE MATTER? ♡

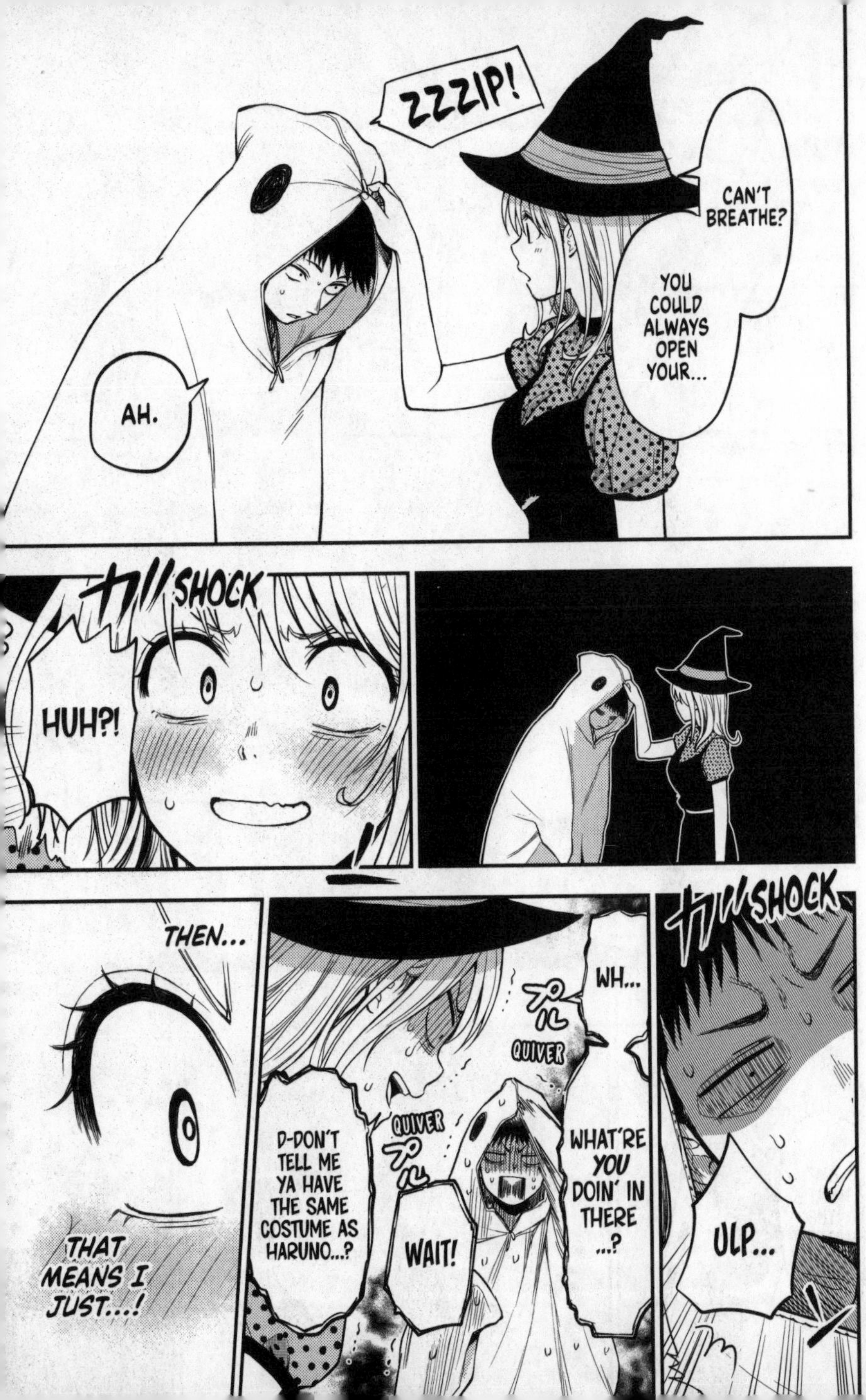
CAN'T BREATHE?
YOU COULD ALWAYS OPEN YOUR...
ZZZIP!
AH.
SHOCK
HUH?!
SHOCK
ULP...
WH...
QUIVER
WHAT'RE YOU DOIN' IN THERE ...?
D-DON'T TELL ME YA HAVE THE SAME COSTUME AS HARUNO...?
QUIVER
WAIT!
THEN...
THAT MEANS I JUST...!

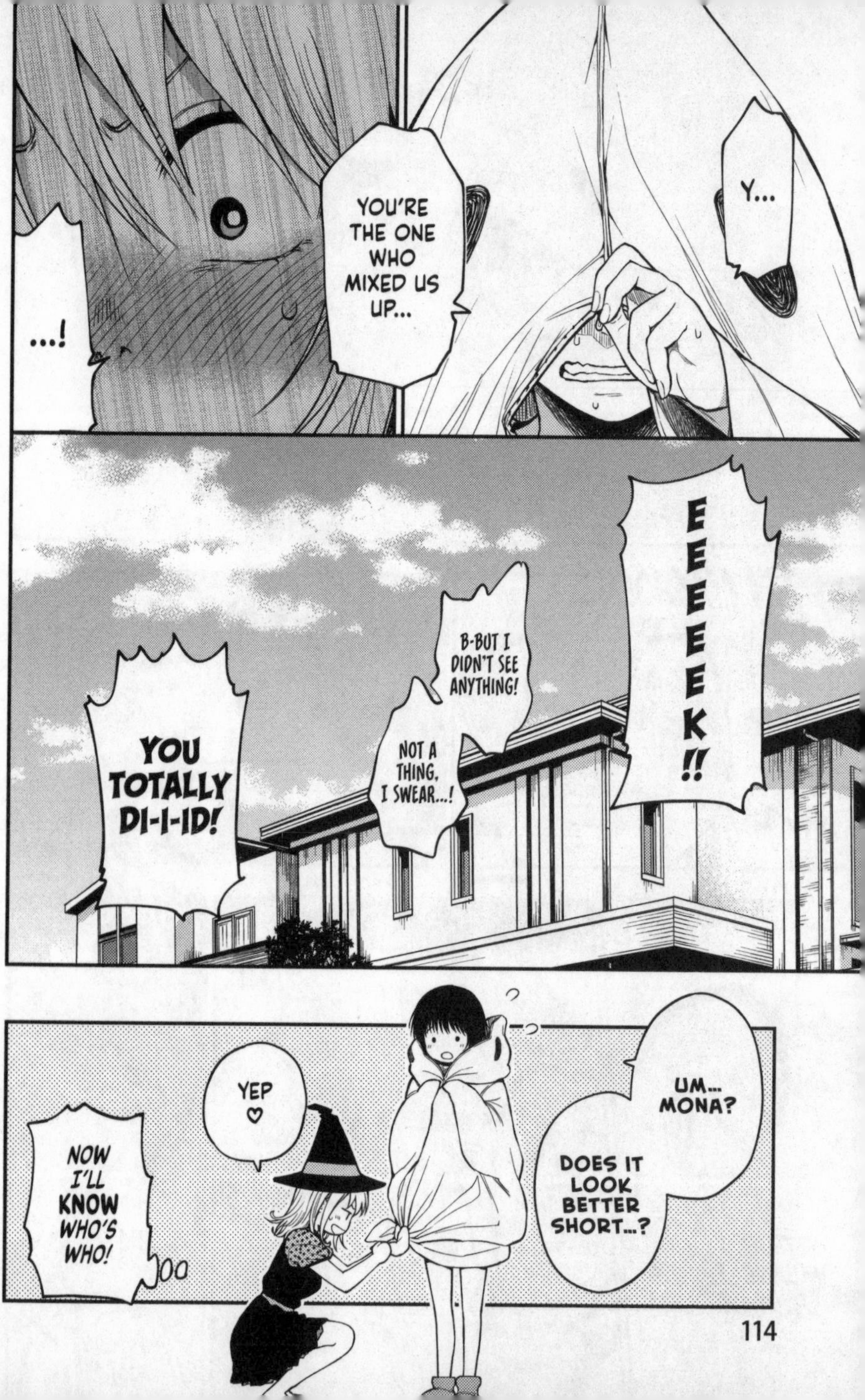
Y...
YOU'RE THE ONE WHO MIXED US UP...
...!
EEEEEK!!
B-BUT I DIDN'T SEE ANYTHING!
NOT A THING, I SWEAR...!
YOU TOTALLY DI-I-ID!
UM... MONA?
DOES IT LOOK BETTER SHORT...?
YEP ♡
NOW I'LL KNOW WHO'S WHO!

Chapter 27 ★ Game Time with That Jerk

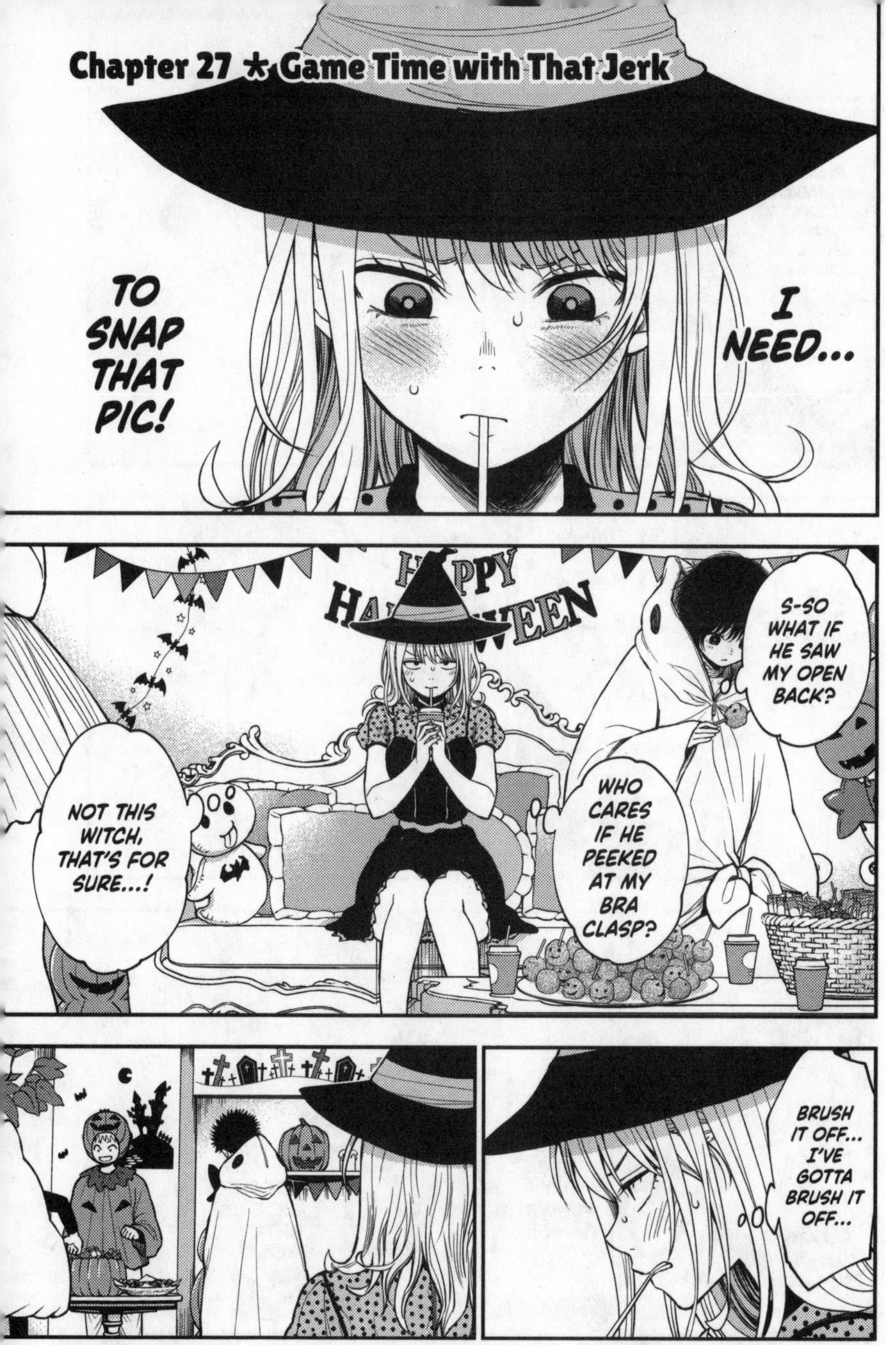

I NEED...
TO SNAP THAT PIC!
S-SO WHAT IF HE SAW MY OPEN BACK?
WHO CARES IF HE PEEKED AT MY BRA CLASP?
NOT THIS WITCH, THAT'S FOR SURE...!
HAPPY HALLOWEEN
BRUSH IT OFF... I'VE GOTTA BRUSH IT OFF...

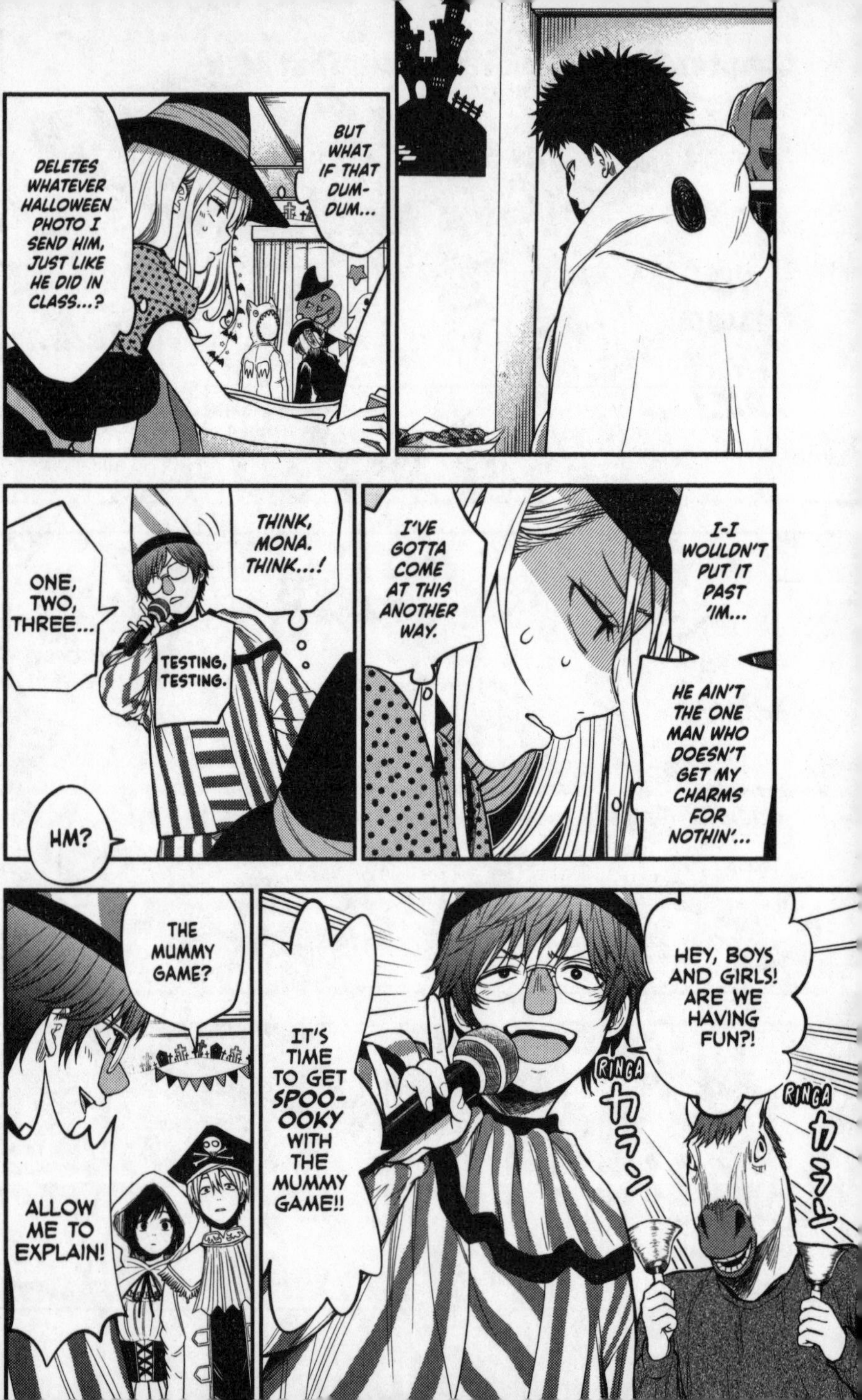

BUT WHAT IF THAT DUM-DUM...
DELETES WHATEVER HALLOWEEN PHOTO I SEND HIM, JUST LIKE HE DID IN CLASS...?
I-I WOULDN'T PUT IT PAST 'IM...
HE AIN'T THE ONE MAN WHO DOESN'T GET MY CHARMS FOR NOTHIN'...
I'VE GOTTA COME AT THIS ANOTHER WAY.
THINK, MONA. THINK...!
TESTING, TESTING.
ONE, TWO, THREE...
HM?
HEY, BOYS AND GIRLS! ARE WE HAVING FUN?!
RINGA カラ～ン
RINGA カラ～ン
IT'S TIME TO GET SPOOOOKY WITH THE MUMMY GAME!!
THE MUMMY GAME?
ALLOW ME TO EXPLAIN!

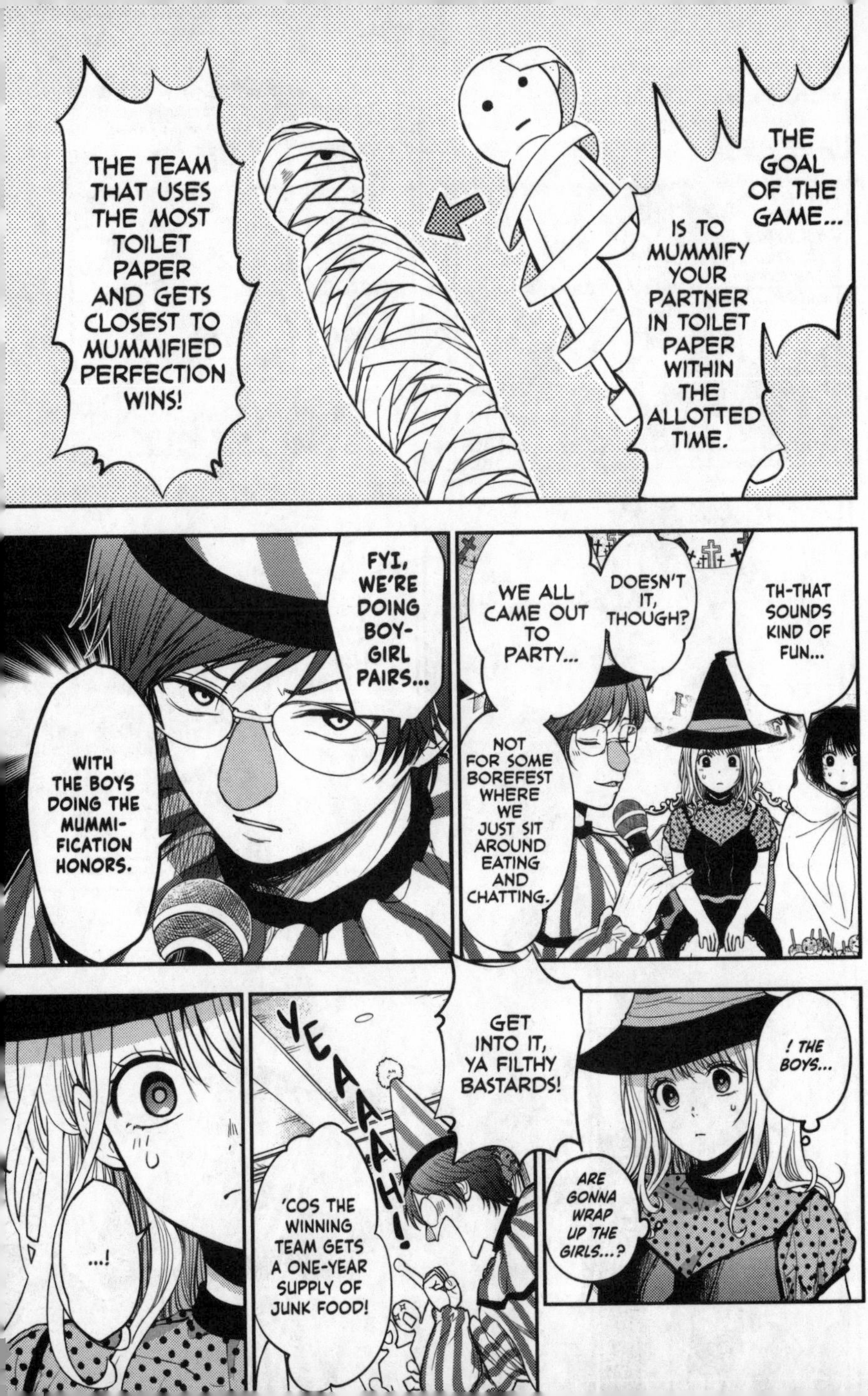
THE GOAL OF THE GAME...
IS TO MUMMIFY YOUR PARTNER IN TOILET PAPER WITHIN THE ALLOTTED TIME.
THE TEAM THAT USES THE MOST TOILET PAPER AND GETS CLOSEST TO MUMMIFIED PERFECTION WINS!
TH-THAT SOUNDS KIND OF FUN...
DOESN'T IT, THOUGH?
WE ALL CAME OUT TO PARTY...
NOT FOR SOME BOREFEST WHERE WE JUST SIT AROUND EATING AND CHATTING.
FYI, WE'RE DOING BOY-GIRL PAIRS...
WITH THE BOYS DOING THE MUMMIFICATION HONORS.
! THE BOYS...
ARE GONNA WRAP UP THE GIRLS...?
GET INTO IT, YA FILTHY BASTARDS!
YEAAAAH!
'COS THE WINNING TEAM GETS A ONE-YEAR SUPPLY OF JUNK FOOD!
...!

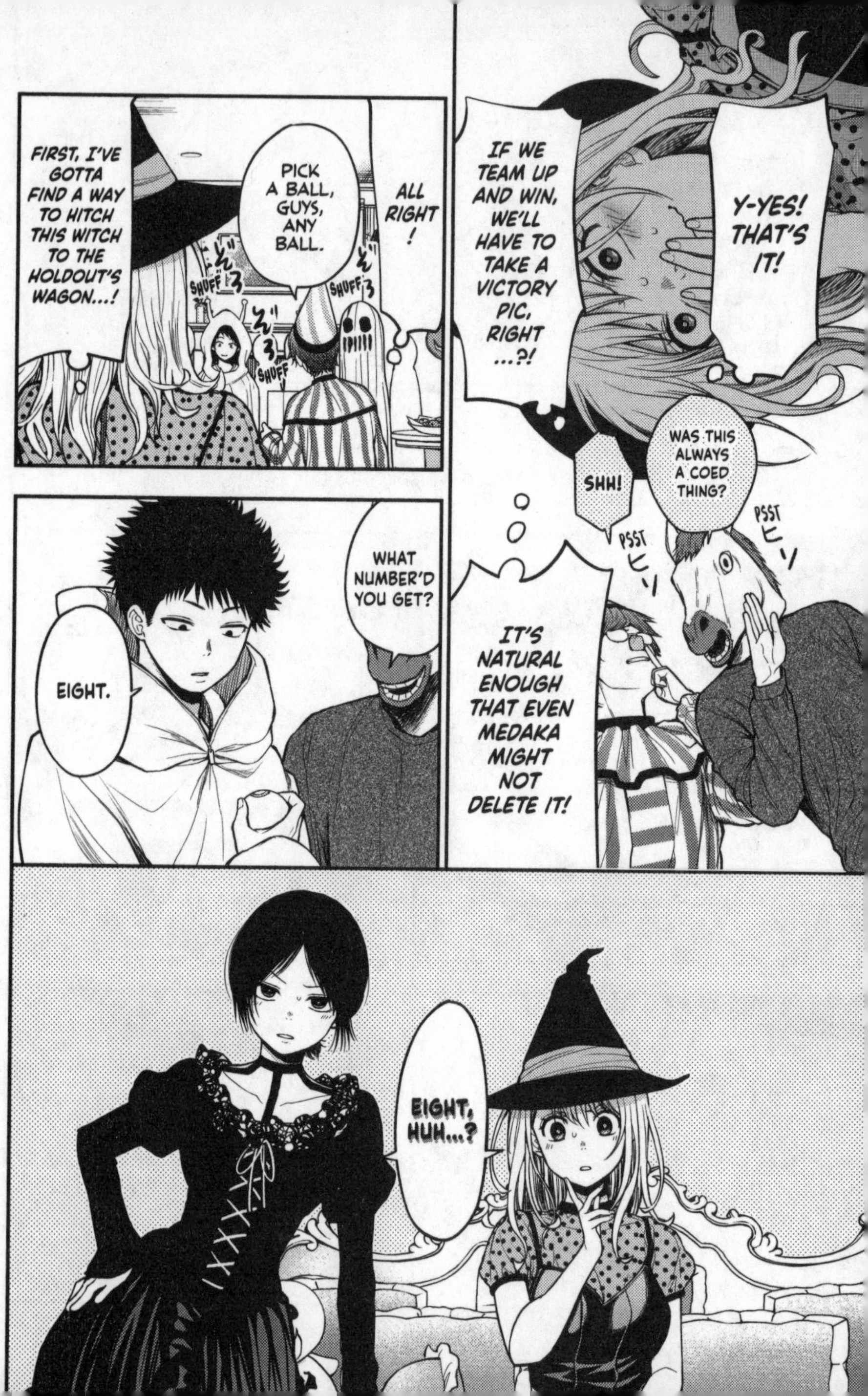
Y-YES! THAT'S IT!
IF WE TEAM UP AND WIN, WE'LL HAVE TO TAKE A VICTORY PIC, RIGHT...?!
WAS THIS ALWAYS A COED THING?
SHH!
PSST ヒソ
PSST ヒソ
IT'S NATURAL ENOUGH THAT EVEN MEDAKA MIGHT NOT DELETE IT!
ALL RIGHT!
PICK A BALL, GUYS, ANY BALL.
FIRST, I'VE GOTTA FIND A WAY TO HITCH THIS WITCH TO THE HOLDOUT'S WAGON...!
SHUFF
SHUFF
SHUFF
WHAT NUMBER'D YOU GET?
EIGHT.
EIGHT, HUH...?

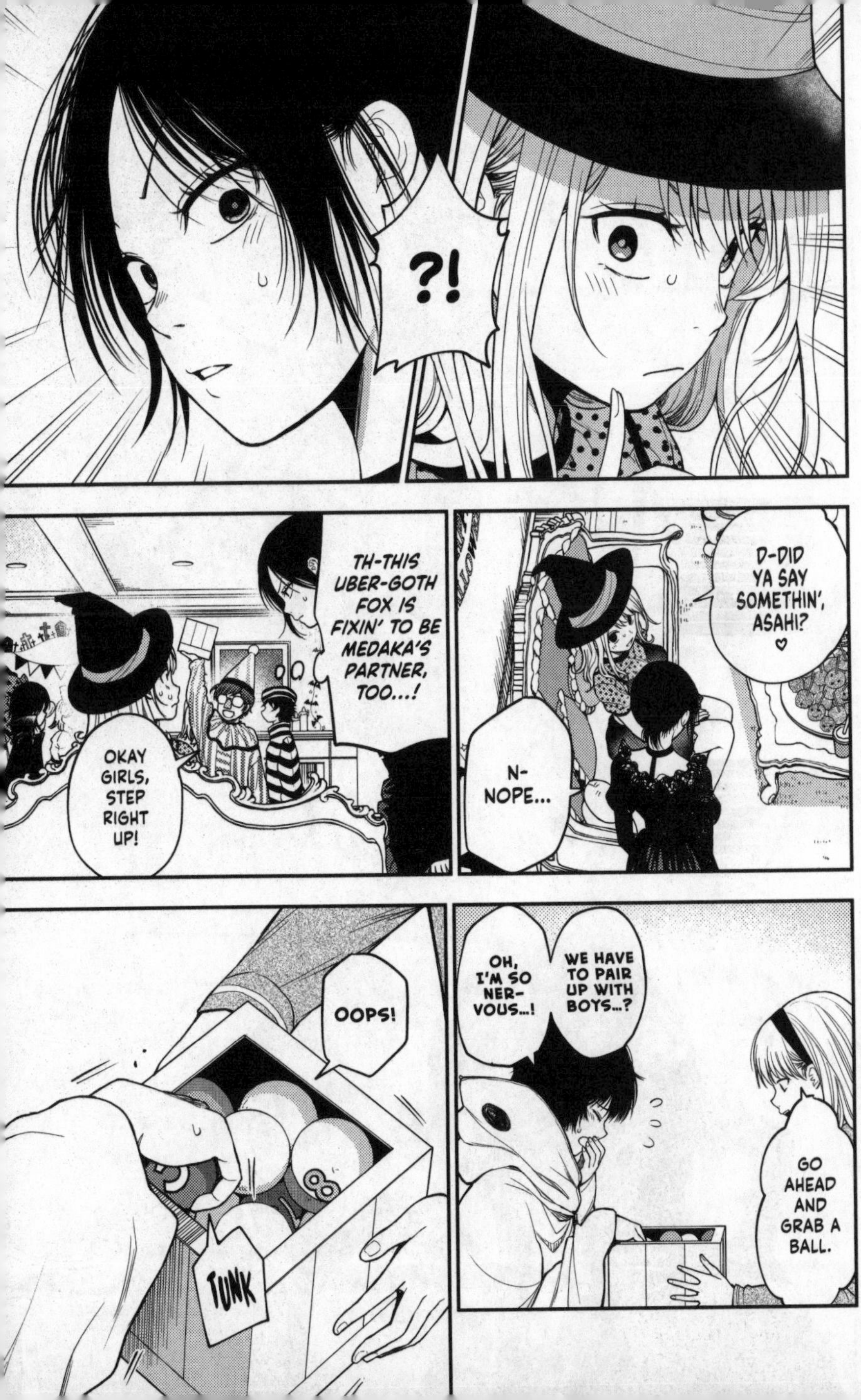
?!
D-DID YA SAY SOMETHIN', ASAHI? ♡
N-NOPE...
TH-THIS UBER-GOTH FOX IS FIXIN' TO BE MEDAKA'S PARTNER, TOO...!
OKAY GIRLS, STEP RIGHT UP!
WE HAVE TO PAIR UP WITH BOYS...?
OH, I'M SO NER-VOUS...!
GO AHEAD AND GRAB A BALL.
OOPS!
TUNK

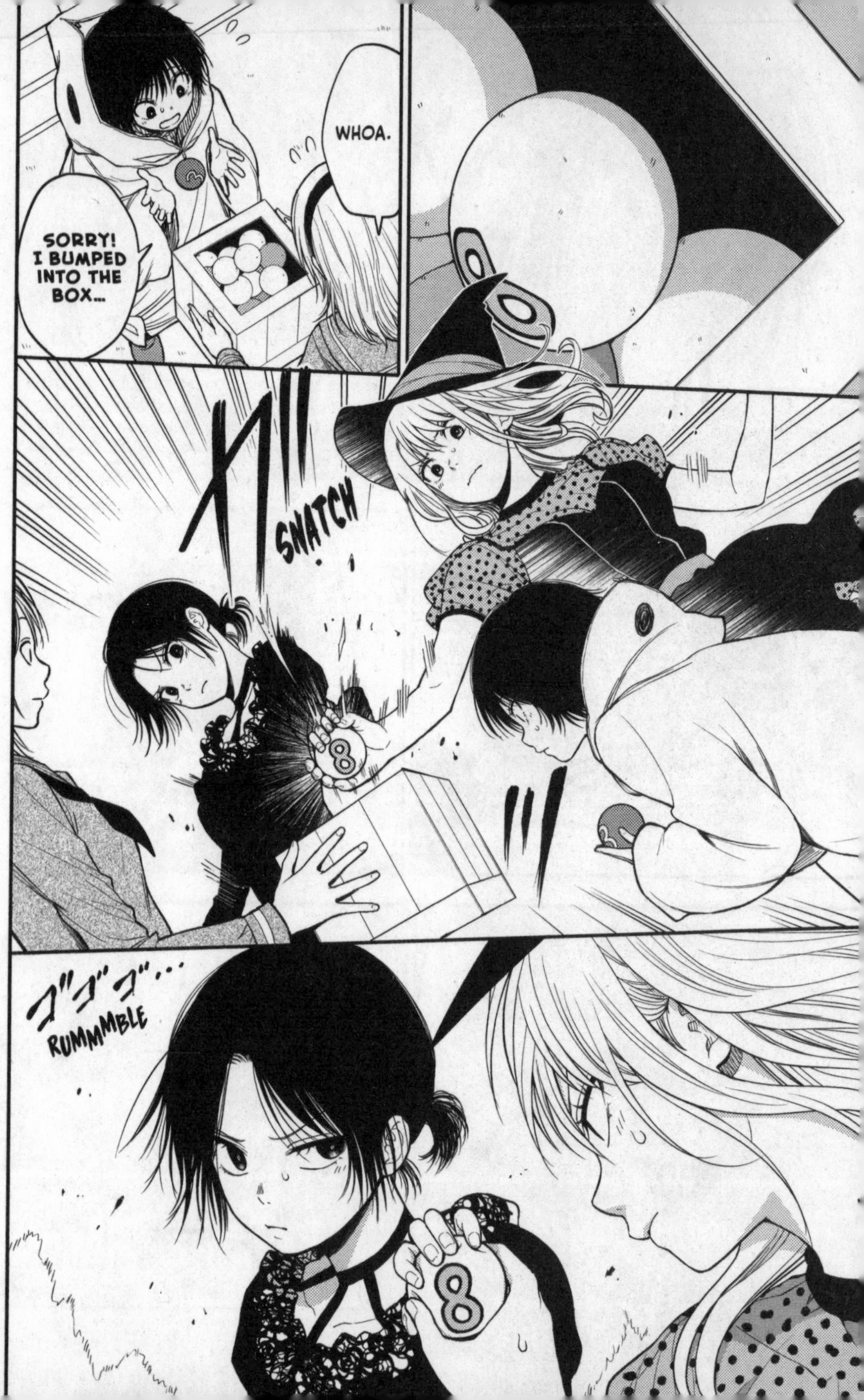
WHOA.
SORRY! I BUMPED INTO THE BOX...
SNATCH
ゴゴゴ...
RUMMMBLE

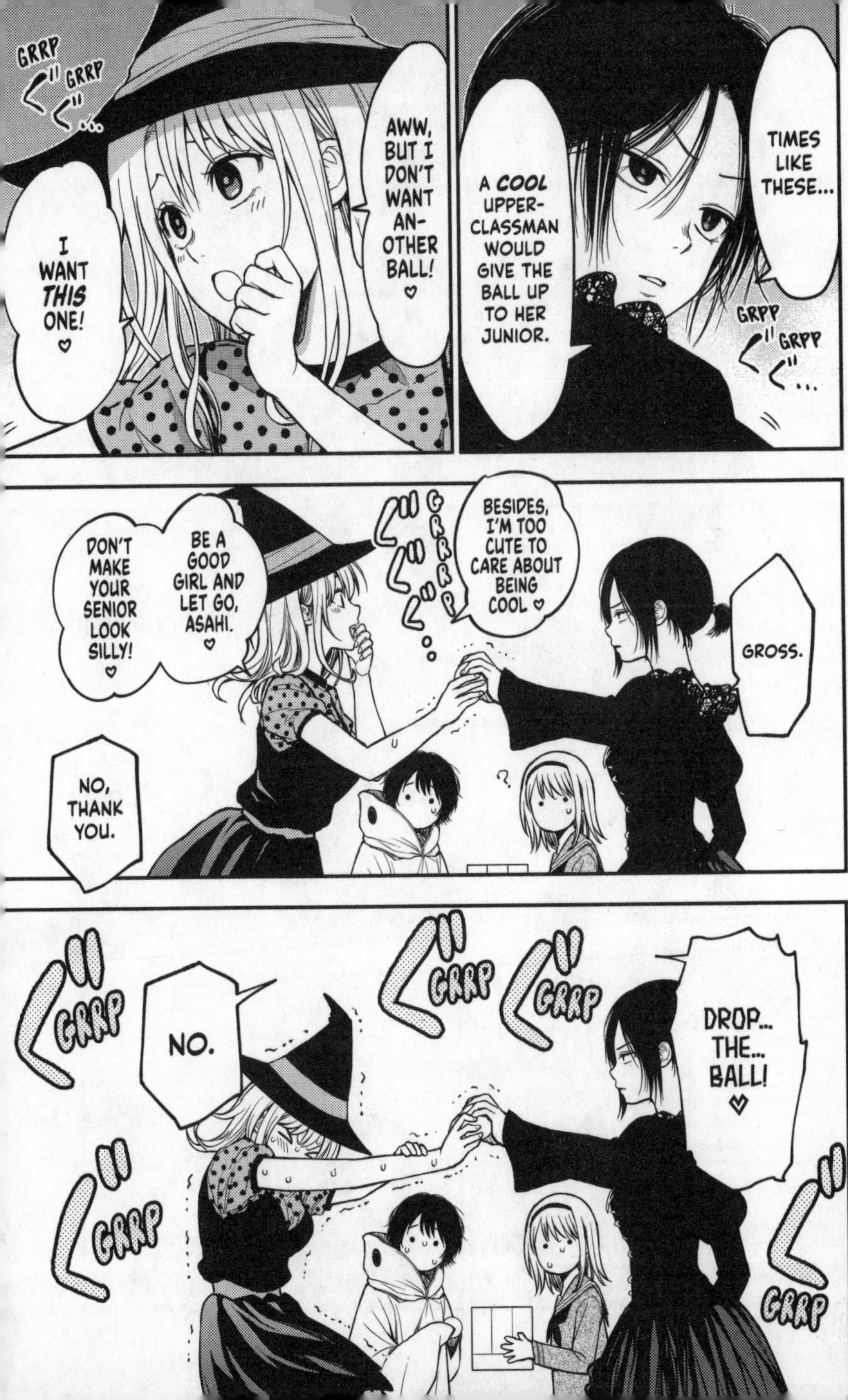
TIMES LIKE THESE...
A COOL UPPER-CLASSMAN WOULD GIVE THE BALL UP TO HER JUNIOR.
GRPP GRPP
AWW, BUT I DON'T WANT AN-OTHER BALL! ♡
I WANT THIS ONE! ♡
GRRP GRRP
GROSS.
BESIDES, I'M TOO CUTE TO CARE ABOUT BEING COOL ♡
GRRRP
BE A GOOD GIRL AND LET GO, ASAHI. ♡
DON'T MAKE YOUR SENIOR LOOK SILLY! ♡
NO, THANK YOU.
DROP... THE... BALL! ♡
GRRP
GRRP
GRRP
NO.
GRRP
GRRP

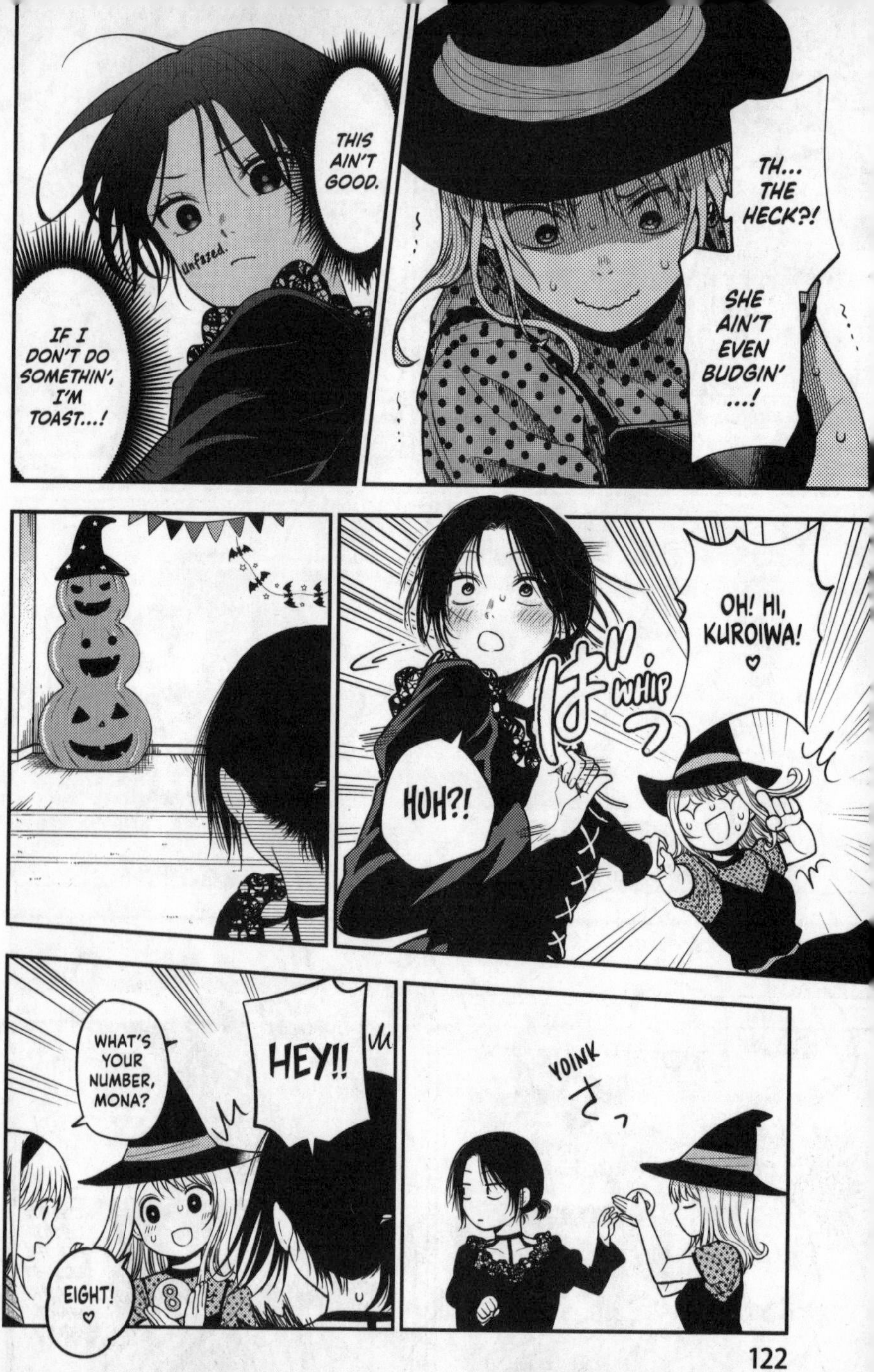
TH... THE HECK?!
SHE AIN'T EVEN BUDGIN' ...!
THIS AIN'T GOOD.
Unfazed.
IF I DON'T DO SOMETHIN', I'M TOAST...!
OH! HI, KUROIWA! ♡
WHIP
HUH?!
YOINK
HEY!!
WHAT'S YOUR NUMBER, MONA?
EIGHT! ♡

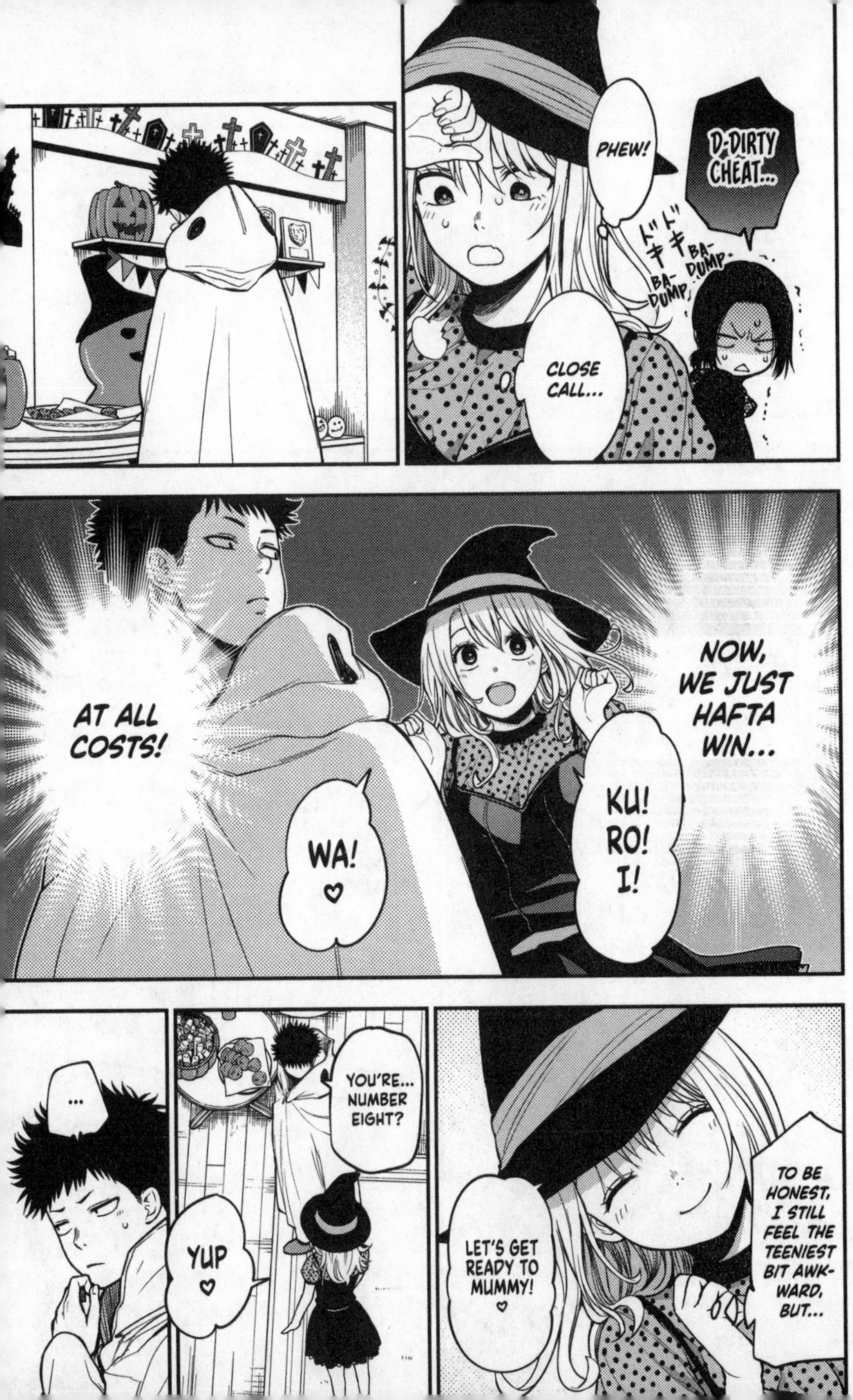
PHEW!
CLOSE CALL...
D-DIRTY CHEAT...
ドキドキ
BA-DUMP BA-DUMP
NOW, WE JUST HAFTA WIN...
KU! RO! I!
WA! ♡
AT ALL COSTS!
TO BE HONEST, I STILL FEEL THE TEENIEST BIT AWK-WARD, BUT...
LET'S GET READY TO MUMMY! ♡
YOU'RE... NUMBER EIGHT?
YUP ♡
...

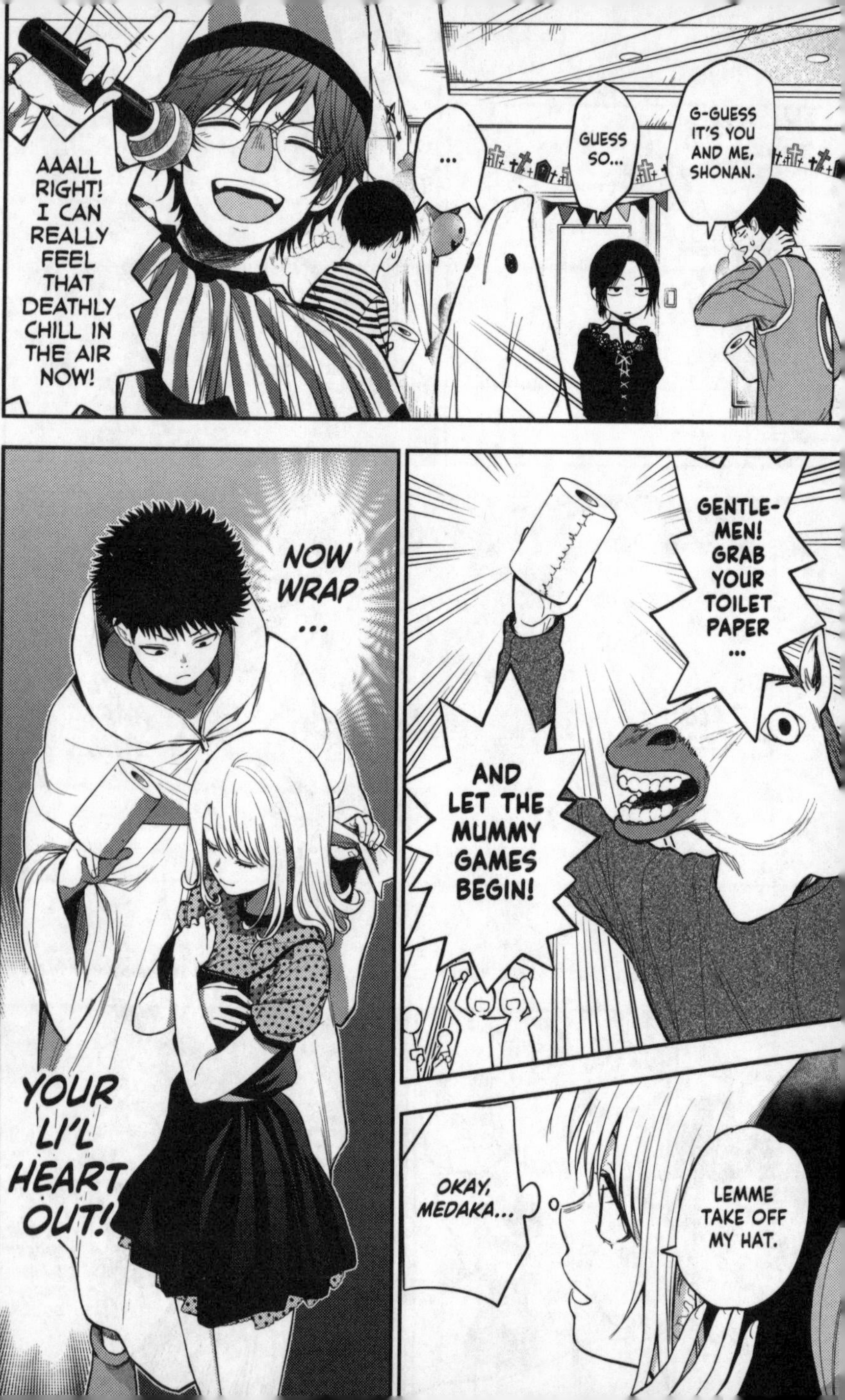
G-GUESS IT'S YOU AND ME, SHONAN.
GUESS SO...
...
AAALL RIGHT! I CAN REALLY FEEL THAT DEATHLY CHILL IN THE AIR NOW!
GENTLE-MEN! GRAB YOUR TOILET PAPER ...
AND LET THE MUMMY GAMES BEGIN!
LEMME TAKE OFF MY HAT.
OKAY, MEDAKA...
NOW WRAP ...
YOUR LI'L HEART OUT!

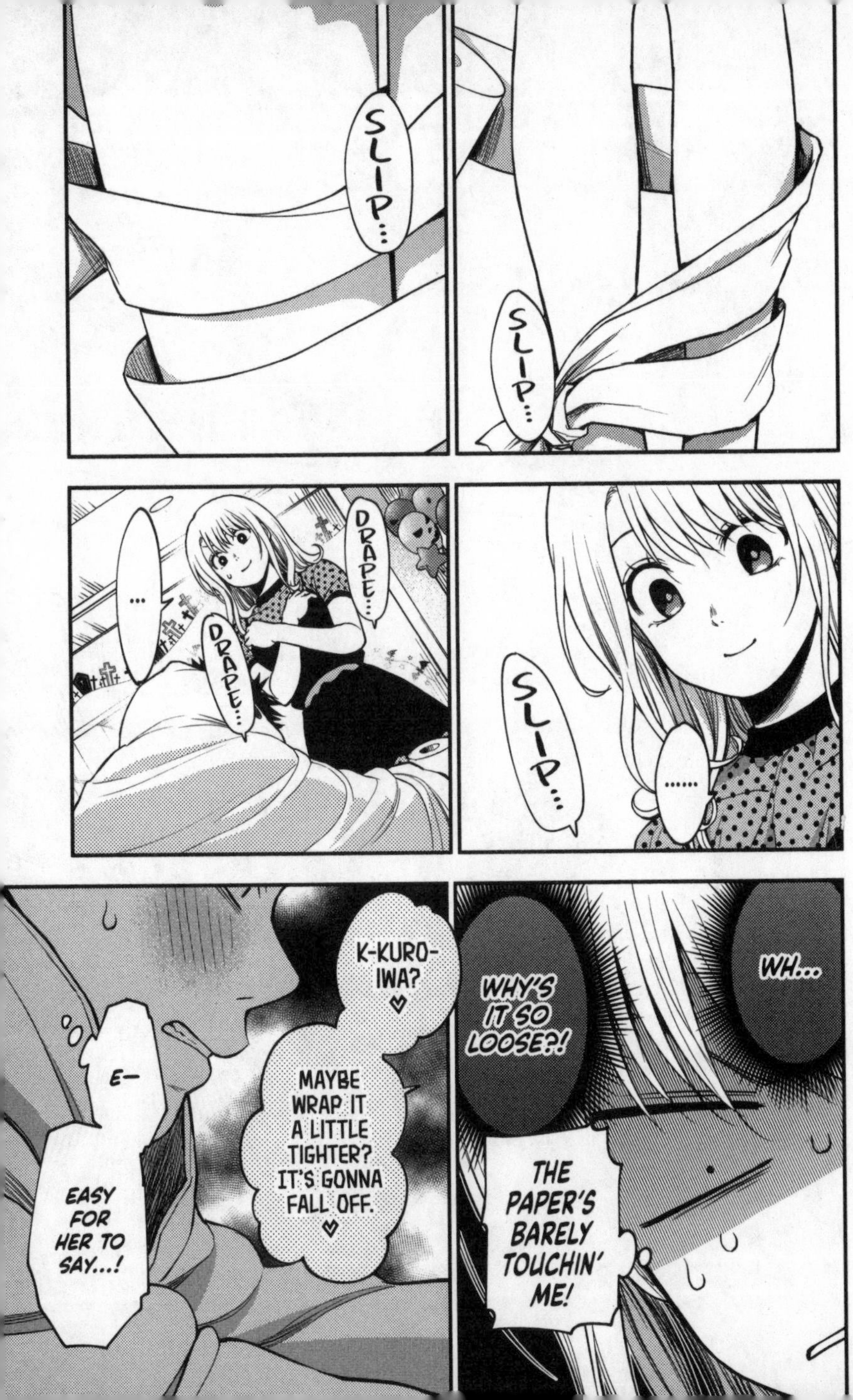
SLIP...
SLIP...
SLIP...
......
DRAPE...
DRAPE...
...
WH...
WHY'S IT SO LOOSE?!
THE PAPER'S BARELY TOUCHIN' ME!
K-KURO-IWA? ♥
MAYBE WRAP IT A LITTLE TIGHTER? IT'S GONNA FALL OFF. ♥
E—
EASY FOR HER TO SAY...!

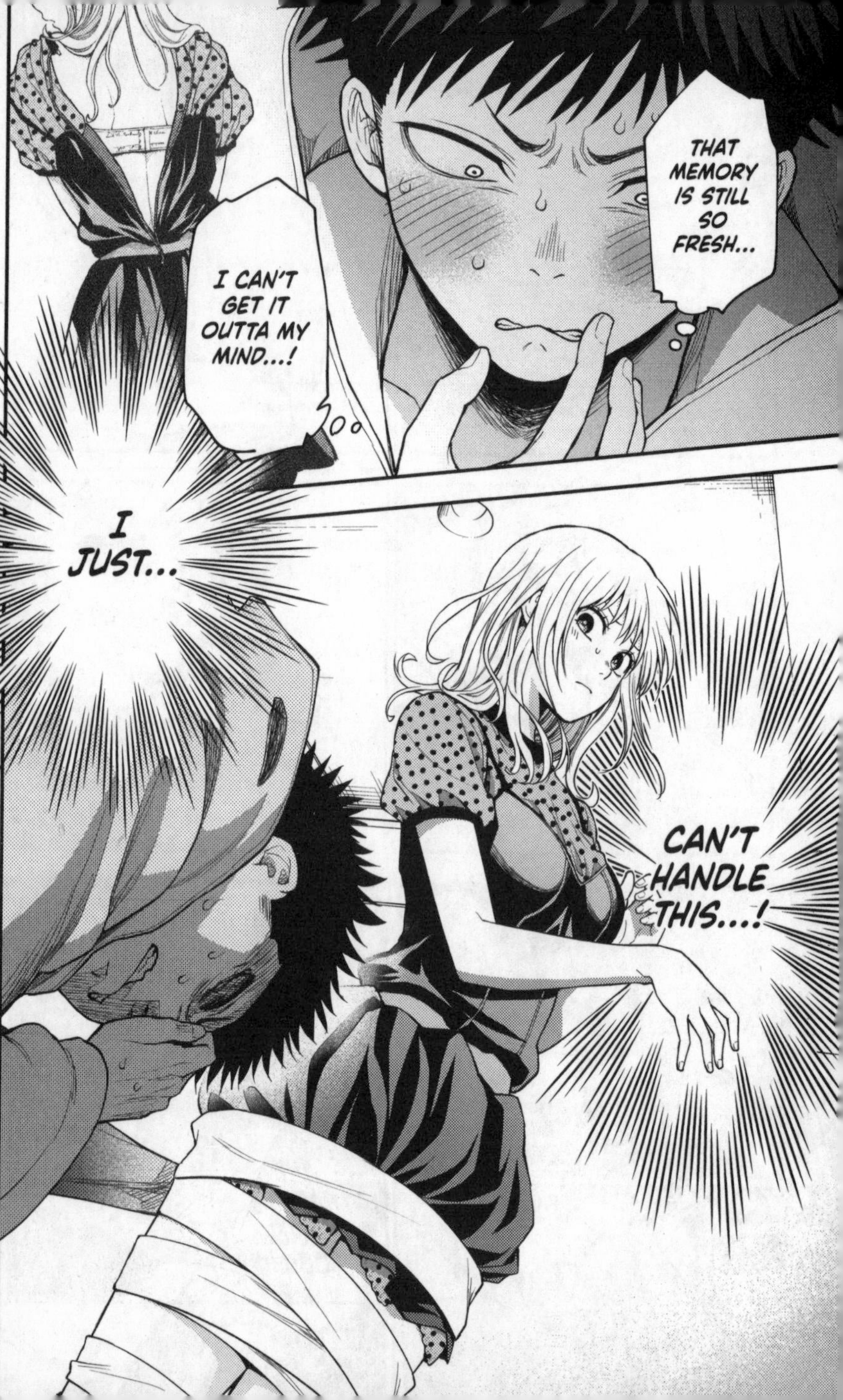
THAT MEMORY IS STILL SO FRESH...
I CAN'T GET IT OUTTA MY MIND...!
I JUST...
CAN'T HANDLE THIS...!

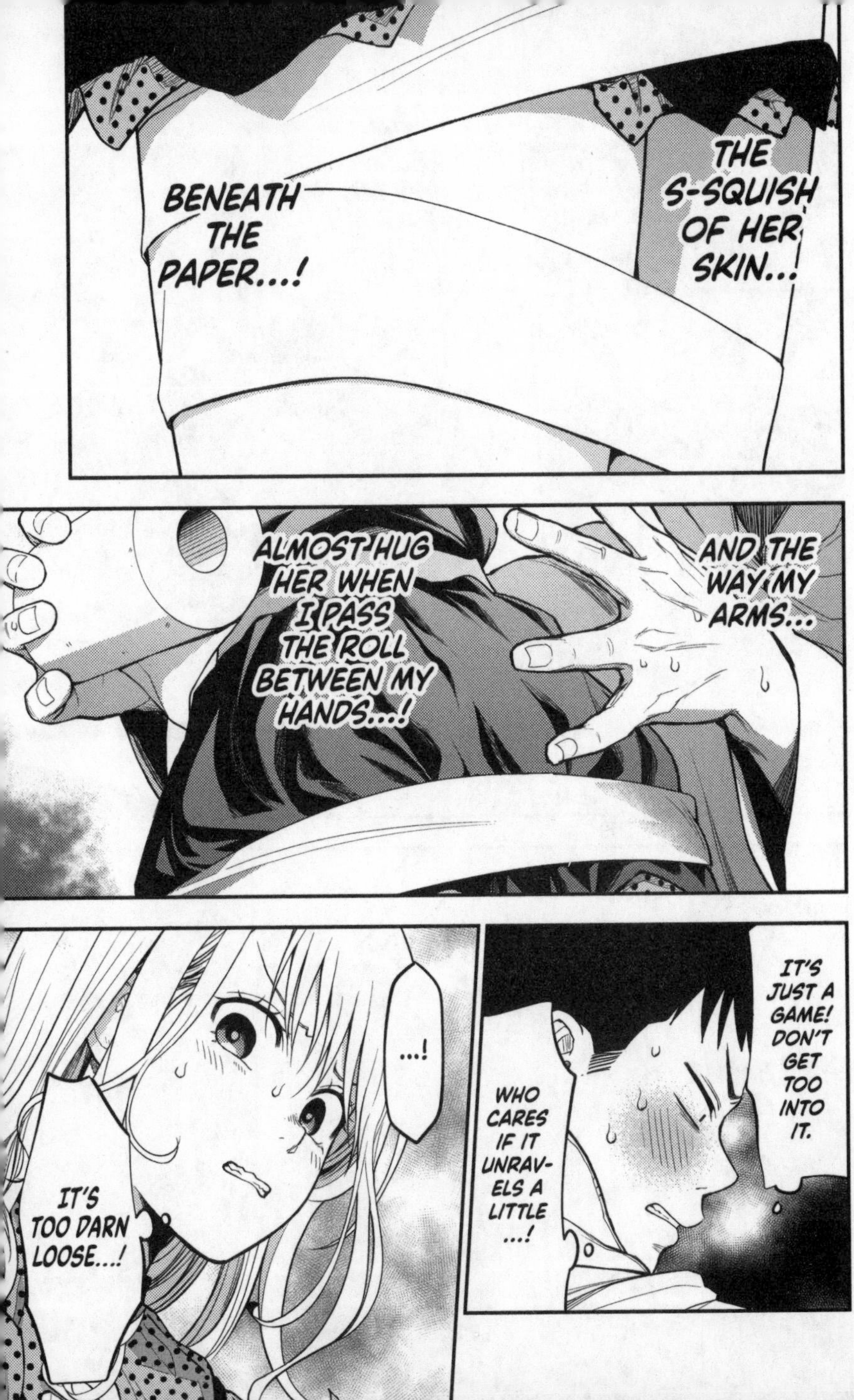
THE S-SQUISH OF HER SKIN...
BENEATH THE PAPER...!
AND THE WAY MY ARMS...
ALMOST HUG HER WHEN I PASS THE ROLL BETWEEN MY HANDS...!
IT'S JUST A GAME! DON'T GET TOO INTO IT.
WHO CARES IF IT UNRAVELS A LITTLE ...!
...!
IT'S TOO DARN LOOSE...!

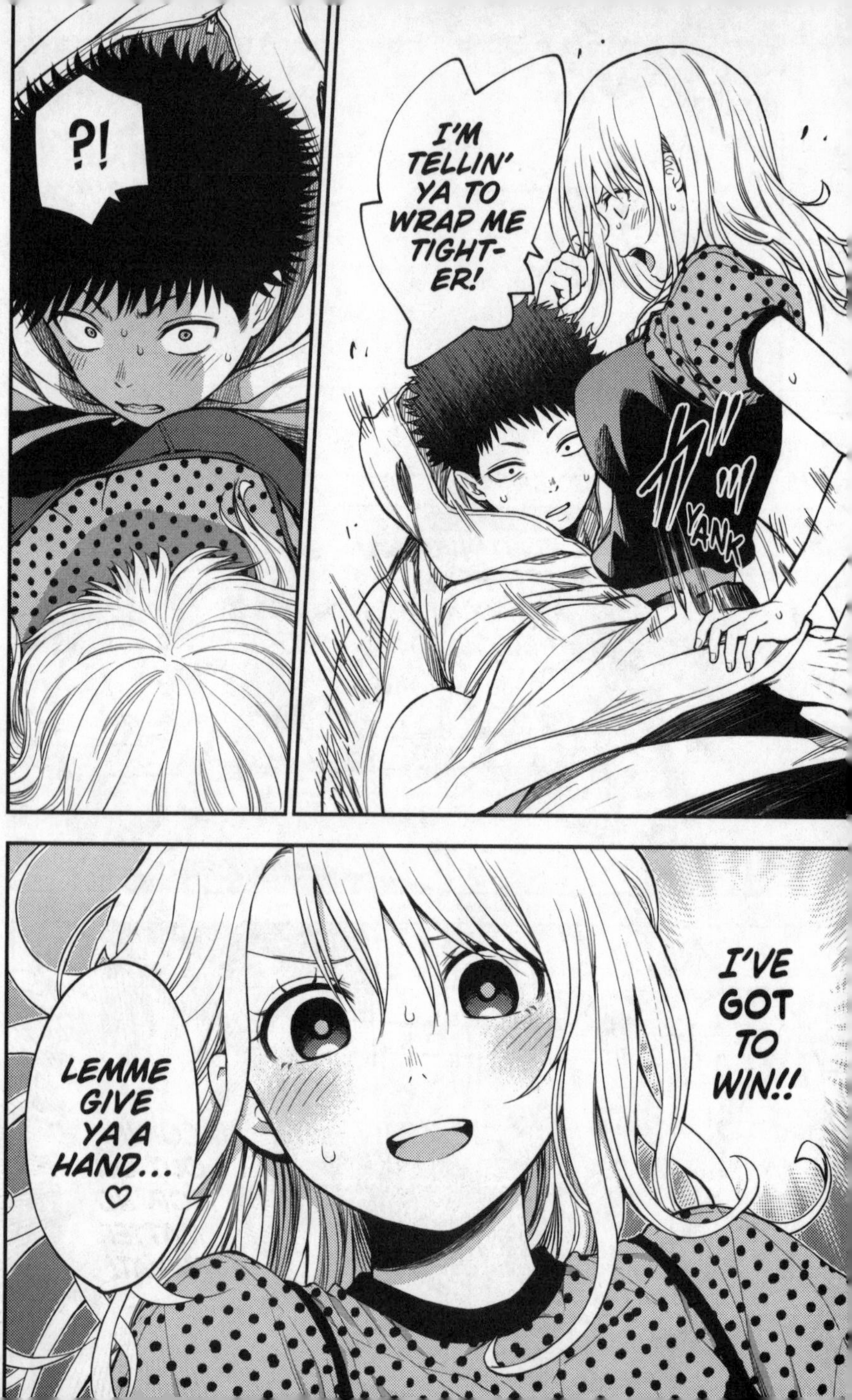
I'M TELLIN' YA TO WRAP ME TIGHTER!
YANK
?!
I'VE GOT TO WIN!!
LEMME GIVE YA A HAND... ♡

Chapter 28 ★ Photo Shoot with That Jerk

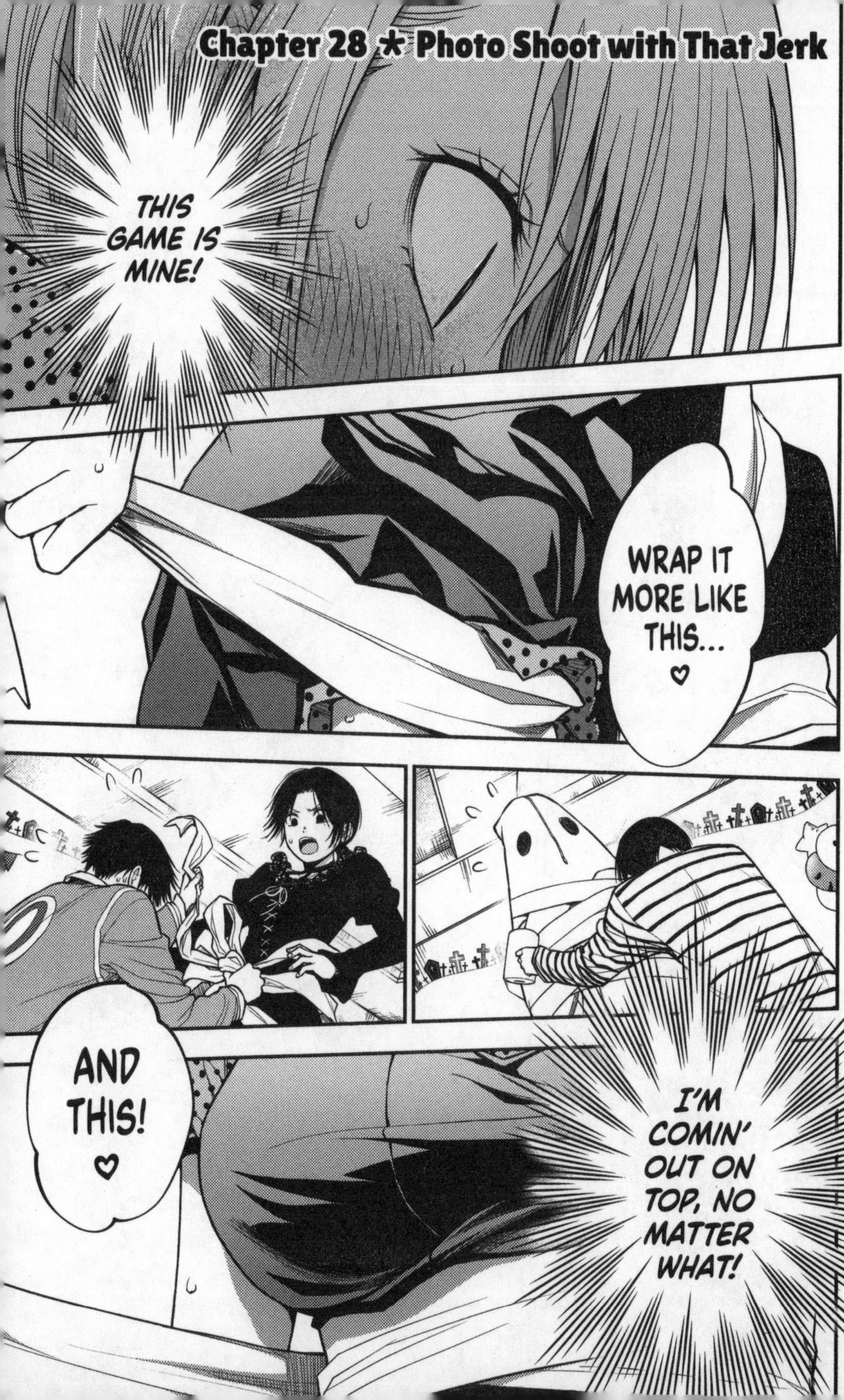
THIS GAME IS MINE!
WRAP IT MORE LIKE THIS... ♡
AND THIS! ♡
I'M COMIN' OUT ON TOP, NO MATTER WHAT!

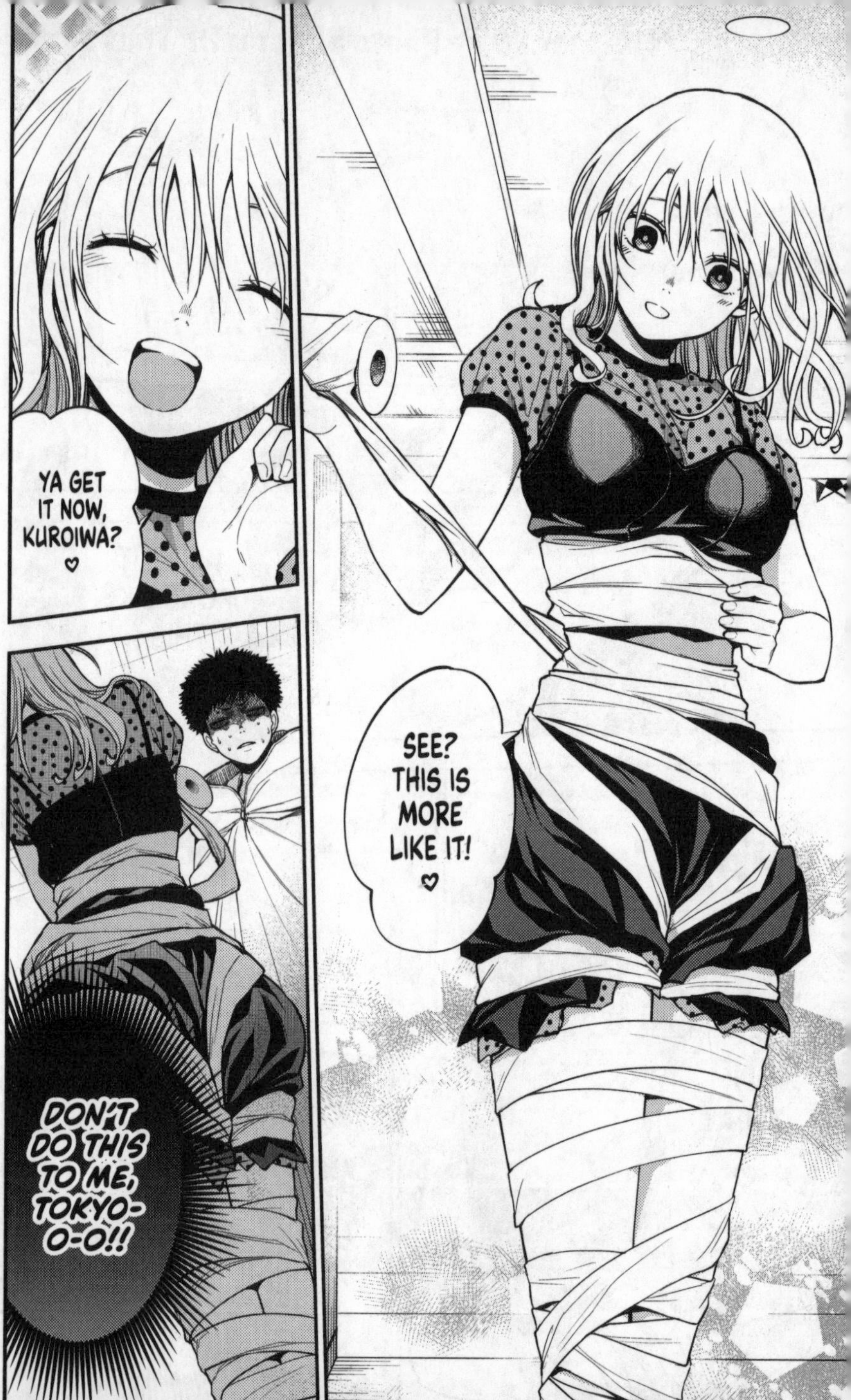
SEE? THIS IS MORE LIKE IT! ♡
YA GET IT NOW, KUROIWA? ♡
DON'T DO THIS TO ME, TOKYO-O-O!!

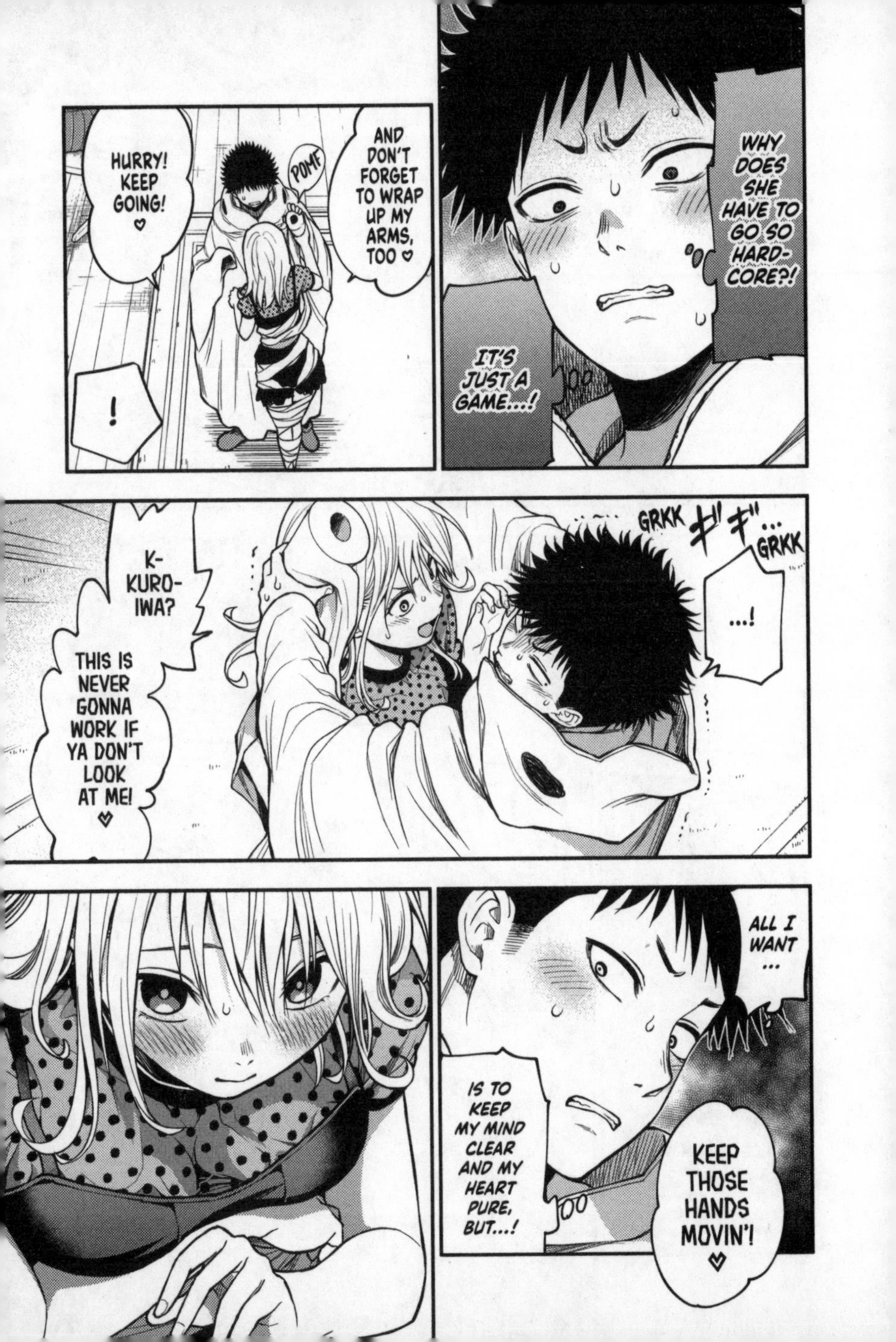
WHY DOES SHE HAVE TO GO SO HARD-CORE?!
IT'S JUST A GAME...!
AND DON'T FORGET TO WRAP UP MY ARMS, TOO ♡
POMF
HURRY! KEEP GOING! ♡
!
GRKK
ギギ
...GRKK
...!
K-KURO-IWA?
THIS IS NEVER GONNA WORK IF YA DON'T LOOK AT ME! ♡
ALL I WANT ...
IS TO KEEP MY MIND CLEAR AND MY HEART PURE, BUT...!
KEEP THOSE HANDS MOVIN'! ♡

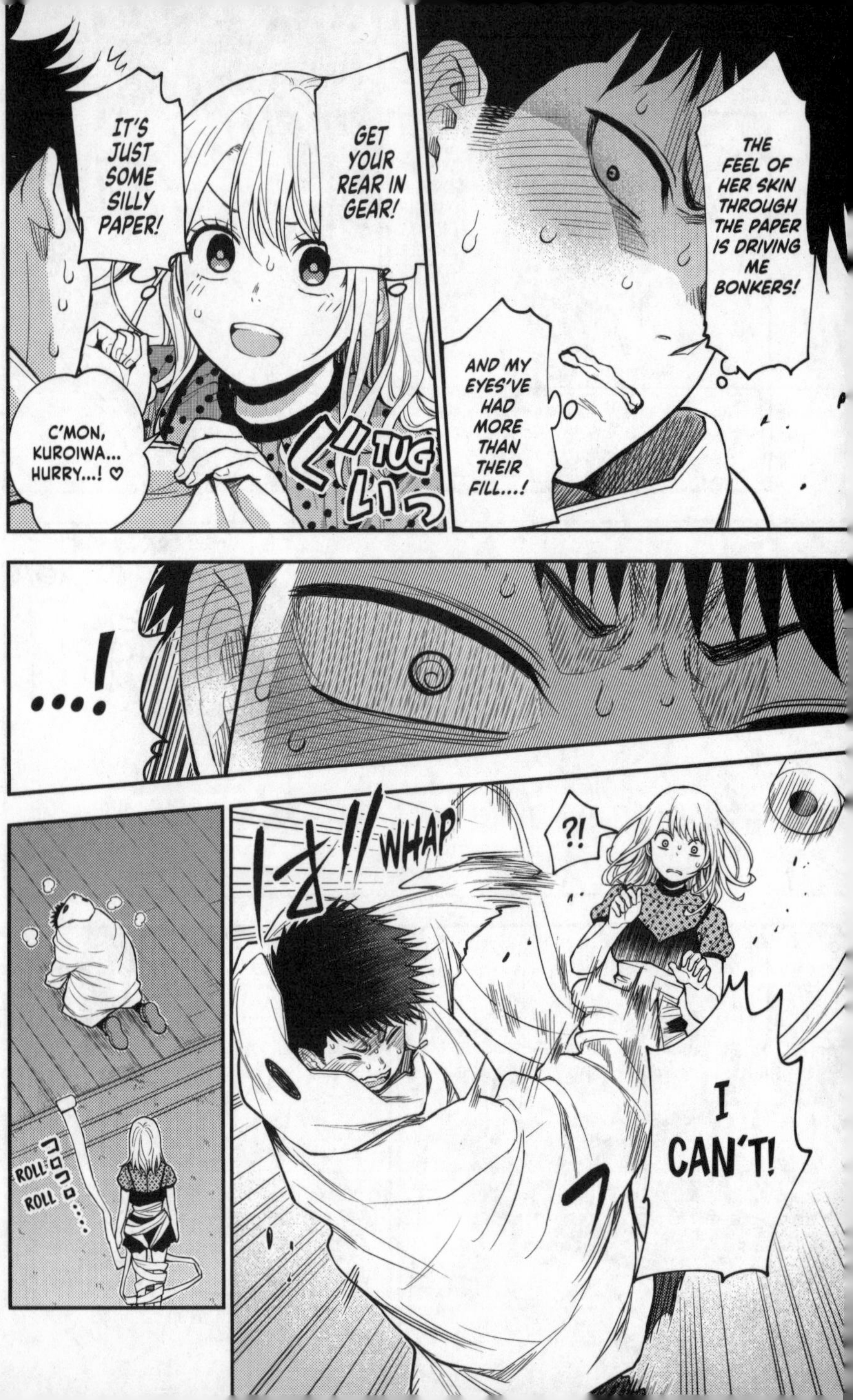
THE FEEL OF HER SKIN THROUGH THE PAPER IS DRIVING ME BONKERS!
AND MY EYES'VE HAD MORE THAN THEIR FILL...!
GET YOUR REAR IN GEAR!
IT'S JUST SOME SILLY PAPER!
C'MON, KUROIWA... HURRY...! ♡
ぐいっ TUG
...!
?!
はっ WHAP
I CAN'T!
コロコロ... ROLL ROLL

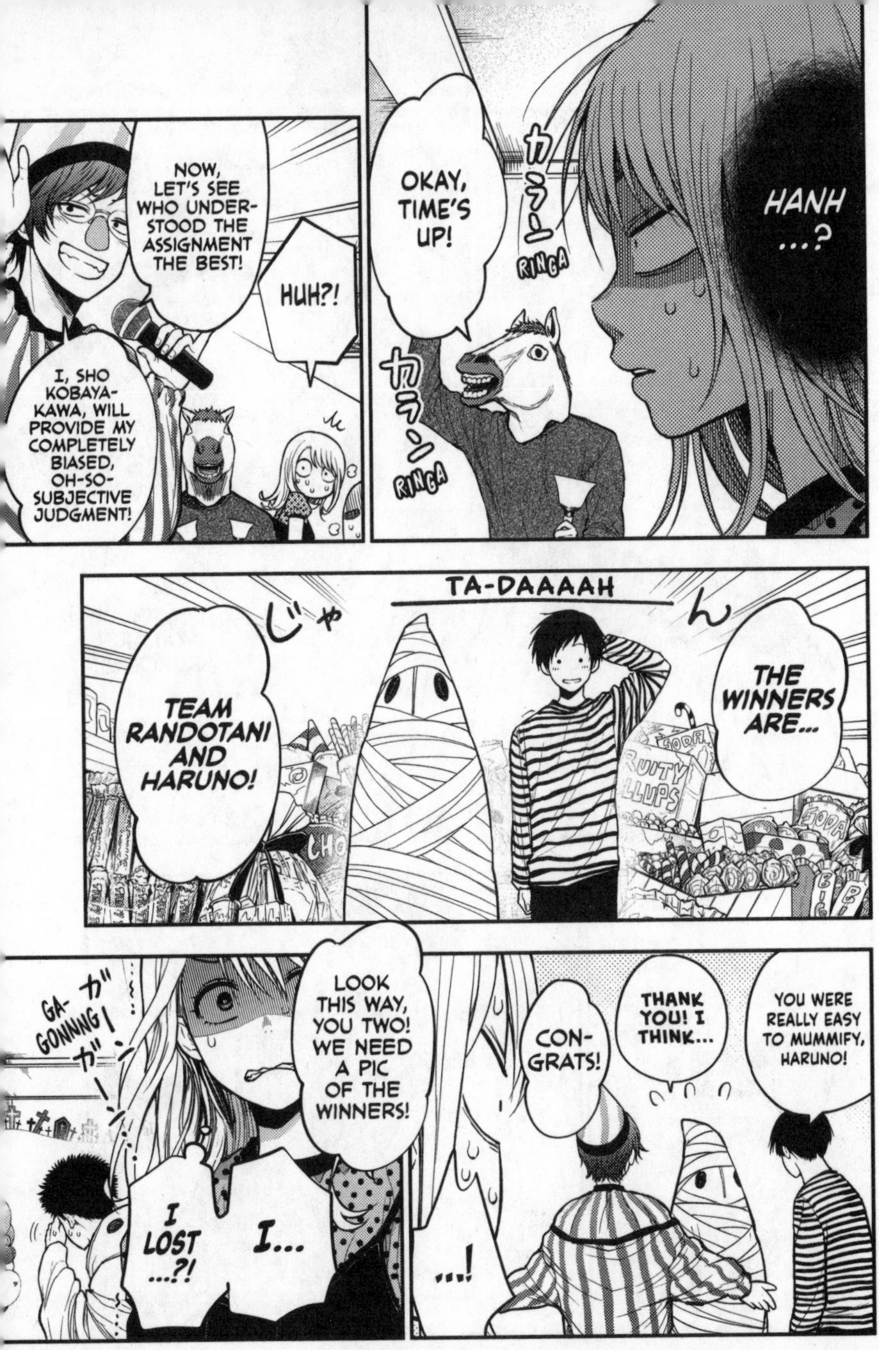
HANH ...?
OKAY, TIME'S UP!
カラン
RINGA
カラン
RINGA
NOW, LET'S SEE WHO UNDER-STOOD THE ASSIGNMENT THE BEST!
HUH?!
I, SHO KOBAYA-KAWA, WILL PROVIDE MY COMPLETELY BIASED, OH-SO-SUBJECTIVE JUDGMENT!
THE WINNERS ARE...
ん
TA-DAAAAH
じゃ
TEAM RANDOTANI AND HARUNO!
YOU WERE REALLY EASY TO MUMMIFY, HARUNO!
THANK YOU! I THINK...
CON-GRATS!
...!
LOOK THIS WAY, YOU TWO! WE NEED A PIC OF THE WINNERS!
I...
I LOST ...?!
ガ
GA-GONNNG
ガ

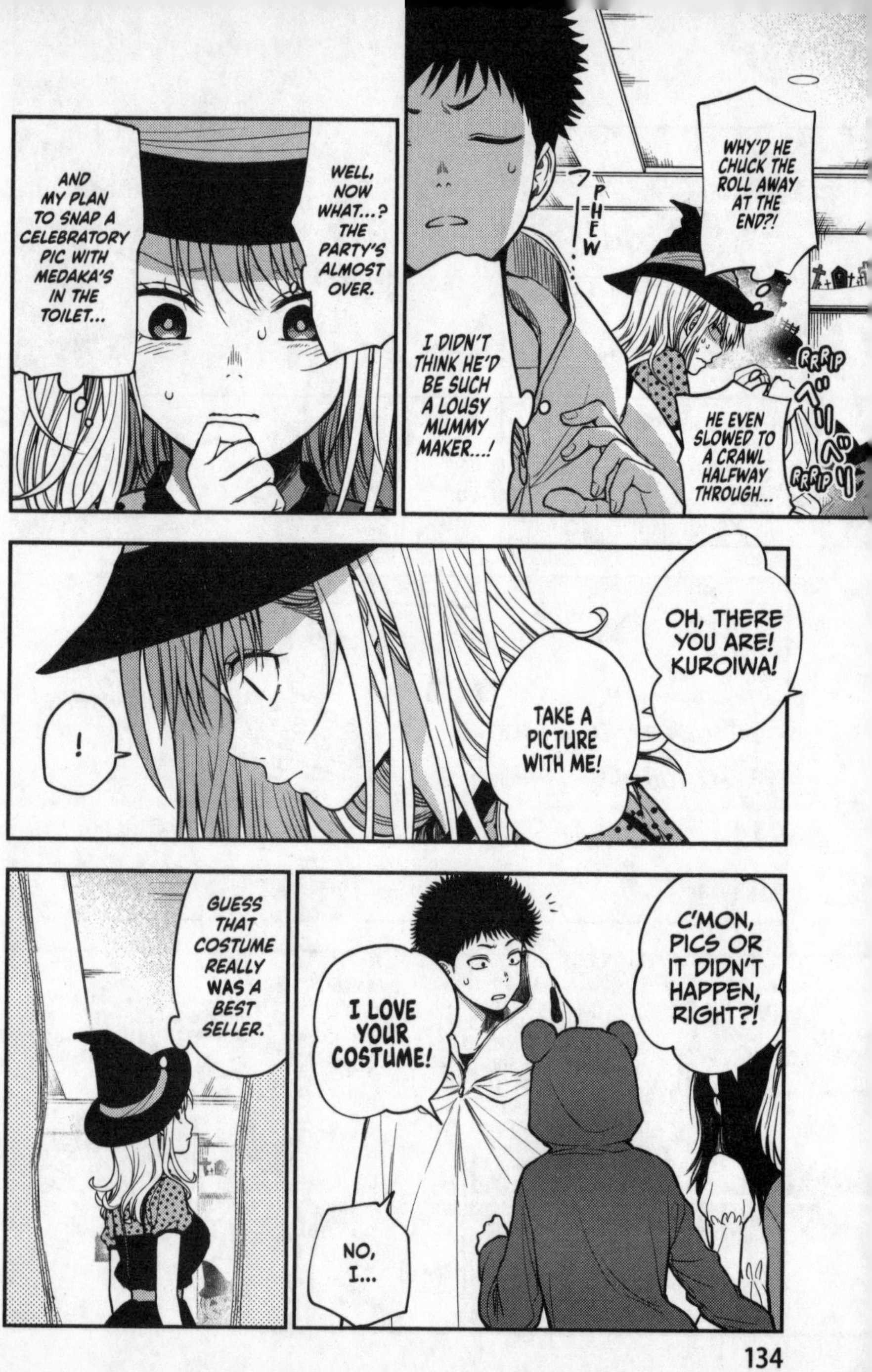
WHY'D HE CHUCK THE ROLL AWAY AT THE END?!
RRRIP
HE EVEN SLOWED TO A CRAWL HALFWAY THROUGH...
RRRIP
PHEW
I DIDN'T THINK HE'D BE SUCH A LOUSY MUMMY MAKER...!
WELL, NOW WHAT...? THE PARTY'S ALMOST OVER.
AND MY PLAN TO SNAP A CELEBRATORY PIC WITH MEDAKA'S IN THE TOILET...
OH, THERE YOU ARE! KUROIWA!
TAKE A PICTURE WITH ME!
!
C'MON, PICS OR IT DIDN'T HAPPEN, RIGHT?!
I LOVE YOUR COSTUME!
NO, I...
GUESS THAT COSTUME REALLY WAS A BEST SELLER.

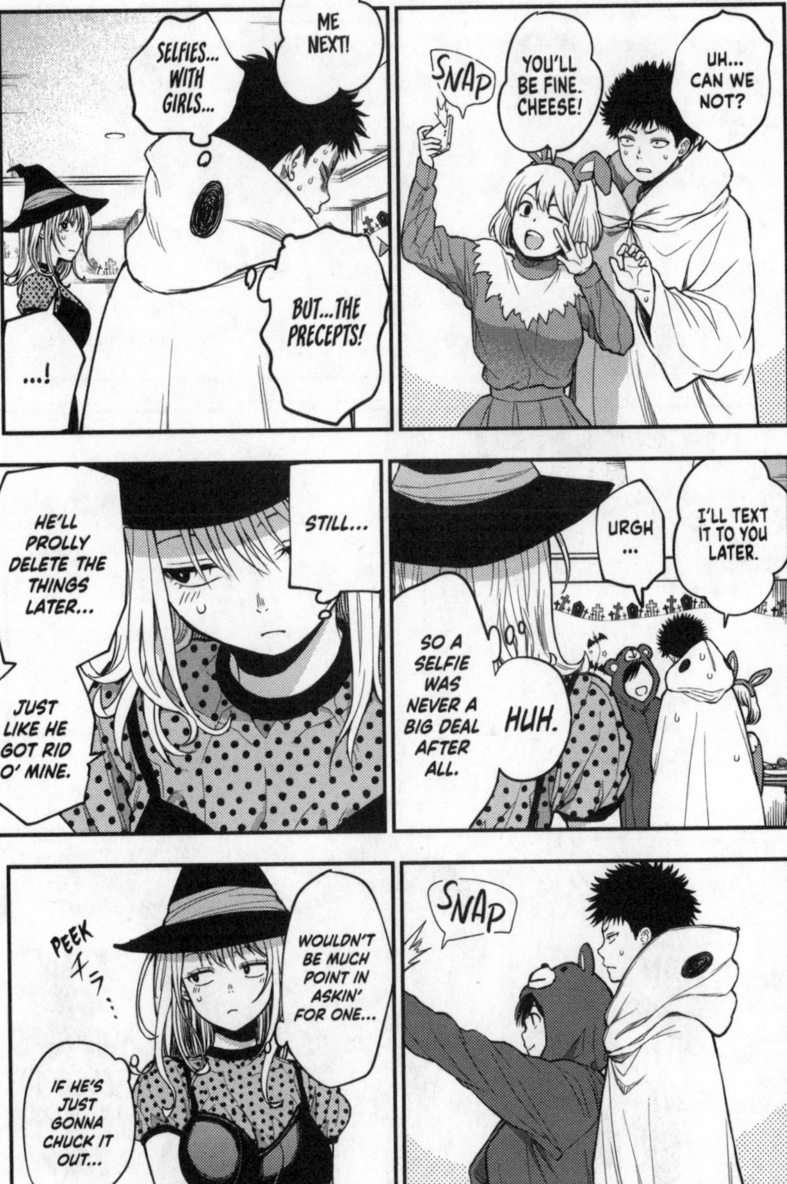
UH... CAN WE NOT?
YOU'LL BE FINE. CHEESE!
SNAP
ME NEXT!
SELFIES... WITH GIRLS...
BUT...THE PRECEPTS!
...!
I'LL TEXT IT TO YOU LATER.
URGH ...
HUH.
SO A SELFIE WAS NEVER A BIG DEAL AFTER ALL.
STILL...
HE'LL PROLLY DELETE THE THINGS LATER...
JUST LIKE HE GOT RID O' MINE.
SNAP
WOULDN'T BE MUCH POINT IN ASKIN' FOR ONE...
PEEK
チラ...
IF HE'S JUST GONNA CHUCK IT OUT...

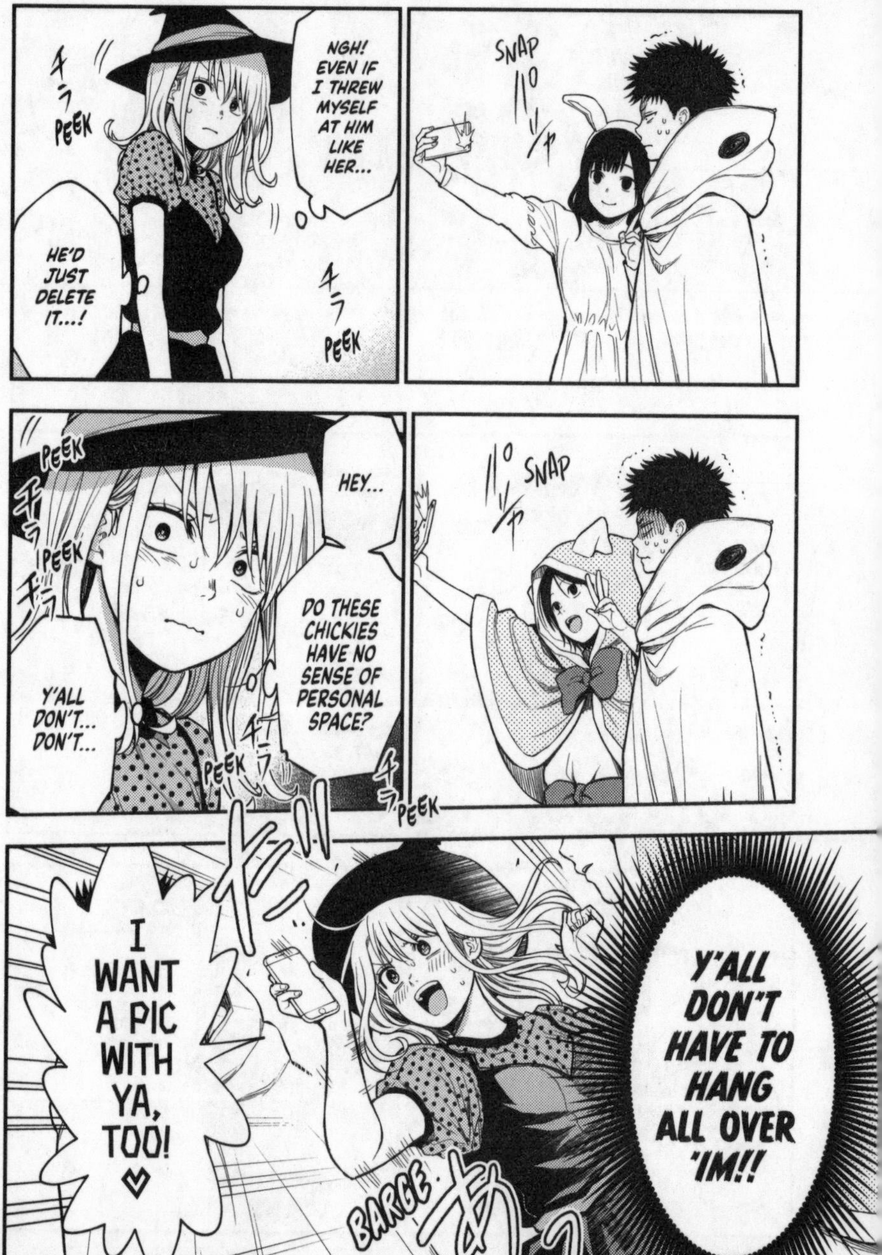
SNAP
NGH! EVEN IF I THREW MYSELF AT HIM LIKE HER...
HE'D JUST DELETE IT...!
PEEK
PEEK
SNAP
HEY...
DO THESE CHICKIES HAVE NO SENSE OF PERSONAL SPACE?
Y'ALL DON'T... DON'T...
PEEK
PEEK
PEEK
PEEK
Y'ALL DON'T HAVE TO HANG ALL OVER 'IM!!
I WANT A PIC WITH YA, TOO! ♡
BARGE

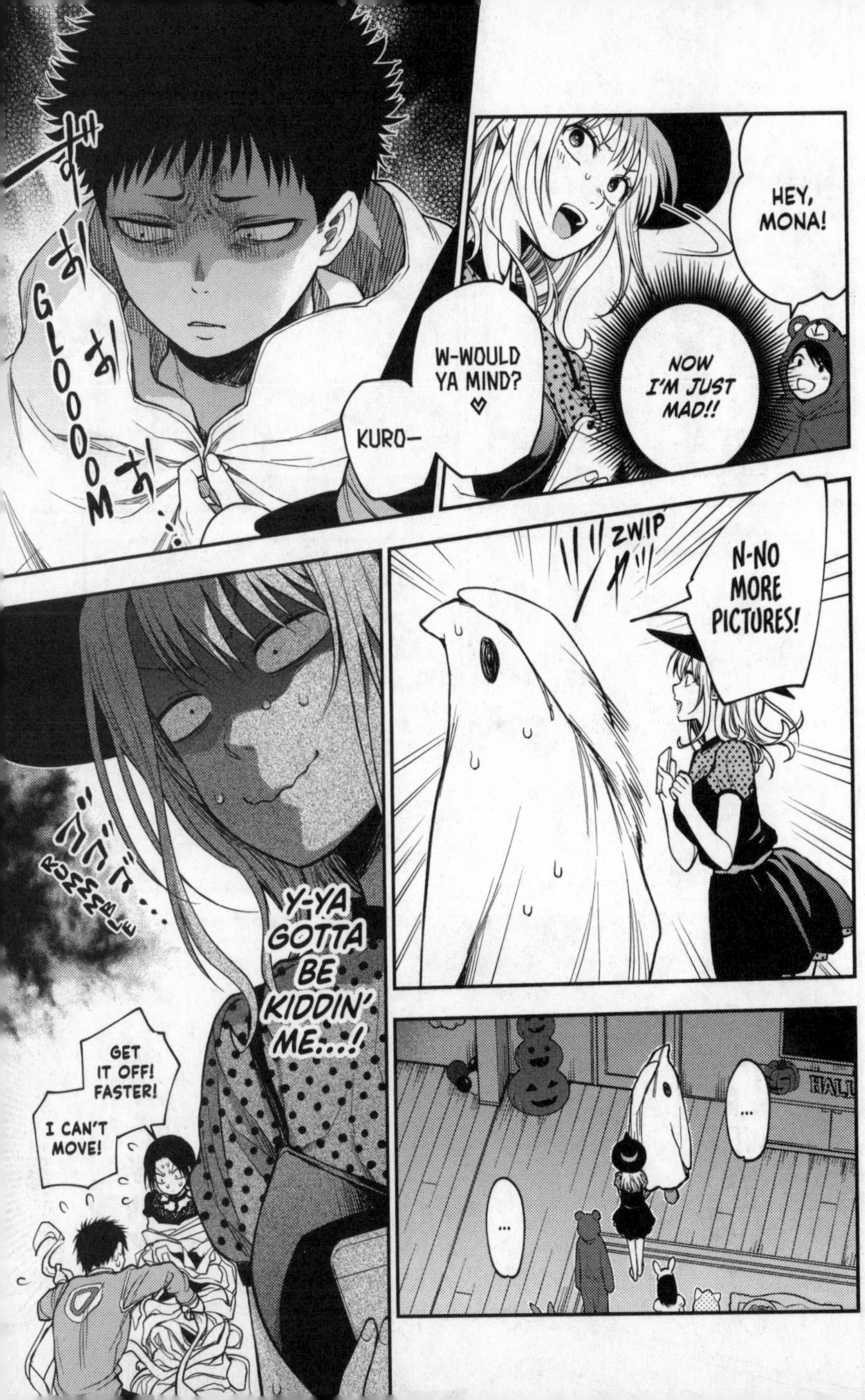
HEY, MONA!
NOW I'M JUST MAD!!
W-WOULD YA MIND?
KURO—
GLOOOOOM
N-NO MORE PICTURES!
ZWIP
...
...
Y-YA GOTTA BE KIDDIN' ME...!
RUSSSSLE
GET IT OFF! FASTER!
I CAN'T MOVE!

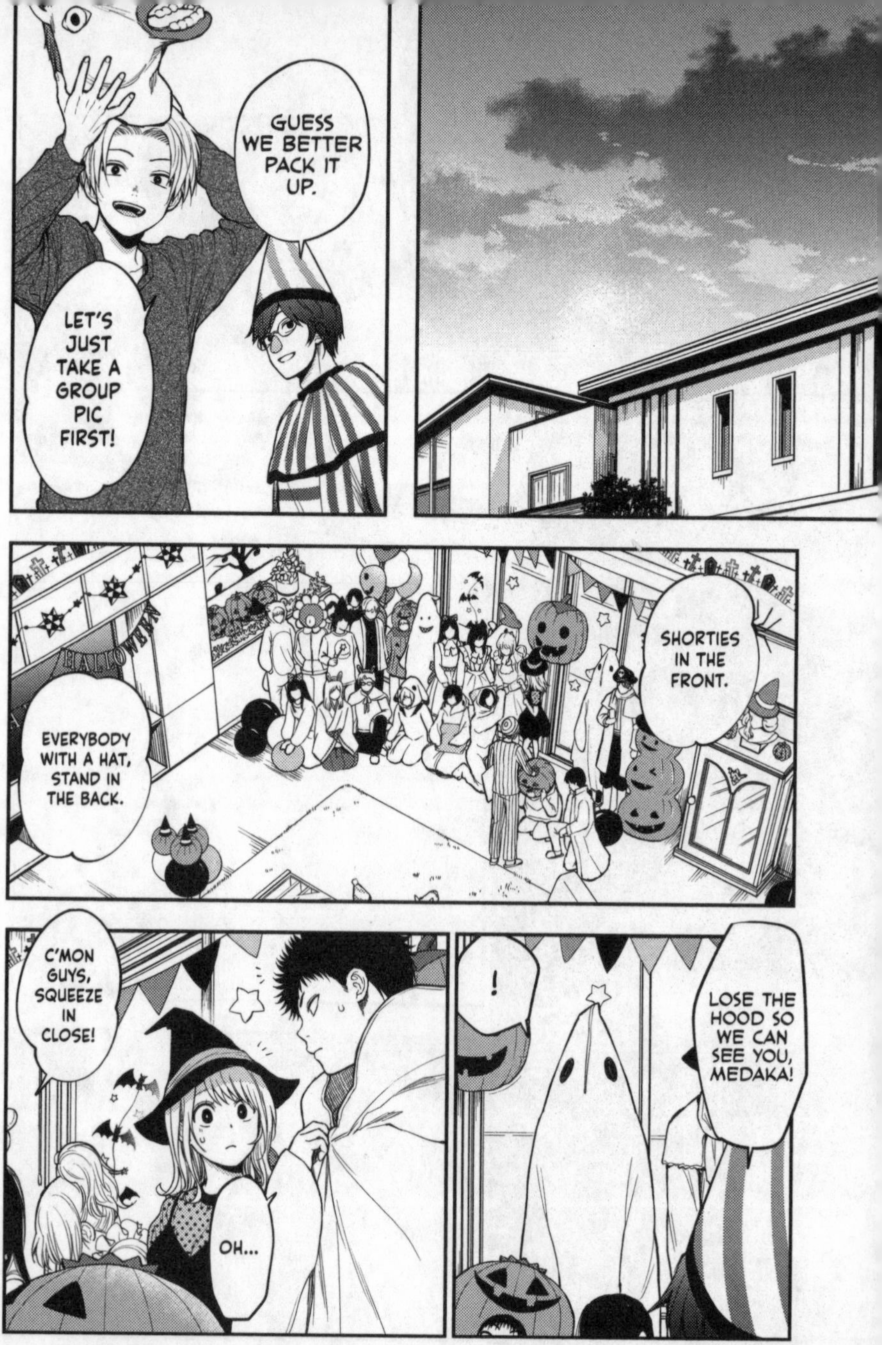
GUESS WE BETTER PACK IT UP.
LET'S JUST TAKE A GROUP PIC FIRST!
SHORTIES IN THE FRONT.
EVERYBODY WITH A HAT, STAND IN THE BACK.
LOSE THE HOOD SO WE CAN SEE YOU, MEDAKA!
!
C'MON GUYS, SQUEEZE IN CLOSE!
OH...

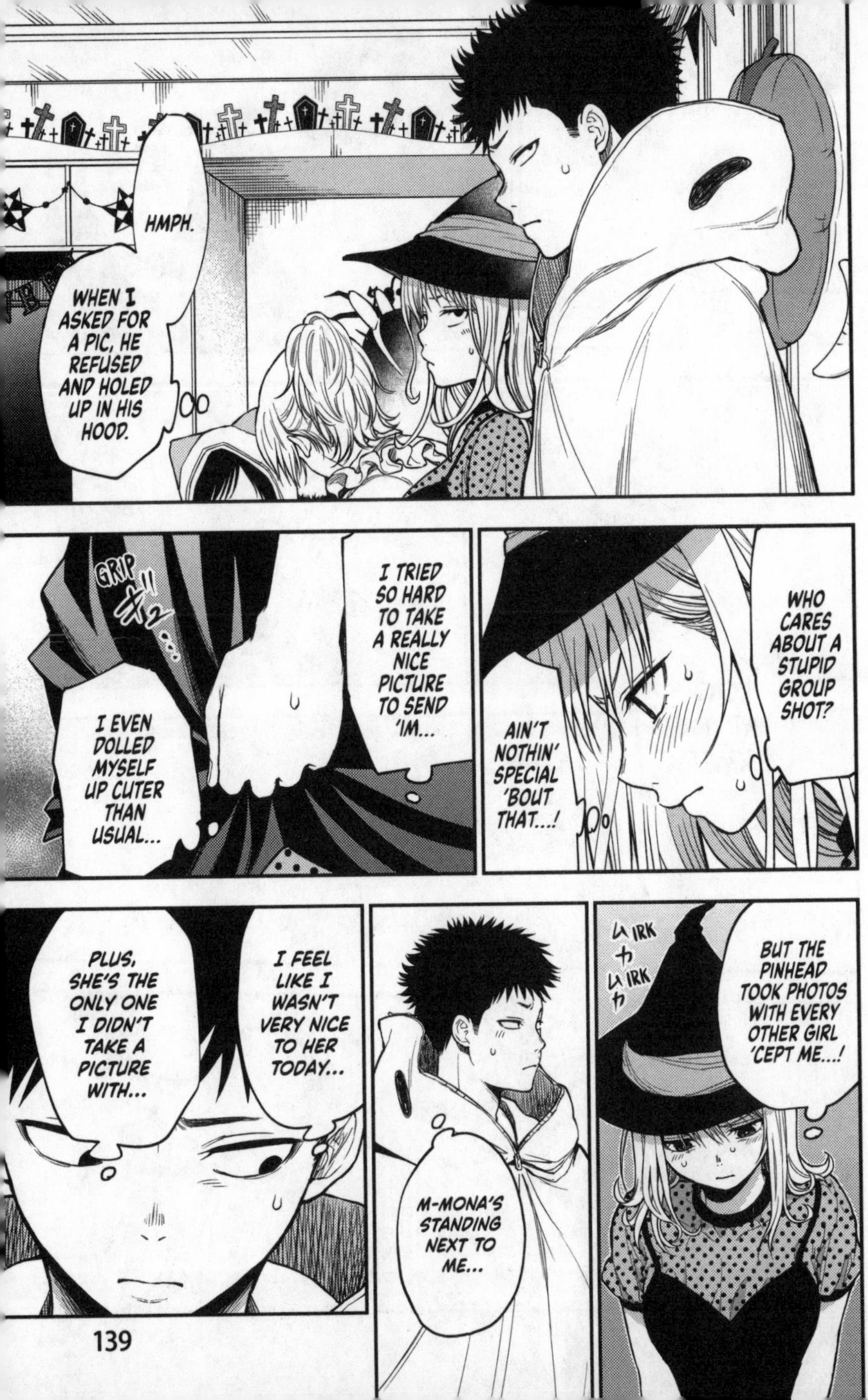
HMPH.
WHEN I ASKED FOR A PIC, HE REFUSED AND HOLED UP IN HIS HOOD.
WHO CARES ABOUT A STUPID GROUP SHOT?
AIN'T NOTHIN' SPECIAL 'BOUT THAT...!
I TRIED SO HARD TO TAKE A REALLY NICE PICTURE TO SEND 'IM...
GRIP
I EVEN DOLLED MYSELF UP CUTER THAN USUAL...
IRK
IRK
BUT THE PINHEAD TOOK PHOTOS WITH EVERY OTHER GIRL 'CEPT ME...!
M-MONA'S STANDING NEXT TO ME...
I FEEL LIKE I WASN'T VERY NICE TO HER TODAY...
PLUS, SHE'S THE ONLY ONE I DIDN'T TAKE A PICTURE WITH...

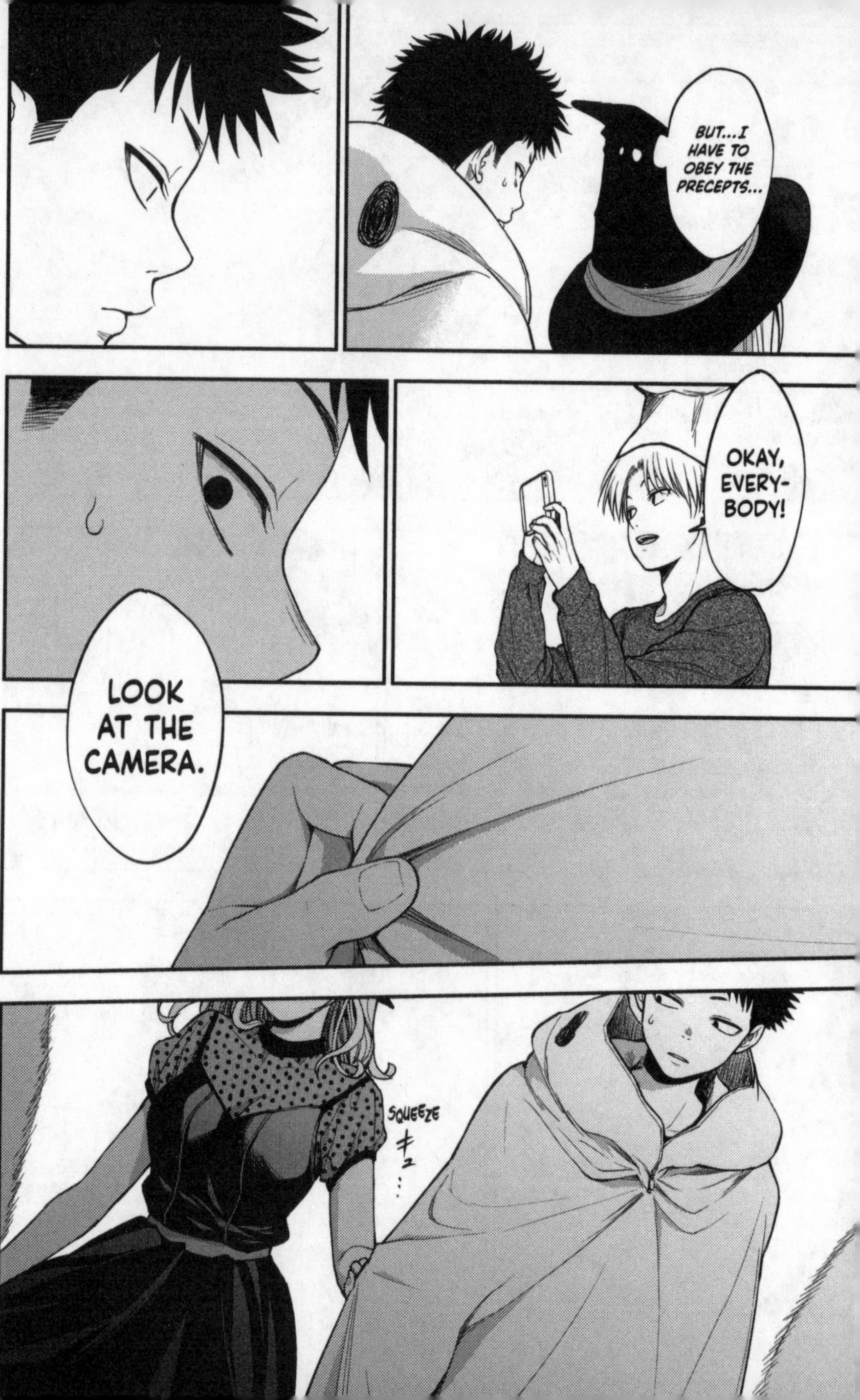
BUT...I HAVE TO OBEY THE PRECEPTS...
OKAY, EVERY-BODY!
LOOK AT THE CAMERA.
SQUEEZE
キュ…

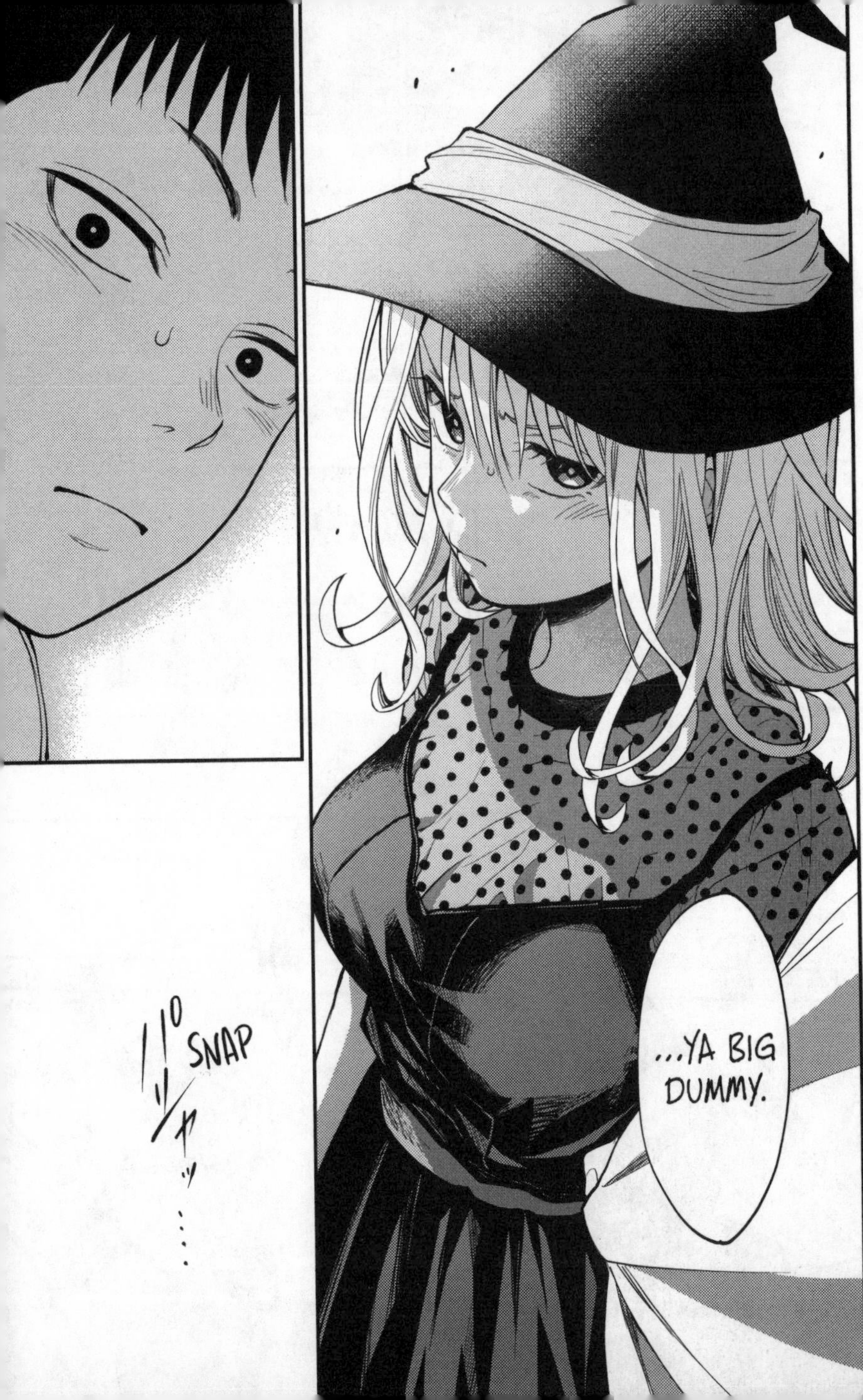
...YA BIG DUMMY.
SNAP

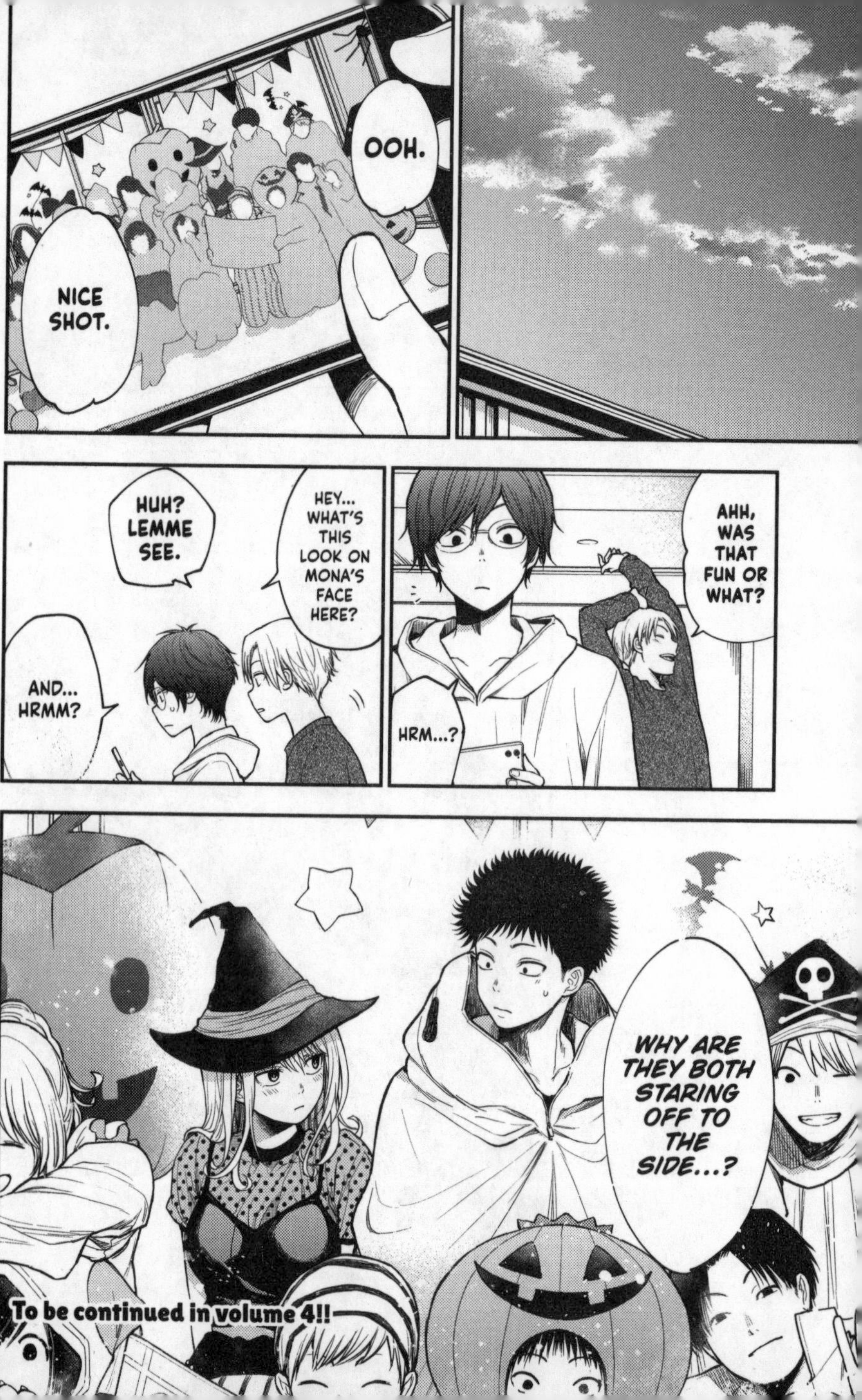
OOH.
NICE SHOT.
AHH, WAS THAT FUN OR WHAT?
HRM...?
HEY... WHAT'S THIS LOOK ON MONA'S FACE HERE?
HUH? LEMME SEE.
AND... HRMM?
WHY ARE THEY BOTH STARING OFF TO THE SIDE...?
To be continued in volume 4!!

PREVIEW

MONA'S SASSY INNER CRITIC SLIPS OUT...

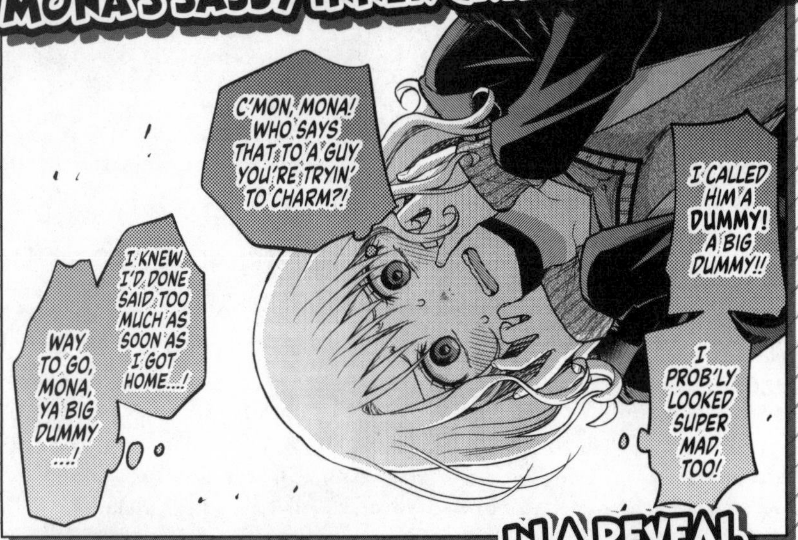
I CALLED HIM A DUMMY! A BIG DUMMY!!
I PROB'LY LOOKED SUPER MAD, TOO!
C'MON, MONA! WHO SAYS THAT TO A GUY YOU'RE TRYIN' TO CHARM?!
I KNEW I'D DONE SAID TOO MUCH AS SOON AS I GOT HOME...!
WAY TO GO, MONA, YA BIG DUMMY...!

IN A REVEAL OF OSAKAN PROPORTIONS!

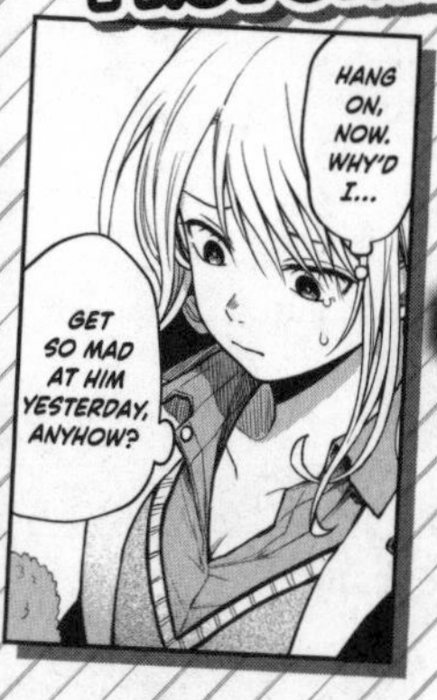
HANG ON, NOW. WHY'D I...
GET SO MAD AT HIM YESTERDAY, ANYHOW?

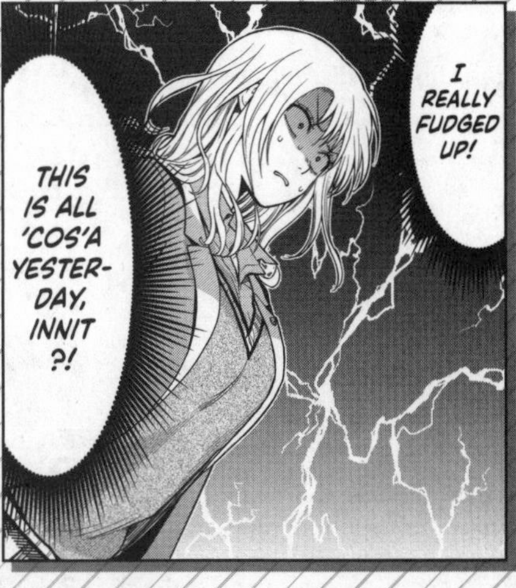
I REALLY FUDGED UP!
THIS IS ALL 'COS'A YESTERDAY, INNIT?!

Plus revelations of the heart...?

Irritation is the herald of infatuation! New developments are on the horizon!

Medaka Kuroiwa is Impervious to My Charms

Volume 4, Coming Soon!!

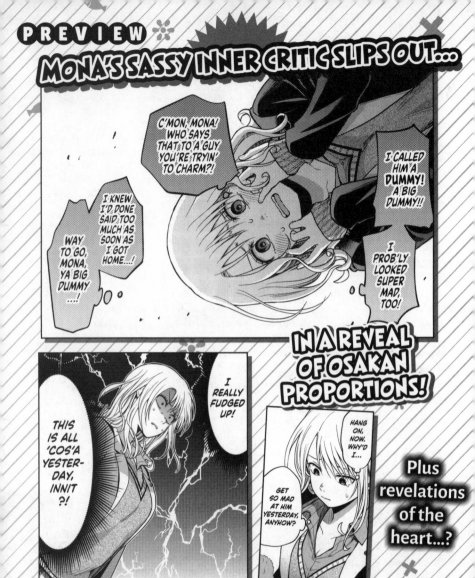

Medaka Kuroiwa is Impervious to My Charms 3

A VERTICAL Book

Translation (Original Digital): Anh Kiet Pham Ngo
Translation (Print): Nicole Frasik
Editor (Original Digital): Thalia Sutton
Editor (Print): Alexandra McCullough-Garcia
Production: Risa Cho, Pei Ann Yeap (print)
Letterer: Arbash Mughal
Proofreading: Kevin Luo (print)
YKS Services LLC/SKY JAPAN, Inc. (original digital)

First published in Japan in 2022 by Kodansha, Ltd., Tokyo
Publication rights for this English edition arranged through Kodansha, Ltd., Tokyo
English language version produced by Kodansha USA Publishing, LLC, 2023

Originally published in Japanese as *Kuroiwa Medaka ni Watashi no Kawaii ga Tsūjinai 3* by Kodansha, Ltd.
Kuroiwa Medaka ni Watashi no Kawaii ga Tsūjinai first serialized in *Weekly Shonen Magazine*, Kodansha, Ltd., 2021-

This is a work of fiction.

ISBN: 978-1-64729-307-9

Printed in the United States of America

First Edition

Kodansha USA Publishing, LLC
451 Park Avenue South
7th Floor
New York, NY 10016
www.kodansha.us

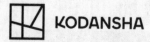